International Political Theory

Agency and Ethics: The Politics of Military Intervention. Albany, NY: State University Press of New York, 2002

Punishment, Justice and International Relations: Ethics and Order after the Cold War. London: Routledge, 2008

International Political Theory

An Introduction

Anthony F. Lang, Jr

 palgrave

First published 2015 by
PALGRAVE

Palgrave in the UK is an imprint of Macmillan Publishers Limited, registered in England, company number 785998, of 4 Crinan Street, London N1 9XW.

Palgrave Macmillan in the US is a division of St Martin's Press LLC, 175 Fifth Avenue, New York, NY 10010.

Palgrave is a global imprint of the above companies and is represented throughout the world.

Palgrave® and Macmillan® are registered trademarks in the United States, the United Kingdom, Europe and other countries.

ISBN: 978–0–230–29203–1 hardback
ISBN: 978–0–230–29204–8 paperback

This book is printed on paper suitable for recycling and made from fully managed and sustained forest sources. Logging, pulping and manufacturing processes are expected to conform to the environmental regulations of the country of origin.

A catalogue record for this book is available from the British Library.

A catalog record for this book is available from the Library of Congress.

Typeset by Aardvark Editorial Limited, Metfield, Suffolk.

Printed in China

Contents

List of Boxes   vii
Preface and Acknowledgements   ix
List of Abbreviations   xii

Introduction   **1**
International political theory   2
Four strands   8
Chapter outline   15
Further reading   19

1 Authority   **20**
Two versions of authority   21
Problem(s) of international or global authority   31
The authority of the UN   38
Conclusion   41
Further reading   42

2 Rules and Laws   **43**
Rules   44
Natural law   48
Positive law   53
International law   58
Kant and law   62
Responsibility to protect   68
Conclusion   70
Further reading   71

3 Rights and Responsibilities   **72**
Rights   74
The history of human rights   76
Foundations of human rights   79
Politics and human rights   84
Responsibilities   87
The United Nations, rights and responsibilities   89
John Stuart Mill and rights   92
Conclusion   97
Further reading   98

4 Wealth **100**
Justice and equality 102
Adam Smith and the invisible spectator 103
Karl Marx and the liberation of the human person 107
Rawls and global justice 111
Peter Singer and global utilitarianism 115
Rules and authority in the global political economy 116
Conclusion 119
Further reading 120

5 Violence **121**
The politics of war and violence 122
Classical approaches 126
The just war tradition 134
Making judgements about war 138
Hugo Grotius 146
Conclusion 152
Further reading 154

6 Nature **155**
Nature and politics 158
The environment and politics 164
Aristotle, nature and virtue 168
Some international political theories of climate change 174
Conclusion 178
Further reading 179

7 Belief **180**
Belief, religion and relativism 183
The right to recognition 188
The politics of pluralism 192
Conclusion 195
Further reading 197

Conclusion **198**

Bibliography 201

Index 231

List of Boxes

I.1	Norms, rules and laws	5
I.2	Agency	6
I.3	Theory and ideology	9
I.4	'Debates' in IR theory	10
1.1	The social contract tradition	27
2.1	The Valladolid debate (1550–1)	59
2.2	Customary law	61
3.1	Greeks and Romans on citizenship and rights	77
4.1	Neoliberal theory	104
4.2	Marx and Marxism	111
5.1	The just war: tradition or theory?	134
6.1	Causation	170
6.2	*Phronesis* in IR theory	171

List of Boxes

Preface and Acknowledgements

The central aim of this book is to show how political theory, broadly conceived, can inform our understanding of international affairs. In order to do this, it draws on the work of a range of different authors and intellectual traditions to explore some complex political problems at the international level. Its aim is to provide the tools to make judgements about the moral and political dilemmas that face us today.

The chapters of the book are organized around a key theme, with the Introduction providing a context by introducing the nature of international political theory and its relationship to other approaches and related fields of study. Chapters 1–3 introduce core themes that structure global political life: authority, rules, laws, rights and responsibilities. Chapters 4–7 provide insights into issues in the global political order in which these core themes play a crucial role: wealth, violence, nature and belief. The Conclusion brings these themes back together and suggests how international political theory can inform international political practice.

Learning features include text boxes in the chapters, which provide some additional background material, and Further Reading at the end of each chapter, comprising some of the most useful works to follow up on the themes addressed in the chapter. The Bibliography is an extensive list of all the materials cited in the text, along with other important references in the field. The Index uses bold print to indicate where important terms are most substantially explained or defined.

While all the material in this book is new, it draws on certain works I have published in the past.

The book was originally conceived as a collaborative project with Nick Rengger and Will Bain but by the time the opportunity arose to write it, they had moved onto other projects. With the encouragement of Steven Kennedy at Palgrave Macmillan, I persisted with it as a solo project. I am indebted to them for starting me down the path that led to this book and grateful to Will for his suggestion (perhaps it was an insistence at the time?) that the topic of authority be one of the chapters in this book. That chapter, in my view, differentiates this text from others on the normative dimensions of international affairs, and I am thankful to Will for proposing it.

Nick Rengger has continued to be a central influence on this book. He has read some of the material and discussed all of it with me over the course of the past few years. His early input along with his own scholarship has vastly improved my understanding of the topics explored here. More importantly, his friendship has made working as an academic in

British higher education much more of a joy than it otherwise might be (especially when we are drinking *my* coffee).

Patrick Hayden is another colleague and friend who has been instrumental in the process of writing this book. Patrick has read more than anyone else (sometimes more than once), and his comments and criticisms – on substance, grammar and style – have improved it immensely. Every time he read a chapter, I learned more. Thanks to him, Kant's idea of freedom, Rawls' difference principle and Hegel's theory of recognition are better explained. Maybe now that this book is finished, I can devote more time to my short game so that I don't have to tell my children that, once more, Patrick beat me at golf.

Other colleagues in the School of International Relations have read or discussed material in this book, including John Anderson, Sally Cummings, Karin Fierke, Caron Gentry, Gabriella Slomp, Bill Vlcek, William Walker and Ali Watson. In particular, Gabriella has been a great help in understanding the 17th-century context of thinkers such as Hobbes, Locke and Grotius, and Sally gave me helpful feedback on the chapter on authority. PhD students at St Andrews have also read some of this material; David Miles and John-Harmen Volk both offered perceptive comments on Chapter 7. Other colleagues around the world have been helpful in reading draft chapters or listening to presentations of them: Chris Brown, Toni Erskine, Harry Gould, Brent Steele, Terry Nardin, Jennifer Sterling-Folker, John Williams and Alexander Wendt, along with many others, have greatly improved the arguments herein. Matthew Slaughter, an old friend from undergraduate days and now an established economist at Dartmouth University, corrected my mistaken assumptions about global equality in Chapter 5. Richard Flathman, whose work features in Chapters 1 and 7, kindly read some of the material, which reminded me how helpful he was as part of my dissertation team many years ago. Palgrave Macmillan's anonymous reviewers were very helpful; one of them made comments on the entire text, correcting my mistaken assumptions about issues such as the social contract theory of Hobbes and Locke.

Steven Kennedy at Palgrave Macmillan has been one of the most helpful (and persistent) editors with whom I have had the pleasure to work. He did not let me give up on this book when I wanted to, and demonstrated the patience of Job in dealing with my continued failures to complete the manuscript on time. I hope it lives up to his expectations, and I owe him more than one drink at future academic conferences for all the work he has done on this. Maggie Lythgoe, the copyeditor, has been helpful in improving the text.

My family continues to be a source of comfort, support and inspiration. My brother Jim Lang has been an important figure in shaping this book, although he has read little of it. His work on teaching and learning in higher education has had a huge impact on me, but I may not have conveyed this to him. His publications, blog posts and discussions on Skype remind me that teaching is not as simple as filling students heads with information. Hopefully, this book, which raises more questions than answers, will capture the kind of active learning approach that Jim and others have shown to be so useful. My other siblings, their spouses and children and my dad keep me grounded in the reality of everyday life.

I have dedicated other books to my wife and children, so I'm not doing that here. But they are the most important people in my life and without them I would probably care less about things like climate change, global poverty and war. Seeking to make the world a better place by getting students to ask the deep questions will, I hope, help give families everywhere the peace and joy I have found in my own.

Finally, the people to whom I do dedicate this book are my students. I have inflicted chapters of this book on undergraduate and postgraduate students studying International Political Theory at the University of St Andrews. My struggles to turn lectures into chapters, the questions they have asked in tutorials and seminars, and the extended discussions during my office hours have been the single most important influence on the shape of this book. I have learned more from them than they can imagine. Thank you.

List of Abbreviations

EU	European Union
GRD	global resource dividend
ICC	International Criminal Court
ILT	international legal theory
IPCC	Intergovernmental Panel on Climate Change
IPT	international political theory
IR	international relations
LGBT	lesbian, gay, bisexual and transgendered
NGO	nongovernmental organization
OHCHR	Office of the High Commissioner for Human Rights
R2P	responsibility to protect
UN	United Nations
UDHR	Universal Declaration of Human Rights
UNGA	UN General Assembly
UNHRC	United Nations Human Rights Council
UNSC	UN Security Council
WTO	World Trade Organization

Introduction

On 17 June 2011, the United Nations Human Rights Council (UNHRC) passed a resolution expressing grave concerns about discrimination and violence on the basis of sexual orientation and gender identity. The resolution, proposed by South Africa, passed on the basis of a 23–19 vote. It called upon the UN High Commissioner for Human Rights to examine the laws and policies of states concerning the rights of lesbian, gay, bisexual and transgendered (LGBT) persons. As a result, the UN High Commissioner has been actively engaged in support of LGBT rights, which led to the creation of a dedicated website, UN Free & Equal (www.unfe.org), to disseminate information about such rights and promote a greater awareness of them.

However, such a resolution was not accepted by all member states, with a number of countries from Africa and the Middle East voting against it. A map posted on the UN website indicates that five countries impose the death penalty for same-sex consensual relations, while numerous others mandate imprisonment for such activities (UNFE n.d.). The position of some of these states, for instance Iran and Saudi Arabia, is that homosexuality is morally wrong according to the teachings of Islam, the religious tradition that frames their legal codes. Other states, such as Uganda, have argued that the promotion of homosexuality is an effort by the 'West' to interfere in their society.

This is just one instance of the kinds of moral, legal and political dilemmas that exist in the current world order. On the one hand, there exists a robust international legal structure to promote human rights, which includes an institutional framework designed to advance rights in different ways. On the other hand, there are well-developed historical, religious and moral views that stand in opposition to such legal structures. Importantly, it is not just religious traditions like Islam or African cultural norms that stand in opposition to such global human rights institutions. The US has refused to sign the Treaty on the Rights of the Child because its military recruitment system recruits teenagers under the age of 18 (through visits to high schools). Various Christian groups in the US also argue that the UN is an institution designed to undermine not only American sovereignty but also its moral beliefs concerning issues like abortion.

These are only a few of the issues that illustrate important problems in the international legal and political order. What kind of authority structure is most legitimate for addressing such issues? Should institutions at the international level be more authoritative than domestic authorities? Are

1

there universal rights that no state should be able to violate? What is the source of those rights? Can rights that arise from a particular modern-day liberal context be applied globally? What responsibilities do the states have to enforce rights, especially outside their own borders? What kinds of rules should govern the global realm? And what happens when those rules are violated?

This book will focus on these and other related questions. The questions have been addressed in different ways by ethicists, lawyers, political and social scientists, and a host of others. This book demonstrates how international political theory (IPT) uses political theory – a body of normative and ethical theory that concerns itself with politics – in order to explore these global issues.

International political theory

Before defining IPT, it is useful to say a few words about the theory and its uses in the social and political world. One of the most important functions of any theory is to provide a critical perspective on what we think to be 'normal' in political life. Social and political theory interrogates this normality in a number of ways:

- demonstrating the heritage of the ideas we think are new
- revealing the assumptions that underlie our political practices
- forcing us to think through the consequences of our political practices
- holding up clearly articulated standards against which our political practices can be evaluated
- connecting disparate locations and traditions in conceptualizing our politics.

These functions can disabuse us of the assumption that our politics should go on as they have while also helping us to refine existing arrangements such that they are more just and peaceful for all peoples.

The most common sort of theories encountered in the social and political sciences are explanatory ones, for example theories of comparative politics or international relations (IR), which use social scientific modes of analysing data such as hypothesis formation, testing and falsification. Robert Keohane (2009), a leading IR theorist, has argued that this sort of theory is the 'vocation' of the political scientist, playing upon Max Weber's idea of the vocation of the politician (Weber 1994 [1919]). IPT has a similar aim to this sort of political science theory – informing political practice by raising important questions about its assumptions and consequences. But unlike political science, IPT uses historical narratives and normative argument to raise questions about political life.

This book adopts the following definition of IPT:

> IPT includes 1) justificatory arguments for certain types of authority, rights, rules and responsibilities that apply to individuals and communities qua political agents in a political order structured by the sovereign state system; and 2) critical and historical investigations of how individuals and communities qua political agents shape and are shaped by authority, rights, rules and responsibilities of a political order structured by the sovereign state system.

Why these particular themes? Authority and rules have been central to organizing political life in domestic contexts, and they have, as a result, been the central preoccupation of political theorists since the classical period. The two concepts are often addressed together; for instance, an authority creates rules to govern, but is also bound by those rules if it is to be a political order that is just. The focus on these concepts within IPT challenges the idea that neither rules nor authority have any relevance at the global level. When great powers run roughshod over international law, it would seem that naked power is the most important concept for understanding IR. But while this may be true at times, even great powers find themselves subject to various kinds of rules and their power only works if it is considered to have some legitimate authority status.

Rights and responsibilities result from the exercise of authority and the implementation of rules. Individuals have the responsibility to live according to the rules that authorities establish. At the same time, when authority structures violate those rules, individuals have rights to ensure that they will not be subject to the whims of those authorities. At the global level, these notions of rights and responsibilities are more complicated, primarily because the very status of authority and rules at the global level is more open to question. But, we also speak of states having responsibilities, for example the responsibility to protect, and rights (non-intervention). Individuals also have certain responsibilities – such as not to kill outside the boundaries of organized military activity, that is, not be a terrorist – and rights, as in the UN Declaration on Human Rights.

As the above definition suggests, IPT can operate in two ways, both of which will be used in this book. One is to provide justificatory arguments for particular configurations of authority, rights, rules and responsibilities. For instance, one might argue that only through an international office, like that of the UN High Commissioner for Human Rights, can universal rights be advanced. To make this claim, one must clearly present an understanding of rights, universality and the nature of international authority. In the chapters that follow, I present different justificatory arguments drawn from historical and contemporary figures. I do not necessarily advance any single justificatory argument on these themes, but seek to provide an overview of some of the most important.

Two, IPT is about putting into particular contexts the types of positions and principles that are operative in the international order. This second function is not a directly normative one, in that it does not advance justificatory arguments. Rather, it tries to reveal why we have the assumptions about the world in which we live. So, for example, IPT can reveal how competing assumptions about what is 'natural' might provide greater understanding of why some believe that homosexual conduct should not be legal because it is not 'natural'; indeed, proponents and opponents of LGBT rights often turn to science to support their justificatory claims. In opposition to this view, one might examine the history of sexuality to reveal a multiplicity of sexual identities that can help locate arguments for and against LGBT rights. In this sense, IPT is not about justifying anything but is instead about revealing how individuals exist within and make claims about the world in some deeper context.

IPT, then, allows us to advance and understand normative arguments about world politics. By normative, I mean that IPT is concerned with the norms, rules and laws that govern political life (see Box I.1). One might note that the term 'normative' privileges its alternative 'empirical' by setting up a world in which investigations of how the world ought to be are distinct from investigations of how the world actually is. This distinction is, admittedly, a contested one; some have argued, for instance, that a true social science is inherently normative, especially in the issues it wishes to engage and the conclusions to which it comes as they might have some sort of political relevance in the world around us (Smith 2004). One extreme version of this argument would be that all social and political analysis is ethical. This book does not assume this, for it posits that certain concepts and methods address the world of 'ought' more than the world of 'is'.

The 'international' in IPT is also important to explain. First, unlike in a domestic political community where theorists either share a set of normative standards at the outset or speak to the same set of political practices, at the international level there is much less agreement on who 'we' are, what 'we' do, and what assumptions 'we' share. The historical narratives that inform international political practice become much wider and more global. The normative standards employed by participants in international politics and observers reach into a broader diversity of traditions. Yet, such political critique and theorizing is most certainly taking place. Political theorists and political philosophers are turning their attention to internat-

BOX I.1   Norms, rules and laws

Norms are those assumptions about the proper behaviour for agents with a particular identity. Norms can be regulative (telling us what to do) and constitutive (telling us who we are). The concept of a norm is etymologically linked to the idea of normal, although normal has a much more general set of assumptions that may not be the same for everyone.

Rules are related to norms, but rules differ from norms in that they are consciously constructed, whereas norms arise from social interactions over time and may not have any specific origin. Rules are guidelines about how a group of individuals ought to act. Rules can be formal or informal depending on their origin and the context in which they function.

Laws are rules that arise from a political structure, either domestic or international. Domestic laws arise from a legislative process, while international laws arise from a much broader set of political interactions. Laws generally have sanctions attached to them when they are not obeyed, although this is not necessarily the defining feature of laws, since rules and norms may also have sanctions attached to their violations.

See: Hart 1994; Katzenstein 1996; Lang and Beattie 2008; Onuf 1989.

ional matters, international legal scholars are asking more fundamental questions about the relationship of law to politics, and IR theorists are realizing that their work has an inherent normative component that they are struggling to articulate.

In addition, unlike political theory in a domestic context, IPT assumes that individuals are not the only agents. This means that states, persons, companies, nongovernmental organizations (NGOs), terrorist organizations and religious traditions can all be subject to investigation. This distinguishes IPT from those theories that assume only the individual person is the subject of concern. Certainly, all politics is about people. What IPT emphasizes is that people cannot be considered as individuals, but can only be understood in terms of the political communities of which they are a part. Moreover, those political communities become 'agents' that can be held responsible and even sanctioned for their actions in the international realm. This focus on multiple agents differentiates IPT from certain kinds of moral philosophy that address only the individual person (Box I.2).

Related to these points is the question of why the term used here is 'international' rather than 'global'. As used in this book, IPT theorizes politics in a world in which states retain the ability and responsibility to use coercive force in pursuit of interests, justice and order. Moreover, the sovereign state

---

BOX I.2   Agency

Agency, at its most basic level, is the ability to change the world around oneself. But agency is more complicated than this; a tornado can change the world, but we do not normally say that tornadoes have agency. Instead, agency requires a certain level of intentionality, which is then connected to our ability to hold agents responsible. Sometimes, agency arises from a formal process, as in a contractual situation when someone acts as an agent for someone else, or in a political situation, where a government formally recognizes individuals or groups as agents, either citizens or corporations. Agency is also understood in the social sciences in relation to structure. In this understanding, structures are institutional arrangements within which agents operate. In IPT, the idea that there are multiple agents relies on these ideas of agency, drawing on the moral, political and sociological.

See: Arendt 1959; Lang 2002; Wendt 1999.

---

system is one in which no single agent can claim to be the sole legitimate authority, which some IR theorists claim makes the system formally anarchic (Waltz 1979), although others would contest this view (Lake 2009). Importantly, certain cosmopolitan theorists argue that the sovereign state system is not the morally preferable way to orient world politics (Caney 2005), while others argue that there is movement towards a larger global political community (Hayden 2005). This book explores cosmopolitan theory but it does so in the context of an international order that remains tightly bounded by the power of sovereign states to structure the international order in their interests. Much takes place outside or in response to this structuring, but it remains a central background condition. So, for instance, the UNHRC resolution described above takes seriously the fact that different communities have different traditions and moral standards, but also acknowledges that international institutions are constructing new authority systems and will have greater say in those communities.

Another clarification to make is that this book, while drawing on the past, is concerned with the present. There is in this work a dialogue between the past and the present. The question of what constitutes the history of ideas and how it should relate to current political concerns and needs has long been one of debate (Skinner 2002). But, at the same time, IPT can only engage with this history from a particular perspective, one shaped by our presence in the modern-day international order. One may approach that history to discover why we have the system we have today (Keene 2005), how we can see alternatives to the system we have today (Lang 2009a), or in order to appreciate what we unconsciously assume from the past (Bain 2007). All these approaches to the past are instances of IPT, because they are driven in part by concerns of the present, concerns which the authors believe are best addressed by turning to specific thinkers or the broader history of ideas.

Some of the historical theorists on which I draw in Chapters 1–3 – John Locke, Thomas Hobbes, Immanuel Kant and John Stuart Mill – have been the most systematic interpreters of the themes explored here. These individuals are often located within a broadly defined 'liberal' tradition. But, this book is not informed only by the liberal tradition, for the thinkers explored in Chapters 4–7 see important limits on the liberty of the individual, limits that arise from the constraints imposed by nature (Aristotle), the centrality of material need (Karl Marx), the challenge of political violence (Hugo Grotius), and the constitution of the individual through their place in national and global communities (Georg Hegel). In this text, then, the problem of liberty for natural persons, states and other agents will be a core concern, although it will be addressed through the ideas of authority, rules, rights and responsibilities.

This book assumes that the current international order can be described as one that is broadly liberal, so it is logical to use these thinkers and the themes they found to be central. The general presumptions of statehood, international human rights, international economics and war revolve around themes that arose in 19th-century liberal thought. International law, as the language through which international affairs take place, best captures this latent liberalism (Koskenneimi 2001). Realist theorists, whom one would assume are most often opposed to liberalism, accept key tenets of liberalism as the political structure that great powers should safeguard in their own political orders (Morgenthau 1960). Naturally, not all states are liberal, nor are all international interactions liberal; rather, the point here is that a vague liberalism operates in the background of our shared global life, a liberalism that is rarely articulated but is often the point of intense criticism.

In the international realm, dilemmas relating to authority, rules, rights and responsibilities are constantly arising; the UNHRC resolution noted above is an example of just such a dilemma. This book will not resolve this dilemma or the others presented here, but it will give you a way of approaching these questions that should give you some confidence to make judgements. This does not mean giving you factual information, although it will point to where you can find some of that information. Rather, it will identify theorists who have considered related problems in the history of political thought. In so doing, you will recognize that while the details of a particular problem are novel, the basic moral and political questions that underlie it are not new.

Four strands

The body of literature that I draw on here does not arise from any one approach or disciplinary background. I suggest that there are four disciplinary strands that constitute the field of IPT: political theory, IR theory, international legal theory, and moral philosophy. Admittedly, some of the authors I cite here may not think of themselves as contributing directly to IPT. Rather, I am using these broad traditions of thought to highlight some of the concerns and backgrounds of those who have written important works that address the problems of politics and ethics at the international level.

Before describing these individual strands, it is important to note that some theorists do see themselves as contributing directly to IPT. Chris Brown has helped shape the field in important ways, first by posing the idea of communitarians against cosmopolitanism (1992), then by exploring the nature of rights and justice within a sovereign state system (2002), and recently by developing an account of international affairs that draws on the Aristotelian conception of judgement (2010). Others have sought to draw on a wide range of intellectual resources to make contributions to IPT, ranging from Terry Nardin's (1983) use of Michael Oakeshott to Molly Cochran's (1999) use of John Dewey. Toni Erskine (2008, 2009) has sought to develop an account of international ethics that she calls normative IR theory. This approach straddles the cosmopolitan and communitarian elements of much of IR theory and moral philosophy, but proposes ways to negotiate that space. David Boucher (1998) has explicitly employed the history of political theory to engage explanatory theories of IR. Kimberly Hutchings (1999, 2010) has creatively combined feminist thought and theorists such as Hegel to develop her understanding of IPT.

Others might also see their work as part of IPT. The list of resources in the next few pages suggest that rather than narrowly delimiting the field of IPT, one effort of this book is to highlight scholarly work that can contribute to IPT by engaging with issues of normativity at the international level.

Political theory

Traditionally, political theorists have tended to address their analyses to specific, bounded communities. As noted above, IPT differs from political theory, in that it engages some of the core questions of political life but in the context of a world in which the boundaries of the state can neither contain nor protect citizens from wider political practices (Box I.3).

Political theory, as a formal disciplinary activity, can be located as a response to the ways in which the general study of politics changed into political science. However, to say that the study of political theory is

BOX I.3 **Theory and ideology**

Political theories and ideologies are often used interchangeably, but it is important to keep them distinct. For example, Marxism, like liberalism and feminism, is both a theory and an ideology. The meaning of 'ideology' has changed over time, but it originates around the time of the French Revolution as a way to label a programmatic approach to the political realm. Prior to this, politics was not understood through a set of actionable ideals that could be put into place; the advent of the Enlightenment and the idea that the political realm (as with the rest of the world) could somehow be controlled gave rise to the concept of ideology. Today, an ideology is understood as an internally coherent set of ideas that have practical application either at the domestic or international level and usually has programmatic policy prescriptions. A theory could draw on an ideology, and vice versa, but theories have a more critical purchase on the political realm. Rather than leading to specific proposals about how to act in the public realm, political theory provides critical and evaluative tools for how to better understand the social and political realm.

somehow new or a 20th-century invention would be absurd. The point here is that something called 'political theory' as distinct from other ways to study politics did not arise until the 20th century. In the early and mid-20th century, the study of politics sought to become more 'scientific', which meant trying to find causal explanations of individual behaviours that can be turned into law-like generalizations. Alongside this effort at finding causal patterns, political scientists sought to remove normative judgements about political life and instead engage in purely descriptive or explanatory accounts. These efforts to become more scientific in the study of politics are sometimes categorized as the rise of 'behaviourism' or 'positivism' (Hollis 1994). In response to these changes, a number of thinkers tried to rescue what they believed to be the preferred mode of study, that is, reading classics of the past for insights into the present, especially because these texts did not assume a rigid scientific approach nor did they banish normative or ethical theory from their study of politics. As a result, in the mid-20th-century American context, thinkers such as Leo Strauss, Hannah Arendt and Eric Vogelin 'invented' a particular tradition to resurrect some classical thinkers (Gunnell 1987, 1993). Some approaches to IPT have mirrored this approach by turning back to the classics of political theory for insights into the international realm, in critical and sympathetic guises (Boucher 1998; Brown et al. 2002; Jahn 2006a; Keene 2005; Pangel and Ahrensdorf 1999; Williams 1992).

Some political theorists address the international dimensions of political life (Derrida 1992, 2001; Habermas 2006; Rawls 1999). In some cases, figures from the mid-20th century have become important sources for reflection on the international. For instance, the work of Carl Schmitt has become an important inspiration for a number of thinkers (Agamben 2005; Hooker 2009; Odysseos and Petito 2007; Slomp 2009a). Hannah Arendt has been a source for others who wish to reflect on the international realm (Hayden 2009a; Lang and Williams 2005; Owens 2008).

International relations theory

IPT arose in part from trends in IR theory, although IR theory initially sought to distinguish an international order from a domestic one, a process that partly undermined the potential for a truly international political theory to develop. IR theory turned away from substantive normative issues towards questions of epistemology and ontology in the mid-20th century (Box I.4). The anarchic nature of international politics certainly reinforced this tendency, but it does not entirely explain it. As this section will suggest, however, the narrative about IR that has excluded ethical and political theory can be challenged from different perspectives. This section highlights contributions to IPT from within the major IR theories: realism, liberalism, constructivism, critical theory and poststructuralism.

BOX I.4   'Debates' in IR theory

Some IR theorists understand the history of IR theory as structured around a series of debates. The first debate was between idealist or utopian thinkers and realists, launched by the critical readings of interwar scholarship from E.H. Carr and Hans Morgenthau. The second debate emerged in the 1950s and 60s, and posed behaviouralists against 'classical' IR theorists. This paralleled the rise of political theory in the context of political science mentioned above, although this debate took on an Anglo-American cast. Those writing from Britain, particularly Martin Wight and Hedley Bull (actually an Australian) took the classical approach of more history and law, while Americans tended to the more behaviouralist tradition, captured in the work of James Rosenau. The third debate resulted from the efforts of poststructuralist theorists to interject more critical perspectives on IR theory, focusing on debates in modern and structural theory. The idea that the field has progressed through these debates, however, is more problematic. It does not necessarily capture the full range of thinking in the field. The recent historical studies of Brian Schmidt (1998) and Duncan Bell (2009) have demonstrated very different theoretical heritages for the study of IR theory, both of which more clearly locate the place of normative issues.

See: Knorr and Rosenau 1965; Lapid 1989; Smith 2004.

Realist and liberal theory, the two dominant strands in IR theory, have contributed to IPT. Realism assumes the following key points: states are the primary agents in the international system, states pursue power and seek to secure their interests, and efforts at cooperation in international affairs are less likely to succeed. Liberalism argues that cooperation is possible in the international order and that explanations of international affairs should include not just states but a wider range of agents. There has been a 'recovery' of the normative dimensions of realism in recent years, with special attention to the classical realist tradition. Thinkers who have been explored here include Hans Morgenthau and E.H. Carr (Bell 2008; Hom and Steele 2010; Lang 2007; Williams 2007). Liberal theory has seen some theorists proposing institutional change that would reinforce a liberal international order, although there is much debate about what kind of liberalism this will be (Hovden and Keene 2002). For instance, Robert Keohane has proposed a series of institutional reforms that are based on explicitly normative ideas (Buchanan and Keohane 2004, 2006, 2011; Grant and Keohane 2005).

A newer strand in IR theory, constructivism, has also contributed to IPT. Constructivism highlights the constructed nature of reality that can be found by investigating the norms, rules, ideas or discourses that structure global political life. Constructivists can be classified into two basic types, positivist and legal/linguistic. Positivist constructivists have sought to demonstrate the importance of ideas or norms in international politics, although their approach tends not to be normative so should not really be considered part of IPT (Steele 2007; Sterling-Folker 2000). Legal constructivists differ in that they argue that norms are not social facts but part of the rules that constitute the world in which we live in a more direct action-guiding way and thus provide a closer connection to theories of IPT (Kratochwil 1989; Onuf 1989). Other constructivist theorists have engaged more seriously the dilemmas generated by ethics, seeking to establish the impact of norms but also critically evaluating them (Crawford 2002; Lang 2002; Price 2008; Thomas 2001).

The critical theory that has arisen in IR has made an important contribution to IPT. Critical theory in IR emphasizes the centrality of the material conditions of global politics and explores the potential of reconfiguring global social and political life to achieve emancipation for those who are marginalized. One of the most well-known critical theorists is Robert Cox (1981, 1996, 2002). Andrew Linklater (1982, 1990, 1997, 2011) has also contributed to IPT from within a critical theory perspective. Poststructural IR derives from the social theory that seeks to advance beyond structural arguments by focusing on the discursive dimensions of social and political life, and which resists grand narratives, either political or explanatory. In terms of its contribution to IPT, poststructural theory seems at first to fit less easily within IPT, primarily because many of its adherents eschew any attempt to create a 'better' world. This scepticism derives in part from the view that there exists no foundational starting point from which a normatively driven analysis might be undertaken (Zehfuss 2009). Ironically, IR theorists not sympathetic to normative theories have argued that poststructuralism is immoral (Krasner 1996). Important theorists here include R.B.J. Walker (1993, 2010) and David Campbell (1992, 1993, 1998; Campbell and Shapiro 1999).

International legal theory

International law as a field of study predates the formal creation of IR or IPT, although not political theory. This book will explore this material in more depth in Chapter 2, which focuses on rules and laws as sites of normative theory at the global level. Only recently have theorists of IPT begun to appreciate the important theoretical insights that international law brings to understanding the global order.

International legal theory (ILT) has contributed in two significant ways to IPT. First, along with an appreciation of the resources that natural law provides for a universal ethic, natural law theorists have looked to the history of ILT for insights into two important issue areas: the use of force and human rights. Second, some works have sought to connect international law with broader trends in international affairs and constitutional theory.

Natural law theory is a broad conceptual category that encompasses Christian religious thought and more secular, Enlightenment-based conceptions of law. Its basic assumption is that the law that governs human conduct is somehow internal to the human condition and so can be known either through an understanding of the human person or through an observation of human conduct in community over the centuries, sometimes summarized in the idea that natural law can be found through the use of 'right reason'. The central writings in natural law theory arise from Christian, specifically Catholic political philosophy (D'Entreves 1951; Finnis 1980; George 1999; Maritain 2001), although there are also strands that draw on early modern and Enlightenment theorists (Haakonssen 1996, 1999). A number of theorists have demonstrated the relevance of natural law theory for international ethics, particularly because its normative guidelines do not depend on any particular national or cultural context but are, supposedly, universal in reach (Boyle 1992; George 1998). Some theorists have connected natural law to IR as a formal discipline, but these interventions are rare (Beattie 2010; Midgley 1975). Work in this area has contributed to theories of the use of force and human rights, ideas explored more fully in the chapters that follow.

Legal theorists have developed important accounts of the rules that structure the international order. Some international lawyers see their role as reinforcing these rules. This effort to promote clearer rules for the international order, while an admirable effort, is also problematic in that it fails to appreciate what rules can and cannot do (Lang and Beattie 2008). The idea that international law is a set of rules rather than an authoritative law reflects, to some extent, a limited view of international law. Indeed, Jan Klabbers (2009) has argued that the power of IR theory has overwhelmed the impact that ILT might make in the study of international affairs. This view of IR theory's appropriation of ILT through the liberal and constructivist frameworks may well have some merit. Many theorists working on ILT, however, are considered to be important contributors to IPT. This may be because the study of law assumes the importance of ethics, even for those writing from within a positivist framework. In other words, if IR theory has unfairly incorporated ILT, IPT provides a way for those interested in law, its politics and history, to explore the ways in which the rules of the international order play a central role in its processes. One area of recent exploration that links rules, laws and politics is the idea of global constitutionalism (Weiner et al. 2012).

Moral and ethical philosophy

The last strand that contributes to IPT is that of moral philosophy. This literature comes in two modes, which I will call 'global ethics' and 'international ethics'. The former employs an analytical philosophical method, or what Hutchings (2010) calls a 'rationalist' method. These scholars focus on the individual person as a rights-bearing individual with responsibilities that cross boundaries and national traditions. International ethics, on the other hand, tends to focus on the morality, responsibilities and rights of states as members of an international society, along with the way in which the state tends to constrict and confine the options and obligations of individuals in the modern international order. Global ethicists tend to see the world as a single large community in which all individuals have equal standing, while international ethicists tend to see the world as divided up into specific communities in which rights may differ depending on the circumstances of those communities.

Global ethicists focus on a wide range of issues, from global distributive justice to the just war tradition. Those who focus on global distributive justice – literature explored in more detail in Chapter 4 – draw on either a Rawlsian institutional approach or a utilitarian approach. The former is led by scholars such as Thomas Pogge (1989, 2008), Henry Shue and Charles Beitz (1999 [1979]). Many of these scholars draw on the work of John

Rawls (1999) for inspiration, although not on Rawls' own efforts to construct a theory of justice at the global level. Instead, they argue that Rawls failed to develop his detailed account fully enough. Utilitarian accounts are exemplified in the work of Peter Singer (2002, 2009), who has made a strong case for individual responsibilities for alleviating global poverty.

In the just war tradition, theorists such as David Rodin (2002) and Jeff McMahan (2009) have argued strongly for an individualist-based approach to questions of war. They have claimed that only a liberal, justice-based account can truly capture the legitimacy of war. Cécile Fabre (2012) has suggested that there can be such a thing as 'cosmopolitan war', one that draws on the application of cosmopolitan liberalism to the practices of conflict and violence. These and other theorists of war and violence are addressed more fully in Chapter 5.

In contrast, those who write from an international ethics perspective come from two different approaches. The first is an older tradition, one that stretches back into antiquity and could be called the 'morality of statecraft'. It focuses on the responsibilities of leaders to their communities, and points to how those responsibilities result in a different set of standards than those that apply to individual citizens. Reinhold Niebuhr's *Moral Man and Immoral Society* (1934) proposes that groups – from states to classes – could not be held to the same standards as individuals, for group dynamics create different dilemmas and tensions than daily life for the individual person.

One strand of this literature that is not so apologetic towards great power leaders, yet still grapples with the question of responsibility of great powers, has focused on the ethics of foreign policy. This has been primarily addressed to American foreign policy (Harbour 1999), although the 'ethical diplomacy' of the British New Labour government of the late 1990s also prompted analyses of British foreign policy in terms of ethics (Chandler and Heins 2007; Smith and Light 2001). Some of this literature seeks to critique the pretensions of being able to talk about ethics in foreign policy, while others seek to promote possible ethical modes of engagement for great powers.

A second approach to international ethics can best be described as the society of states or international society. Molly Cochran (2009) has argued that this tradition provides what she calls a 'middle ground ethics', which can provide a way of linking the practices of international affairs with normative theory (see also Navari 2013). Andrew Linklater and Hidemi Suganami (2006) present an account of international society that reflects their orientation in critical theory.

A third approach is the quasi-Hegelian tradition found in the work of theorists such as Mervyn Frost. Frost (1996, 2009) proposed a constitutive theory of international ethics, one in which the world is constituted by our overlapping ties to each other and, at the international level, to a state-based system that is devoted to peace and justice. This is not the international lawyer's positivist world, but a Hegelian world in which the nation-state provides an ethical ideal that, if followed by all persons in all contexts, would create a world in which peaceful interactions would be the norm. Kim Hutchings (1999) has argued for a theory of IPT that also draws broadly on Hegel, but focuses more on his ethical theory of recognition.

A wide range of works have tried to put these different ethical traditions into dialogue with each other (Coicaud and Warner 2001; Commers et al. 2008; Hayden 2009b; Rosenthal and Barry 2009; Rosenthal and Kapstein 2009; Seckinelgin and Shinoda 2001; Valls 2000). Those that have arisen from the Ethikon Institute (www.ethikon.org) are an attempt to put different religious and philosophical traditions in dialogue and have been influential in shaping the debate about the potential for ethics in a multi-cultural world (Nardin 1996; Nardin and Mapel 1992). All these attempts to think through the ethical dimensions of IR have been fundamental in clarifying how authority, rights, rules and responsibilities apply to states and individuals as moral agents.

Chapter outline

Each chapter is organized around a concept that elucidates its core ideas through an overview of key theorists. This method or approach of taking different theorists to explore global issues outside their historical and/or national context presents problems of interpretation, ones that have been subject to debate in the history of political thought. My approach mirrors that of a leading political theorist who has contributed to international political theory in important ways, William Connolly, who describes his approach as follows:

> I read and teach classic political thinkers as if they were interesting strangers who have moved in next door (or down the hall). One engages them, thinks about the conversation for a while, and then returns to continue it at a more refined level. Commentaries on the particular circumstances in which a thinker wrote or, more pertinently, the contexts which give specific meaning to the concepts deployed, are helpful to political thinking of this sort. But they are also insufficient to it. World historical thinkers need not be confined to the context of their thought because, first, thought itself is a creative response to particular conditions irreducible to particular conditions of existence, second, highly

creative thinkers transcend and transfigure understandings of their own time and, third, those in other times and places who use these texts as a prod to their own thought often come to them with questions, interests, and anxieties divergent from those which governed the composition of the texts. Thinking is often advanced by lifting theories out of contexts in which they were created. (Connolly 1993 [1988]: vii–viii)

As the chapters that follow make evident, I read political theorists in precisely this way. The chapters include different theorists whose works do not necessarily answer the questions posed at the outset of each chapter, but rather provide new ways to see and understand international political life.

Chapter 1 examines the concept of authority. Most accounts of authority in international affairs rely on Thomas Hobbes, the 17th-century author of *Leviathan*. Hobbes argued that without the security of an all-powerful authority to reinforce rules and protect rights, there could be no political order. Many IR theorists see in Hobbes everything that is missing from the international realm; without a leviathan-like figure, the international realm is anarchic. This chapter addresses Hobbes but also compares him to John Locke, another 17th-century thinker. Locke's core idea on authority is that it is given conditionally, and can be taken back if the authority structure fails to live up to its obligations. This means that agents with differing interests can come together to create an authoritative structure, but it will always be subject to their approval and, potentially, resistance. Both Hobbes and Locke are helpful thinkers to explore because they were writing at a time when the traditional markers of political and religious authority were being challenged, leaving a conceptual vacuum in terms of what constitutes a just authority structure. The chapter highlights other key theorists, but focuses primarily on the debate between these two. The practical issue explored in this chapter is the authority of the UN in the current international order.

Chapter 2 examines the topic of rules. All political and social life is rule governed, although some types of rules are closer to social norms, while others are more law-like. In international affairs, both kinds of rules play key roles in political life, so understanding the varying roles of rules at the global level is the focus of this chapter. The chapter uses the moral philosophy of one of the most famous philosophers of the modern era, Immanuel Kant. Kant represents what has come to be called a 'deontological' approach to ethics, the view that morality is about obeying rationally derived rules, no matter what the outcome. Kant has become known in IR theory for proposing a solution for war; make all states democratic (or what he called 'republican') and they will not go to war with each other. They will form a rule-governed international order that will eventually move towards a cosmopolitan one in which all persons will live under a single rule of law. Kant's theories point to the importance of constitutionalism as the framework from within which rules need to arise; if there is no larger political structure, rules become nothing more than regulations without any political force. The practical issue that is the subject of this chapter is the idea of the responsibility to protect, which began as a norm, moved to something like a rule, but does not yet seem to be a law. The critical commentary surrounding this effort to shift the discourse around humanitarian intervention demonstrates the importance of understanding clearly the relationship between rules and laws.

Chapter 3 examines the twin concepts of rights and responsibilities at the global level. This chapter uses another famous philosopher, John Stuart Mill. Mill is considered one of the founders of liberal political thought, especially because of his famous short book, *On Liberty*. The chapter draws on this and other works by Mill to explore whether or not the invocation of rights at the global level should also be accompanied by responsibilities. Much of the rights literature leaves out the fundamental relational context of rights claims, as will be demonstrated in reviewing certain practices of the UN rights regime. The chapter also explores the extent to which rights are inherently international rather than somehow derivative of a liberal individual who has no grounding in the global political order.

Chapter 4 explores the problem of wealth. The problem of wealth and how to distribute it fairly and justly has long been an issue in the modern world. Global poverty has become an issue in recent years, as theorists have pointed out that the existence of vast disparities of wealth are not the result of national economic decisions but arise from the global distribution of resources. This chapter examines this problem by focusing on the two representatives of modern political economy, Adam Smith and Karl Marx. The fathers of capitalism and Marxism were responding to national and international economic issues, so their theories are directly relevant for understanding how an international economic order should be shaped. More importantly, both were fundamentally concerned with ethics, with Smith being a professor of moral philosophy and Marx drawing on classical philosophy to construct his theory. The chapter examines the global financial and economic crises that began in 2008 as a way to flesh out these problems in more detail.

Chapter 5 turns to the problem of political violence, which stretches from war to terrorism. Political violence has long been the core problem of IR, and has too often been absent from theories of politics, where, for many, it is seen as outside the realm of the political. The chapter surveys the just war tradition and international legal rules on violence, exploring how these ideas have shaped our understandings of when violence can be justified. The chapter focuses on one central figure in the development of the just war tradition, the 17th-century Dutch thinker Hugo Grotius. Grotius played a key role in reviving the just war tradition and turning it from a largely theological debate to one that was more widely accessible. He is considered the 'father' of international law and was a key theorist of the just war tradition. Rather than explore traditional war, this chapter examines if these theorists of traditional warfare can speak to more recent developments in the use of military force.

Chapter 6 explores the theme of nature, a concept that has a wide range of meanings in IR. Many arguments about human rights rely on an unarticulated idea of 'human nature' as providing a foundation for the protection of all persons. What is 'natural' has also served as an important justification for various positions in debates about reproductive rights, sexuality and animal rights. This chapter teases out the various meanings of this term and tries to put them into dialogue with one of the most important political theorists of all time, Aristotle. Aristotle argued that political life relies heavily on an account of a particular kind of natural order, one that includes the world along with the human person. He proposed that politics is 'natural', although his conception of nature is much different from modern usages of this term. Aristotle's use of nature led to various forms of inclusion and exclusion from the political sphere. His use also connected to his understandings of knowledge and science. The chapter turns to the politics of climate change and its impact on communities around the world as a problem that Aristotle may help us reconsider.

Chapter 7 turns to the issue of belief, particularly contrasting belief systems that are often at the core of objections to any form of shared normative order at the global level. These competing belief systems include religious and cultural sources of belief. The chapter explores these systems in terms of how they shape communal and personal identities through an engagement with the work of the 19th-century philosopher G.W.F. Hegel. Hegel's work provides the foundation for what is sometimes called a 'theory of recognition', an alternative to a focus on liberal rights and responsibilities as a way to see how a dialectical process allows individuals to engage with each other. The chapter also explores the idea of pluralism, which is a traditional liberal response to difference and disagreement. Rather than the standard liberal form of pluralism, however, the book returns to the idea of belief by looking at the work of the philosopher William James, whose writings on religion and pluralism provide an alternative way to see the dilemmas of the modern world.

The Conclusion provides a brief overview of the arguments made and points the reader to possible ways to think critically about IPT. This textbook introduces readers to a wide range of issues that arise at the global level. As noted above, though, it does not give final answers to these questions but invites readers into a conversation about them. It presents a work in progress, for no political theory is ever finished, but is always in the process of making and remaking in response to ideas and events in the international realm.

Further reading

David Boucher. 1998. *Political Theories of International Relations*. Oxford: Oxford University Press.
   Explores how IR theories, while drawing in some simplistic ways on the history of political thought, often fail to fully appreciate the historical trajectories of ideas. His versatility with IR theory and political theory makes this an excellent introduction to IPT.
Chris Brown. 2002. *Sovereignty, Rights and Justice: International Political Theory Today*. Cambridge: Polity Press.
   Uses the three concepts of sovereignty, rights and justice to frame the complexities of normative thought at the global level. Brown, one of the founders of the idea of IPT, does not seek to transgress the idea of sovereignty as some theorists of global theory do, but instead proposes a way to advance normative goals in the complicated international political order.
Chris Brown, Terry Nardin and Nicholas Rengger, eds, 2002. *International Relations in Political Thought: Texts from the Ancient Greeks to the First World War*. Cambridge: Cambridge University Press.
   This edited collection from a diverse range of thinkers and traditions is essential for any student of IPT. Organized chronologically, it provides short introductions to each era, which locate the thinkers and debates in which they were engaged.
Kimberly Hutchings. 1999. *International Political Theory: Rethinking Ethics in a Global Age*. London: Sage.
   Another excellent introduction to the field of IPT, which precedes Brown's. Hutchings addresses some of the core dilemmas of IR, and brings to bear her longstanding interests in feminist thought, to develop an intriguing argument that uses the political theorist Hegel to understand how states can continue to exist parallel with global normative agendas and institutions.
Edward Keene. 2005. *International Political Thought: An Historical Introduction*. Cambridge: Polity Press.
   Historical introduction to IPT. Not simply a review of thinkers, but a narrative account that demonstrates how events such as the European interaction with the Islamic world shape not only international affairs today but political thought as it relates to matters of war and peace. Its scope and versatility in dealing with a range of complex issues and thinkers make this one of the best historical introductions to the field.

Chapter 1

Authority

The Introduction began with a discussion of the UNHRC passing a resolution in 2011 calling for the UN High Commissioner of Human Rights to investigate the human rights records of all member states. The fact that the particular form of discrimination being investigated concerns sexual orientation has made this resolution more controversial than others. Indeed, any resolution that requests such an investigation could be deemed controversial, for it infringes on the prerogatives of sovereignty, the ability of nation-states to determine their own policies concerning the rights of their citizens. On what basis can an organ of the UN claim such authority?

A realist might argue that any organ of the UN only has the authority that states give to it. The fact that the UN as a whole was created by a treaty and member states do not sacrifice their sovereignty by being a member means its authority is limited by those agents (nation-states) that have consented to belong to it. Others argue, though, that the UN's authority has greatly increased over the years. Even more than the UNHRC, the actions of the UN Security Council (UNSC) and the Secretary-General have made the UN a much more authoritative actor in the international system. For instance, while it is true that states retain their sovereignty, they are bound by UNSC resolutions. Other actions of the UNHRC have also become more intrusive, such as fact-finding missions that theoretically could lead to prosecutions before the International Criminal Court (ICC). Also, the bureaucracy of the Secretary-General's office has been so active that it has, at times, challenged the sovereignty of certain states.

The problem of authority can also be found outside the UN system. For instance, what authority allows some to determine which states can have nuclear weapons? What authority allows credit rating agencies to determine the trustworthiness of national economic structures? What authority gives NGOs the right to determine when a case of political conflict is genocide? Despite all these important and interesting cases, authority has not been the focus of recent attention within IPT. This chapter explores the idea of authority – historically and theoretically. It starts with a debate between two of the most important theorists of authority, Thomas Hobbes and John Locke, both of whom wrote during the religious and political conflicts of 17th-century England. Their efforts to understand the basis of authority produced two very different proposals, even though they started from very similar points of departure. Drawing on the insights of these two theorists, the chapter then turns to more recent theories of authority, in domestic political theory and IPT, using the idea of cosmopolitanism as a way to explore global authority. It concludes by turning to the UN, particularly the Security Council, as an institution of great importance in the current international order, but one whose authority is constantly under attack from various parties in the international order.

Two versions of authority

In the modern world, the first problem with authority is that it is both difficult to understand yet necessary. Hannah Arendt (2006 [1963]) captured this idea in her influential essay, 'What is Authority?' Arendt argued that we can no longer understand authority because its origins are rooted in Roman political thought, particularly in the way in which the Romans linked politics to religion. For the Romans, authority meant to bind oneself to the past, to traditions and standards that find their justification in their link to history rather than in some utilitarian justification. Arendt's argument is that when the modern world tries to use the word 'authority', this connection to the past and to religious faith creates a stumbling block, one that renders the meaning of authority problematic in the modern world. But at the same time, our shared political lives are subject to authority all the time, in ways that we both do and do not recognize. A contemporary of Arendt's, Yves Simon (1980 [1963] argued that a political system or indeed any large-scale activity requires authority to function so that diverse interests can be coordinated and made to work together. That is, we could not make group decisions or conduct group activities without a coordinating structure that links individuals together in some common purpose.

A second problem with authority is that obedience to it seems to violate our freedom to determine our own life plans. An authority structure is designed to keep us safe, for instance, but it results in restrictions that go beyond our safety; an obvious example would be counterterrorism legislation and the powers of security services to intrude upon our lives. There are less obvious ways in which authorities limit freedom. An authority can tell us where we can study, live and work. This happens domestically through various laws concerning property ownership and labour relations. It also impacts education, as we are told where our children can go to primary and secondary school. It happens internationally through laws governing immigration and citizenship laws. Of course, we need some authority to provide guidance on how to organize such complex processes as security, housing, labour and citizenship. More often than not, however, authorities step over those boundaries and begin to interfere in areas of our lives where we would prefer they have no role.

One way to think about the problem of authority is to recognize that the ability to act as we wish is connected to our ability to reason. Hence, an even deeper problem is that an authority can override our *reasons* for acting in certain ways. As one political theorist notes:

> To be subjected to authority, it is argued, is incompatible with reason, for reason requires that one should always act on the balance of reasons of which one is aware. It is of the nature of authority that it requires submission even when one thinks that what is required is against reason. (Raz 1990: 3)

Authority, then, is somehow related to our ability to not only act but to think.

Some philosophers have sought to address this problem by clarifying two distinct types of authority, what they call 'practical' and 'theoretical' authority. Practical authority means being 'in authority', or the fact of authority arising from an agreed upon convention or procedure being followed (such as the social contract, described in more detail below). Theoretical authority comes from the expertise or knowledge of the authority figure, what some might call being 'an authority' (Christiano 2013). For example, the Ancient Greek philosopher Plato in *The Republic* presented a theoretical form of political authority, that is, the philosopher king. Most modern democratic theory assumes practical authority, that is, it is the procedure by which an individual comes to office that gives them authority.

Richard Friedman (1990 [1973]) uses this distinction to argue for privileging the concept of practical authority over theoretical authority in the political realm. In an influential essay, Friedman discusses how conforming to authority means the suspension of private judgement. At the same time, he suggests that authority does not mean the imposition of brute coercion to force compliance. Rather, as Arendt (2006 [1963]) describes it, authority is located somewhere between brute force and persuasion through reason; while it has elements of both, it cannot be reduced to either. Friedman surveys a wide range of theoretical insights about authority, but concludes with a discussion of the problem of theoretical authority in a world fraught by stark moral disagreement. He argues that in such a world, there arises an epistemological problem with theoretical authority; that is, claims to be authoritative in various realms require an agreed upon convention about what constitutes right knowledge. Borrowing from Alasdair MacIntyre's (1981) thesis about the incommensurability of various moral frameworks,

Friedman concludes that in a world where there is no shared moral background, there can be no moral authority. Instead:

> someone who is 'in authority' is not necessarily an authority on anything; his decisions do not have to be presented as authoritative expressions, deliverances, or interpretations of logically prior beliefs. On the contrary, it is precisely the key point about the concept of 'in authority' to be disassociated from any background of shared beliefs. It is, then, in those circumstances in which a society has lost the sense of a common framework of substantive moral beliefs and has grown sceptical of the idea of a homogenous moral community, that the notion of being 'in authority' may present itself as the appropriate form of authority for defining the general rules all men must conform to. (Friedman 1990 [1973]: 84)

For Friedman, then, practical authority is far more important than theoretical authority, a position he draws in part from the Hobbesian idea that the sovereign makes not only the rules by which individuals with contending moral and political visions of the world can live in peace but also the very nature of right and wrong.

Indeed, this condition seems to define the current international order. Some have argued that there exists a basic shared moral core that stretches across global politics (Harbour 1995; Nardin 2002). This argument, while persuasive at the level of more general values, begins to unravel when it comes to more specific political issues. For instance, when it comes to the use of military force, ongoing debates about the definitions of terrorism and aggression suggest that there remains stark moral, legal and political disagreement about these key elements of international affairs. To return to the problem identified at the beginning of this book, there certainly does not seem to be any global consensus on the question of whether or not homosexuality should be protected through rights legislation. Indeed, some have argued that homosexuality is a distortion of what it means to be human, so it cannot be a question of human rights. For others, discrimination of any kind can never be justified, so sexual orientation should be protected through robust human rights structures. If there is a lack of consensus on these basic ideas, then is Friedman correct? Do we simply need to acquiesce to a political authority that will construct the international normative order in such a way that moral and political disagreement will become irrelevant?

In response to Friedman's call for practical authority triumphing over theoretical authority, Richard Flathman has argued that there must be some background of shared beliefs for those in authority to function properly; that is, there needs to be a level of theoretical authority in matters of politics and ethics for practical authority to make any sense. Flathman (1980) introduces two concepts of authority, what he calls the substantive-purposive (SP) and the formal-procedural (FP). This distinction parallels the theoretical/practical distinction, but is not exactly the same. SP authority relies on an overarching goal or purpose guiding it, while FP authority is based primarily on following rules, with no concern for the purpose for which such rules are being followed. Flathman does not accept that there is a complete suspension of reason when one conforms to authority; rather, he argues that there must be some basic agreement on the procedures that create authority, for example elections. This is central for Flathman's (1980: 175–91) arguments, which rely in part on ensuring that individuals subject to authority retain some level of agency, or the ability to determine their actions. As one can imagine, there might well be a direct conflict between the claim that individuals have agency and that they are subject to authority.

The solution to this dilemma for Flathman is that there is a need for some agreement among those who subscribe to authority, an agreement not just that this individual or institution should govern us, but that this individual or institution must somehow reflect out shared beliefs and values about the political realm, beliefs and values that he calls 'authoritative'. These beliefs and values are not the teleological or SP kinds of values that would direct a community towards a specific goal. Instead, these values form a kind of background set of conditions that make authority possible. These conditions include certain broadly defined procedural elements, but they also include values that may reflect principles that define certain realms of life, certain distinctions between people and the rest of the world, or certain kinds of distinctions concerning social practices. In other words, authoritative values are partly procedural, but not entirely so. That is, rather than abandoning theoretical authority, Flathman is proposing a world in which theoretical authority can provide a set of background conditions by which practical authority can effectively function, and on which individuals can place their trust in order to be sure that they do not have to simply follow authority without any reasons for so doing. These background conditions include the procedural ones by which an authority is chosen, but, more importantly for our purposes, norms that, in part, constitute what a community values.

The problem of authority, in other words, might be solved if there were a set of authoritative values that underlay our political lives. What happens, however, when authoritative values begin to unwind? Seventeenth-century Great Britain was just such a time. The debates about authority taking place at this time in history were not simply about politics; religious and scientific authorities were also being subject to contestation. The conflicts that resulted from these debates were ultimately about authority relations, about who could control both thoughts and actions. While such conflicts exist in one form or another in every society, the issues taking place when Hobbes and Locke were writing their works can be traced to Henry VIII's (1491–1547) decision to break with the Roman Catholic Church. When James VI (1566–1625) of Scotland became King of England in 1603, hence becoming James I, the conflicts intensified in part because of James's own ideas about kingship and authority. He believed that kings ruled by divine right, a position he articulated in both political treatises and various speeches to Parliament (Sommerville 1994). Charles I (1600–49), his son, adopted similar views, and his rule led to conflicts with Parliament, which became increasingly assertive under his reign. It was under Charles I that the English Civil War broke out, pitting supporters of the monarchy against parliamentarians.

The war, which lasted roughly from 1640 to 1652 (historians continue to debate the exact dates), resulted in the beheading of Charles and the creation of the Commonwealth, led by Oliver Cromwell, who ruled primarily through the military during the period that is sometimes called the Interregnum (1649–60). During this period, Puritans dismantled much of the established church, pushing for a much more simplified Christian Church, and were especially concerned to undermine the authority of bishops and even priests. After the collapse of Cromwell's rule, Charles's son Charles II (1630–85) returned the monarchy to prominence in the period called the Restoration. While the Church of England and Parliament were restored to their previous roles, ferment continued throughout the country. This erupted again on the ascension of James II (1633–1701), Charles's brother, to the throne in 1685. A Roman Catholic, James II created controversy because of his religion and his political style, which asserted the superiority of the king over all others. He was eventually toppled in what is called the Glorious Revolution, when William of Orange (1650–1702) came to power as William III on the basis of his marriage to James's daughter, Mary. Their rule, from 1689 to 1702, brought to a close a century of religious and political ferment (Ashcraft 1986).

The political realm was not the only place where conflicts over authority were taking place in the 17th century. Knowledge in a wide range of fields relied heavily on the authority of the Christian Church, the Bible and the philosophy of Aristotle. These authorities structured theoretical and practical knowledge across the wide range of human experience. The Renaissance saw advances in knowledge throughout Europe, although by encouraging a return to the classical world of Greece and Rome, certain thought patterns were reinforced rather than freed up. One of the most important intellectual changes that took place in the 17th century was the growth of the scientific method and empiricism, efforts to understand the world through experimentation rather than reliance on authority. Key figures in this effort were Francis Bacon and Isaac Newton. Bacon (1561–1626) was an English nobleman who served as a counsellor to James I and was an acquaintance of Thomas Hobbes. While his political career was not successful, his efforts to create a new scientific method radically altered the way in which the natural and physical world was seen. Newton (1642–1727), also English, generated new insights into mathematics and physics. A friend of Locke's, Newton's ideas about physics remained the orthodoxy until ideas about relativity became the norm in the early 20th century.

Thomas Hobbes and John Locke addressed very similar problems, although they were writing at different points in the English Civil War. Thomas Hobbes (1588–1679) confronted a world in which the old markers of certainty – church and monarch in particular – were being challenged. His life was shaped in many ways by those wars – as a supporter of monarchy, he served as a tutor to Charles II and was forced to live in exile in Paris for some time. Yet, political authority was not the only standard being challenged in Hobbes' time; the sources of knowledge were also under attack, especially the authority of tradition. Hobbes excoriates 'the schoolmen' for their reliance on the authority of Aristotle and church fathers in their philosophy. He concluded that only direct experience and science could lead to truth and he saw geometry as a master science, leading to an approach that focused on defining concepts in order to achieve certainty.

While Hobbes wrote widely on politics in Latin and English, his most well-known work is *Leviathan*, published in 1651. He sought to develop an argument that would explain why individuals should abdicate their rights to a powerful sovereign, or 'leviathan' as Hobbes called it. Hobbes argued that without the leviathan, society could not function. Not only would social and political norms be overridden, normal social intercourse and even language would not be possible – leading to the famous description of human existence as 'solitary, poor, nasty, brutish and short'.

While he emphasized the sovereign's absolute power and authority, it is important to remember that Hobbes' ideas of governance and authority are grounded in a liberal conception of the human person, that is, one that relies on the rights of individual persons (Strauss 1936). The nature of the human person, however, creates the need for a sovereign to whom those rights will be abdicated. Those individuals pursue power in order to protect themselves since they have an equal ability to kill each other (Hobbes 1968 [1651]: 183). This description of the human person leads Hobbes to propose a series of natural laws, the first two of which are the most important. First, every man seeks peace. Second, every man will defend himself (Hobbes 1968 [1651]: 190–3). The result of these natural laws is that man must submit to a sovereign authority that will ensure the protection of all.

That sovereign has authority over all members of the society, the result of a contract of sorts among individuals in a society. That contractual relationship leads members to create an authority to whom they owe their allegiance. That authority manifests itself in the ability of the sovereign to issue commands (see Box 1.1). Commands are orders expressive of the will of the sovereign and are authoritative for this reason. Laws derive their force from being commands of the sovereign, which Hobbes differentiates from counsels, which are orders to obey based on reasons for what would be good for the individual (Hobbes 1968 [1651]: 303). This distinction is central to Hobbes' conception of obligation. I am obliged to follow the dictates of the sovereign not because he gives me reasons to do so, but simply because he has ordered me to do so. If the sovereign is forced to justify his orders and debate with individuals, then his authority is weakened. This obligation to obey the sovereign is, ultimately, grounded in Hobbes' natural law arguments – obedience is necessary to protect us from each other, a point that arises from Hobbes' natural laws, particularly the first two. But, once the contract that creates the sovereign has been put in place and we have entrusted our welfare to the sovereign, we no longer need to have our obedience justified by reference to those reasons but simply because the sovereign wishes it to be that way.

BOX 1.1 The social contract tradition

Some argue that Hobbes and Locke are part of a social contract tradition, one that differed radically from the medieval world they inherited. The basic idea of the contract is that individuals agree to create political authority structures in order to protect themselves. This contractual tradition is sometimes traced back to Grotius and extends through thinkers such as Rousseau and Kant. It became less popular in the 19th and early 20th centuries as alternative theories emerged such as utilitarianism. As an idea, it remerged with the publication of John Rawls' *A Theory of Justice* in 1971. While all these thinkers share a few core ideas, their conceptions of the social contract and its function in creating a civil society are very different. Hobbes sees the social contract as a way to create external political order, while Locke sees the contract as a source of order and as a reflection of a divinely inspired natural law (Forsyth 1994). So, while the term 'social contract' is deployed in interpreting many different figures, it is important to keep in mind some of the variations in its meaning for different political theorists.

For more on the social contract tradition, see: Boucher and Kelly 1994.

Howard Warrender (1957) argued that the foundation for obligation in Hobbes was not in fact a contract but is based on divinely based natural law. Warrender's thesis is not widely accepted by Hobbes' scholars, but it does point to an important debate about the concept of authority. Can authority really be based on an implicit contract formed among members of a society, especially the kind of authority that Hobbes describes? Or does the decision to allow another person to rule over us require something more divinely based?

In part because he argued for the creation of such a strong authority structure, Hobbes has long been claimed by realists as part of their 'tradition'. Reading some of Hobbes' concerns about the perilous nature of life without a strong authority figure, one can hear echoes of realist concerns about the dangers of anarchy. At the same time, more recent work on Hobbes and IPT points to a more nuanced figure, one whose conceptions of authority could well respond to the problems of contract and knowledge that have been identified above (Prokhovnik and Slomp 2011). As noted in the Introduction, Hobbes has been a central figure in political theory and IR theory. But his answer to the problem of authority is not the only one, nor even the only one that arises from the conflicts of the 17th century.

John Locke (1632–1704) provides a different answer to these same questions, although one that begins from similar foundations as Hobbes. Locke also devoted a great deal of his writings to the question of knowledge, work for which he was more well known than for his political writings in his own day. Reading his work on knowledge alongside his work on politics points us towards some ways of understanding the problem of authority.

Locke worked on natural philosophy, which in the 17th century meant a combination of moral, political, scientific and religious studies. Locke was intensely concerned with religious issues and much of his political writing was in response to the debates that swirled about the English Civil War, debates which were primarily about religious worship and authority. Locke's writings addressed a wide range of issues. The work for which he was most famous in his own life was *An Essay Concerning Human Understanding* (1959 [1690]). Here, Locke argued that all our knowledge comes from what we experience through our senses, rather than from some mystical, preordained access to the world. In making this argument, Locke drew on his training in medicine and philosophy, and it became an important part of a philosophical theory that is today called 'empiricism'. Yet while he made this argument, Locke was also an advocate of a kind of natural law, the idea that there are rules and principles concerning our moral and political life that are not simply what governments legislate but are found in the nature of the human person. Our ability to access this natural law is complicated, however, if we take into account Locke's ideas about knowledge. Importantly, natural law is not the same as divine law, or the law given to humanity through specific religious injunctions, such as those found in the Bible. Locke and other natural law theorists kept these laws separate from natural law. At the same time, natural law originates in God, and, as Locke (1997 [1663–64]: 117) pointed out, 'all obligation leads back to God'.

The status of natural law in Locke's work is difficult to appreciate, especially because of the emphasis he placed on liberty and rationality in his political writings, found most clearly in his *Second Treatise on Government*. As the name implies, it is the second of two treatises that Locke published anonymously in 1689; the first was a refutation of Robert Filmer, a well-known writer who had argued in his work *Patriarcha* that politics, and especially authority, should be understood analogously to the role of a father in a family. Locke argued strenuously against this position in the *First Treatise on Government*, and then developed his own account of the basis of government and authority in the *Second Treatise* (1988 [1690]).

It is important to remember that Locke developed his ideas about politics in the context of political and religious upheaval in England. As political authority was in a constant state of flux, Locke proposed ways of understanding what politics is like without authority and yet why it needs some authority. Locke's political theory is premised on the basic fact that 'all Men are naturally in, and that is, a State of perfect Freedom'. This further leads to them being in 'A State also of Equality, wherein all the Power and Jurisdiction is reciprocal, no one having more than another;' (Locke 1988 [1690]: 269). Importantly, this initial state of freedom is one of liberty, not licence; for underlying the original freedom of each person is the natural law that 'teaches all Mankind, who will but consult it, that being all equal and independent, no one ought to harm another in his Life, Health, Liberty, or Possessions' (Locke 1988 [1690]: 271).

This fundamental starting point means that any political structure, and especially any authority structure, must come about through individuals consenting to being governed. Unlike in Hobbes' work, the state of nature that necessitates the creation of government is not necessarily one of war, because of the underlying natural law, but it can certainly lead to conflict and violence when individuals violate the laws of nature. Because humans are indeed prone to violating that law of nature, Locke argues that they need to be governed through some structure. That structure looks like a constitution in the modern sense of the word, one in which legislators and executives create law and in which judges adjudicate where there are disputes. But, crucially, those in that society only grant to the authority the right to govern them based on the contract they have created with each other.

Thus Locke can be understood as providing the basis for a liberal political structure in which the consent of the governed is central for the creation of any authority. Locke privileged liberty as the foundation of politics. But, Locke saw what happens when political authority collapses, as it did during his lifetime. So, he needed a firmer basis for authority than a fictional social contract. That basis rests on natural law, which provides a set of values that all the participants in a society accept as the source of their obligation to authority. As noted in the discussion of Hobbes, some argued that there was a similar foundation in Hobbes' account of authority, although this is much less evident.

As we get to the international level, however, Locke's appeal to natural law becomes more complicated. Especially in an international system in which there are such divergent views on politics and morality, the foundations for natural law become more problematic. As noted above, natural law for Locke is not the same as divine law, but relies on a Christian belief system that had developed over 1,000 years (Waldron 2002; Zuckert 2002). Does this mean one needs to believe in God to accept Locke's formulations of authority? More importantly, in an international system with a diversity of faiths and philosophical views, is natural law inherently Christian?

One possible way around the problem of God and Locke's natural law theory can be found in his ideas about legislation. In a recent analysis of Locke's relevance for modern liberal theory, Alex Tuckness has argued that one way to understand Locke's ideas of politics is to privilege what Tuckness (2002) calls the 'legislative point of view'. Tuckness uses Locke's writings on toleration, for which he was also well known in his day and still is today, as a foundation for this position. Toleration demands that we take into account differing, sometimes strongly differing, moral and political positions when acting in the political realm. How is one to make the distinction between what can be tolerated and what cannot? Tuckness argues that Locke relied on natural law as providing a standard – primarily a standard of reasonableness – to be used when adjudicating between what should be accepted and not accepted in the political realm. Because natural law originates in a divine legislator – God – it has been created such that individuals who are rational should be able to enact it. In other words, a good legislator will not pass laws that are impossible to fulfil.

Tuckness (2002), however, argues that if we reason analogously from this idea about natural law, we do not necessarily need God as the ultimate legislator. What we need to do is to think 'like God', to create political principles that are reasonable and actionable and treat all persons fairly and justly. As a result, we can understand politics through natural law, but not a natural law that relies on a belief in God. The authoritative values that will then undergird our conception of authority can be drawn from a natural law that may or may not rely on a divine source.

Problem(s) of international or global authority

For scholars of IR, the idea of authority has generally been left to one side. The assumption that the international system is anarchic has informed a great deal of the scholarship in IR theory. This assumption could be traced back to realists like Hans Morgenthau, who used the concept of power as his starting point. By focusing on power rather than authority, Morgenthau (1948) reinforced the idea that states have no overarching authority structure beyond them and, instead, need to be understood in the ways they use power to advance their interests. Kenneth Waltz, building on Morgenthau's emphasis on power, presented the clearest statement of the centrality of anarchy in his work *Theory of International Politics* (1979). Waltz drew upon economics to posit that in a situation where there is no structured hierarchy, all the 'units' in a system will act in the same way. More importantly, all those units – or states in the international order – will need to ensure their survival first and foremost. Thus, for Waltz, the formal condition of anarchy results in a state of conflict at the global level.

Among liberal IR theorists, this assumption of anarchy has generally been accepted as true, but they do not think that this fact creates conflict. Instead, liberal IR theorists have argued that in a condition of anarchy, states will realize that it is in their interests to cooperate. One reason relies on the idea of relative versus absolute gains (Baldwin 1993). For a realist, states are interested in their status in relation to other states, or their relative power. Hence, they will act so as to increase their power in relation to other states, even if this means that, in the long term, their own power may be less than it could be otherwise. Liberal IR theorists, on the other hand, argue that if states sought to increase their absolute gains, that is, gain as much power as possible, they would see that cooperating and acting through institutions would be to the benefit of all of them. This would mean that fellow states will increase in power too, but this is worthwhile if the goal is everyone's power and gains increasing.

In terms of authority, this has led to two strands of thought among liberal IR theorists on the question of authority. For one group, the benefits of cooperation will lead to the creation of institutions that enable states to share the benefits and burdens of international life. Once these institutions are created, they have a staying power that reaches beyond their initial foundations, giving them legitimacy for much longer than they might have intended (Keohane 1984). These institutions come to have legitimacy and authority over time as they become more widely accepted by various actors in the system.

A second group of IR liberals have suggested that states will accept the authority of powerful states in the system as their leader. Rather than create new institutions, states will buy into a hierarchy in which some states undertake the responsibilities of leading. This hierarchy can be reinforced by the creation of a set of shared values among members of international society, or it can be based on the goods that such states provide. G. John Ikenberry (2006) has argued that the US provided such values in its position as leader during the Cold War and after, while David Lake (2009) has argued that the sheer power of the US and its role in bearing the burdens of defence spending and international economic governance have made it the hierarchic power in the system, a position other states have come to (grudgingly) accept.

Constructivist IR theorists have also weighed in on the debate about anarchy versus authority. Alexander Wendt (1991) famously argued that 'anarchy is what states make of it'. By this, Wendt meant that anarchy is a socially constructed term, which relies on a shared understanding of power, politics and international order. Wendt proposes that once this idea is understood, it is possible for states and other actors to change their behaviour. He goes further and suggests that the processes of globalization and the recognition of the social nature of our political life will eventually lead to the creation of a 'world state' (Wendt 2003). This more radical conclusion is not shared by all constructivists, but it does demonstrate how the logic of a constructivist theory of IR can result in a very different understanding of authority.

Other constructivists do not go as far as Wendt in their analyses. Instead, a number of these theorists have explored how international organizations become more legitimate and authoritative through bureaucratic or political practices. Drawing on the ideas of legitimacy found in Max Weber's work, Michael Barnett and Martha Finnemore (2004) have demonstrated how the bureaucratic procedures of various international organizations have given them an authority that stands outside the states that constitute them. Some have taken this focus on bureaucratic structures of authority even further, arguing that a wide range of actors in the international system – NGOs, corporations and regional institutions – have all taken on governance roles that give them authority (Avant et al. 2010). Ian Hurd (2007) has explored how the UN Security Council has come to be seen as authoritative through a legitimation process. This means its authority comes from the widespread acceptance of its practices by ensuring a voice for smaller states that may not be able to determine outcomes, but will accept a structure in which they have some role, no matter how small.

Critical and poststructural theorists are more sceptical about the concept of authority. Critical theorists have used the concept of hegemony rather than authority as their way to address these issues. A key concern of critical theorists is identifying how what we believe are legitimate authority structures are, in fact, shot through with power relations that need to be more clearly brought to life – an interesting overlap with realist theories. Relying on Antonio Gramsci, the Italian political theorist, these works argue that there is a hegemonic structure underlying politics that ends up exploiting the weak. Stephen Gill (1993, 2003), for instance, proposes power as a key variable to explore in understanding international affairs. Unlike realists, however, Gill sees power throughout the international system, particularly in the international economic system, and not just in the formal power that states possess.

One body of IR theory that has sought to more formally address the question of authority are those who write within the context of international society theory, or what is sometimes called the 'English School'. These theories begin with the assumption that states constitute an 'international society' of sorts, one that has a shared sense of norms and values that structure their interactions. These values arise from the practices in which states engage to make the world work, such as diplomacy and even war. Hedley Bull (1977), one of the founders of this approach to the study of international affairs, argued that there was an order that arose from anarchy, an order that had important authoritative functions underlying it. This idea has been expanded on by a wide range of scholars, particularly Andrew Hurrell (2007) and Ian Clark (2005, 2007). Both have argued that there exists a constitution of sorts at the global level, one that has legitimacy because the states in the system require it in order to structure their interactions with each other. This notion of a constitution as a potential organizing principle of international affairs is not the same as a single authority structure, for their idea of constitutionalism includes a wide range of practices and values. At the same time, it points to the existence of a set of authoritative values that do structure the way states interact with each other.

International legal theory has also grappled with the concept of authority. Chapter 2 will explain more fully the idea of laws and rules as key elements of the international order. Here, briefly, it is useful to emphasize how the tradition of international law makes certain assumptions about authority in the international order. Like IR theory, most international legal theorists accept that it is states that have this final authority. Indeed, international law emerged in the 19th century with a strong emphasis on states as the key agents in the international order, which may come together to form treaties and conventions but which remain the only authoritative powers in the international order. For international lawyers, the concept of 'sovereignty' has thus been central (as it has for IR theorists). Sovereignty, as it is used in international law, tends to locate final authority for political life in the state. Sovereignty, then, becomes synonymous with authority, but it prevents authority from transcending the state. While the idea of sovereignty as an organizing principle of international affairs has been subject to contestation, it is important to note that its centrality was and is fundamental to much of international law.

This more classical conception of international law came under challenge in the 20th century, especially with the rise of the human rights regime at the close of Second World War. We will return to questions of rights in Chapter 3, but it is important to note that the authority of sovereign states to decide how to treat their populations came under fundamental challenge when human rights norms became part of international conventions and institutions. No longer could states claim that their policies were outside the scrutiny of other states. Coupled with demands for humanitarian intervention, this move towards greater global attention to human rights has been a direct challenge to the traditional conception of sovereignty (Mills 1998).

Within international legal theory, however, one body of work has emerged that addresses the question of authority more directly. Like those writing within the international society tradition, this material has proposed the concept of 'global constitutionalism' as a way to show how authority works at the global level. This concept draws on the history of constitutional thought and transports those ideas to the global level. A few theorists have proposed that the 1945 foundational UN Charter could serve as a global constitution (Fassbender 2009); generally, though, most who have addressed this topic tend to argue that international affairs have become more rule governed and more institutionally integrated through various international organizations. These shifts in world politics have created a global constitutional-like order, one more akin to the unwritten British constitution than the American Constitution (Dunoff and Trachtman 2009; Klabbers et al. 2009).

Identifying such an order is, however, not without difficulty. For most who write within this genre, primarily international legal theorists, global constitutionalism is the increasingly law-governed aspect of international affairs as manifest in different types of international organizations. Some theorists focus on international judicial institutions, such as the International Court of Justice or the ICC, others point to the UNSC as providing evidence of a legalization of international politics, while still others look to institutions like the World Trade Organization as evincing a rule-creating institutional framework.

We might, however, turn away from a purely legal focus towards a political one. Just as constitutionalism includes not only an emphasis on the rule of law, but also a set of institutional limits on power, so the global constitutional order exhibits some of these same characteristics. For instance, constitutional theory includes an emphasis on checks and balances or balance of institutions; that is, a balance between different levels of government (a federal system, for instance) or a balance between different institutions (executive, judiciary and legislature). If we look to the institutional design of the international order, we can see that the relationship between institutions like the UNSC and the ICC manifests a kind of balance of institutional design that may not have been intended but certainly creates a kind of constitutional-like order. The 2008 decision by the European Court of Justice to overrule an attempt to implement a UNSC resolution concerning sanctions – the Kadi case – points to how different institutional actors interact in such a way that no single actor can govern the international system as a whole (Lang 2014). This balance of institutions reveals a proto-constitutional order at the global level.

One way to address authority at the global level is through the idea of 'cosmopolitanism'. Chris Brown (1992), one of the leading figures in IPT, highlighted the challenge of cosmopolitanism to international affairs in *International Relations Theory: New Normative Approaches*. Brown contrasts cosmopolitanism with communitarianism, arguing that these two ethical frameworks capture the different normative assumptions in IR theory. Cosmopolitanism is the idea that 'every person has global stature as the ultimate unit of moral concern and is therefore entitled to equal respect and consideration no matter what her citizenship status or other affiliations might be' (Brock 2009: 4). This core idea is sometimes divided into moral and political cosmopolitanism; moral cosmopolitanism is the idea that equal regard means all persons should be treated equally, while political cosmopolitanism is the idea that political institutions need to be created to form something like a world government in order to enforce this moral ideal. A wide range of theorists have developed and elaborated cosmopolitanism, a body of literature that has grown exponentially over the years (Beardsworth 2011; Brock 2009; Cabrera 2004; Caney 2005; Hayden 2005; Jones 1999).

The opposing idea, according to Brown (1992), is 'communitarianism'. As a political theory, communitarianism arose in opposition to liberalism. It countered the liberal assumption of the individual person as the focus of moral worth and presented the community as just as or more important than the individual. Ultimately, communitarians argued that the community is important because of the allegiances and shared beliefs that shape individuals, but their view is that the community needs to be given a kind of moral status. Some of these views arose from the philosophy of Hegel (Taylor

1979, 1989), some drew on religious traditions (MacIntyre 1981), and yet others from revised versions of nationalism (Miller 2007; Tamir 1993).

Brown (1992) suggests that communitarianism overlaps with realist IR theory. While some have argued that realism has no ethical foundation, others have found in realist thought a moral foundation in the sovereign state. This concern with the sovereign state is sometimes translated as a concern with 'national interest' or national security. For a communitarian, these concerns might be better understood as protecting the sovereign state so that it can create a community in which individuals can flourish. Michael Walzer's (1994) communitarian political theory has played a role in some of his writing on international affairs. Specifically, he has argued that states provide a 'thick' moral framework within which individuals can flourish, while the international political order provides only a 'thin' framework. His writing on just war, which begins from a very different tradition of thought, also touches on communitarian thought when he justifies the use of military force by states (Walzer 1977). Other IR theorists have developed communitarian arguments, specifically drawing on the work of Hegel. One such account comes from Mervyn Frost, whose constitutive IR theory argues that individuals flourish when their specific communities advance their interests, but, crucially, orient individuals towards the importance of global concerns. For Frost (1996), Hegel provides a way for individuals to be both communitarian and cosmopolitan in their regard for individuals throughout the world as mediated by the particular moral and political norms of their own community (see also Hutchings 1999).

While a few theorists have tried to bring the communitarian and cosmopolitan ideals together (Erskine 2008; Tan 2004), much of IPT can be placed on a spectrum that keeps these ideas distinct. What is interesting, and relevant for the purposes of this chapter, is how the question of authority has largely been evaded by those engaged in this debate. For cosmopolitan theorists, especially those who write from a moral cosmopolitan perspective, the concept of authority is not relevant. One way to see this is in debates about warfare. The classical just war tradition, which led to modern international humanitarian law, in many ways presumed that only a 'right authority' could wage war. This question became a heated one in the tradition during the medieval period, when conflicts between the papacy and monarchies over who should be able to authorize war led to a flourishing of the tradition. As the sovereign state system and international law developed, the question of authority receded, with most agreeing that only the nation-state was authorized to wage war.

But globalization and the end of the Cold War challenged this assumption. For some, these developments have meant that only the UN can authorize war, while others have retreated to the nation-state as the only legitimate authority. Some cosmopolitan theorists took these developments even further, arguing that there is no longer any need for authority. Cécile Fabre (2012), a leading cosmopolitan political philosopher, presents this argument most clearly. Fabre argues that if we accept cosmopolitan theoretical assumptions, assumptions that underlie important international norms such as human rights, the idea that a state – the institution that most often violates rights – should be the one to rectify rights through warfare is highly problematic. Especially as state sovereignty is becoming conditional on the basis of criteria concerning rights and support for democratic principles, states cannot be the only agents that can rightfully wage war (Fabre 2012). Fabre draws on classical and modern sources to argue that there is nothing illogical about individuals waging war, especially wars of self-defence (wars of punishment are more problematic on this account). Her claims rely on the fact that anyone can judge the justness of a cause, given that a capacity for judgement has a central place in her understanding of what constitutes a just war. Fabre concludes not simply that the state is not necessary for a just war, but that there is no need for a legitimate authority to wage war, emphasizing the centrality of the individual in a cosmopolitan world order; indeed, her challenge is not simply to the state, but to any institution, including the UN, that might be seen as such an institution

Meanwhile, some cosmopolitan theorists have argued that there are emerging forms of global authority we need to consider. Political cosmopolitanism locates specific practices and institutions that would lead to the creation of a world in which individuals would have shared citizenship rights. Some political cosmopolitans argue that the world is moving towards a more cosmopolitan order by examining changes in the international legal and political framework (Hayden 2005). Others have made more radical proposals for how to construct such a world. One of the most well known comes from Daniele Archibugi (2008), who argues for a cosmopolitan democracy. Archibugi recasts democratic theory so as to see how democracy is necessary and possible at the global level, suggesting a new way of understanding authority in the international realm.

Authority, then, has been approached by a number of theorists, albeit not often directly. Ideas about legitimacy, governance and order within this literature reveal a number of important dimensions of IR. Yet underlying these efforts is the core problem of balancing freedom and authority. Clearly, then, political authority cannot be based purely in power, as much of the IR theory seeks to do. Instead, for authority to truly work, it needs a foundation in something deeper, something more normative. As noted above, the possibility of grounding authority in the authoritative values of the natural law tradition is one possibility. To test out this idea, let's turn to the UN, particularly the Security Council.

The authority of the UN

The UN is an important authority structure in the international system. For some, it is seen as the only authority structure, especially when it comes to the use of military force. Yet, its authority is constantly being contested, by great powers who feel constrained by its judgements and by smaller powers who do not feel it is representative enough. What exactly is the foundation of its authority?

The authority of the UNSC seems grounded in something that combines necessity and values. As mentioned earlier, Hurd (2007) has sought to address the authority of the UNSC. In Hurd's account, however, the UNSC is best understood through the concept of legitimacy. Legitimacy is closely related to authority; we often speak of authorities being legitimate or not as a way to evaluate their claim to authority. This framing of the question, in Hurd's case, draws on the work of Max Weber, the late 19th-century and early 20th-century sociologist who developed a threefold account of what constitutes legitimate authority. For Weber (1994 [1919]), an authority either comes to be accepted through charisma, tradition or bureaucratic effectiveness. Hurd does not borrow directly Weber's threefold distinction to develop his account of legitimacy, but he does draw roughly on the idea of legitimacy that Weber proposed. This is premised on the fact that legitimacy does not rely on any normative evaluation, that is, to be legitimate means simply to be widely accepted. That wide acceptance may include conforming to certain types of values, but it is simply a judgement made on the basis of acceptance and not evaluation. This differs from other interpretations of Weber, which emphasize the importance of a level of acceptance with standards of justice and fairness (Coicaud 2002).

Hurd argues that the UNSC has attained legitimacy as an authority in the international order as the result of its founding and ability to include smaller powers in policy formation. Hurd is focused, in other words, on why states not given the same power as the five permanent members with veto power would accept a situation in which they are manifestly unequal. This framework, while helpful in demonstrating why small powers accept the legitimacy of the UNSC, does not necessarily explain why the great powers would accept it. Especially with the evidence of the US acting without UNSC authorization in the cases of Kosovo and Iraq, we need to have a stronger account of why any state would accept the limits on its powers that the UNSC imposes.

The ideas developed above, on the social contract tradition and the importance of authoritative values, might help here. The UNSC was created to privilege powerful states but also to create a world in which more than one power would be able to act in response to threats to peace and security. The basic premise of collective security, the idea that underlies the UNSC and the defunct League of Nations, is that states have a shared responsibility to govern. They have consented to join the international community and, in so consenting, have agreed to give some of their power over to a political structure that can keep peace. This consent does not simply rely on that initial decision, however; it requires some shared sense of what is right and justified in the international order when it comes to violence, which differs from Hurd's position. Natural law, as manifest in international law and the just war tradition, might provide that structure. One need only look at the responsibility to protect doctrine, first articulated by a Canadian government commission then approved by the UN General Assembly in 2005, for evidence of a movement towards a shared sense of what is right and wrong when it comes not only to war, but a much wider range of international issues, such as the use of force to protect human rights. This is not a natural law that relies on a Christian vision of the world, but one that relies on broadly shared standards concerning the use of force, human rights and international legal obligations.

This is not to say that all agree on the natural law underpinnings of the UNSC. Rather, it is to say that Locke's formulation of a liberal authority structure undergirded by natural law might be a viable justification for the UNSC's legitimacy. It suggests that for all its problems, the UNSC does conform to something like an authority that can allow for the freedom of individual agents to contest its authority if it fails to function in the way it was intended.

Clearly, states are not the only agents in the international order. While the UN as a whole was established as a treaty-based structure through the agreement of states, other aspects of the UN system take seriously the agency of individual human persons through its various human rights regimes. These will be explored in more detail in the chapters to follow, but one institution that is worth highlighting now is the UN Human Rights Council, mentioned in the Introduction as the body that passed the resolution concerning sexual orientation. The UNHRC is an intergovernmental body created by the UN General Assembly in 2006 in order to strengthen and support the protection of human rights around the world. The UNHRC replaced the Commission on Human Rights (Commission hereafter), a body that had been part of the UN since its founding in 1946. The Commission was a subsidiary body of the Economic and Social Council of the UN system, tasked with promoting human rights. At its founding, the Commission was faced with the issue of theoretical versus practical authority. Eleanor Roosevelt and others proposed that the Commission be composed of individual experts on human rights rather than representatives of specific governments. If this proposal had gone forward, the Commission would have been a primary source for the articulation and promotion of the kind of authoritative values that might have given the UN more authority. Instead, as described by Paul Gordon

Lauren (2007: 314), this proposal was knocked back by all the powerful and not so powerful states involved in the creation of the UN, including the US. Instead, members were to be representatives of their governments, following 'highly politicized agendas'.

When the UNHRC replaced the Commission, an attempt was made to redress this problem. Alongside the representatives of states, an Advisory Committee was created, composed of human rights experts, as had first been proposed by Roosevelt. The Committee is tasked with aiding the UNHRC through the promotion of human rights and investigation of various issues. A further attempt to create more theoretical authority has been the creation of specific fact-finding missions, such as the Goldstone Report on the Israeli invasion of the Gaza Strip in 2009. The idea here was not so much ongoing theoretical advice about human rights, but investigations of various problem areas and regional conflicts.

A second aspect of theoretical authority can be seen in the creation of the UNHRC. The biggest criticism of the Commission had been that various governments with poor human rights records were serving on the Commission and using it to deflect criticism of their own regimes. This resulted from a number of factors, including the election of members through slates from regions, the progressive increase in the number of states serving on the Commission and, during the Bush administration, the practical removal of the US from the work of the Commission (Lauren 2007). This included an increasing attention on Israel and its occupation of the West Bank, Gaza and East Jerusalem, which, while certainly raising important human rights questions that demanded attention from the UN system, seemed to be a bit of overkill by becoming the only permanent item on the Commission's agenda. This is a question of theoretical authority because it assumes that a state without a good human rights record would not be able to productively contribute to the evaluation of other state's human rights records.

The creation of the UNHRC sought to allay some of these problems. It introduced requirements that members have positive human rights records, they are elected in a universal and secret ballot, and there is a regular review of each country's human rights record. At the same time, attention has remained focused on Israel, as evidenced by the decision to keep it as a regular item on its agenda.

At one level, then, the UNHRC has the kind of practical authority that Friedman recommends as necessary in a world of conflicting value systems. Yet, as the constant debate about what role experts and expertise should play in the work of the Commission and UNHRC, the role of theoretical authority cannot be so easily divorced from the practical authority. In fact, one of the key reasons that the Commission was seen as so problematic was that it failed to have a set of authoritative values in place that it could use to create a foundation for the evaluation of other states. Instead of simply asserting its authority on the basis of being part of the UN system, the UNHRC needed to do things like include an Advisory Committee to strengthen its authority.

This brings us back to Locke, the social contract and natural law. The social contract concerning human rights might be described as the treaty regimes that almost all states have signed onto. In a way, the formal ascension to a treaty that is so much a part of international relations seems closer to the idea of social contract than what happens in domestic political society. One could argue that when the UN created the Commission and then the UNHRC, it gave member states and their citizens a contract about its role in the protection of their rights. Naturally, the protection of these rights cannot solely be the responsibility of this one institution and, in Chapter 3, I suggest various other institutions that can play this role. The point here is that there is a contract into which states have entered that rests on the protection of rights.

Finally, some have argued that the emergence of human rights as an international issue only makes sense in the context of natural law. C. Fred Alford (2010) has argued this, drawing on Thomas Aquinas and Locke as foundations for this natural law argument. Alford sees the progression of natural law from the theologically grounded Thomistic account to Locke's more secular (although not completely so) account as a foundation for the modern human rights regime. Admittedly, others are more sceptical of this foundational claim. David Boucher's (2009) systemic overview of natural law concludes that it simply cannot provide that basis for human rights. And theorists such as Andrew Vincent (2010) have argued that human rights only make sense in the context of political practices rather than foundations.

Acknowledging these sceptical accounts, though, does not necessarily undermine our turn to Locke. Locke's account of the social contract founded on a set of shared values is put in the context of natural law. But, as Tuckness (2002) reminded us, this natural law might be better understood as a kind of legislative orientation, one that should point us to the importance of creating rules that apply equally across all persons. Authority within the UN system is a contract among states and persons. But it is a contract that requires some form of rules or laws to truly function effectively. It is to this problem that we turn in Chapter 2.

Conclusion

This chapter provided an overview of a concept that remains underdeveloped in the literature on ethics and international affairs and international political theory. A number of theorists have put concepts such as legitimacy and sovereignty at the core of their works (Brown 2002). International relations theorists have long resisted discussing authority because of the power of the realist assumption concerning anarchy. But, as I have suggested here, if we look more widely in law, politics and ethics at the global level, we can find a number of interesting insights into the problems of authority and how confronting those problems gives us access to a deeper understanding of how and why international affairs can lead to conflict or cooperation.

Further, this chapter demonstrated, as will the following chapters, how turning to the history of political thought, in this case the differing positions of Hobbes and Locke, can provide us with insights into how international affairs can be seen differently through themes such as the social contract and natural law. While these are not normal concepts employed at the global level, they provide us with new ways to understand and evaluate institutions such as the UN Security Council and the UN Human Rights Council. By drawing on these theorists, and exploring the nature of Locke's answer to the problem of contested authority, I have not settled the matter by any means. Indeed, one might turn to a range of other figures in the tradition of political theory to arrive at different conclusions. My effort here has been to demonstrate how one might undertake such an analysis using figures from the past whose insights continue to resonant to this day.

Further reading

David Bosco. 2009. *Five to Rule them All: The UN Security Council and the Making of the Modern World*. Oxford: Oxford University Press.
Excellent history of the UNSC and how its formation played a crucial role in how we understand international affairs and global authority structures.

Bruce Cronin and Ian Hurd, eds. 2008. *The UN Security Council and the Politics of International Authority*. London: Routledge.
Includes some excellent papers exploring the nature of the UNSC through the lens of authority. Provides theoretical and empirical insights, giving a much fuller picture of how this institution may or may not be 'authoritative' at the global level.

Joseph Raz, ed. 1990. *Authority*. Oxford: Basil Blackwell.
Has some of the most important pieces from philosophers working on the question of authority. Includes the paper by Friedman mentioned in this chapter, along with responses and developments about the problem of authority in international affairs.

Roger Woolhouse. 2007. *Locke: A Biography*. Cambridge: Cambridge University Press.
Excellent biography, puts Locke's writings in the context of the events of his own life and those of the British Civil Wars in which he was enmeshed. Also reveals his international experience, in his travels to Europe and his role in the British colonial enterprise.

Chapter 2

Rules and Laws

In December 2001, the International Commission on Intervention and State Sovereignty (ICISS), supported by the Canadian government, issued *The Responsibility to Protect*, a report that sought to shift the discourse of international humanitarian action and international security away from debates on the right to intervene towards a discourse of 'responsibility' (ICISS 2001). It arose, at least in part, from the frustration of many that while a serious humanitarian disaster was developing in Kosovo, the UN Security Council would not authorize military action, which led NATO to launch an air war to halt the Yugoslav leadership's attacks on the Albanian/ Muslim community. The release of the document was, however, overshadowed by the American response to 9/11, although it has seen a return in international security debates, particularly those emanating from the UN.

The report attempts to reinterpret the rules to conform to new international security challenges, particularly those concerning humanitarian intervention. It begins with the principle of non-intervention, and then construes its task as being the definition of those circumstances when that 'rule' can be overridden, in other words, the creation of a rule for breaking the rules (ICISS 2001: 31–2). Its section on authority emphasizes that the UNSC must remain the only source of legitimate authority in the international system. Challenging or evading the UNSC will 'undermine the principle of a world order based on international law and universal norms' (ICISS 2001: 48). In 2004, a UN report, *A More Secure World: Our Shared Responsibility,* continued to insist that the current rules of the UN system simply needed to be better enforced rather than abandoned. This report resurrected collective security as a central principle of the international security order. The report's subtitle, 'our shared responsibility', suggests a possible move away from a rule-governed international security order. But, when considering the dangers of preventive military action, the report falls back on the UN Charter, stating boldly: 'We do not favour the rewriting or reinterpretation of Article 51 [states cannot use military force without Security Council authorization]' (UN 2004: 63).

The fact that the UN has had some difficulty integrating this report into its structures and legal frameworks points to the difficulties of making international law. There is no formal legislative body for international law making, which means it arises from a diverse set of sources. These sources, including state practice, treaties and even the opinions of international legal scholars, mean that international law lacks some of the characteristics of domestic law making, such as the fact that it arises from a representative legislature. At the same time, the responsibility to protect (R2P) has generated widespread enthusiasm among global civil society, particularly those concerned about human rights abuses. A website devoted to R2P provides information and context for how to promote the rules more widely (http://r2pcoalition.org).

One of the difficulties with R2P in the current international order is that it has become a focal point for those who want to push for interventions in situations of conflict and human rights abuses even though the idea does not have any clear legal status. So, for instance, when the UNSC invoked the idea in passing resolutions concerning Libya, it was not clear if this was an instance of obligating action or simply justifying action already decided on for other reasons. Aidan Hehir (2012), an expert on humanitarian intervention, has argued that one of the problems with R2P is that it lacks any foundation in international law. As such, it cannot be used in any productive way until it becomes part of the international legal order.

This chapter uses the debate surrounding R2P as one way to explore the relationship of rules and laws to each other and to the international order. The chapter first introduces the idea of rules in international relations, specifically the ways in which rules can be understood as either formal or informal. It then moves to a discussion of laws, examining the ideas of natural and positivist law as ways to understand international legal theory. It then turns to the political philosophy of Immanuel Kant as a way to understand the centrality of legislation as the best mode for law making in any context, while recognizing the lack of an institutional structure in the international order by which representative law making might take place. It concludes with some suggestions for how seeing international law as part of a global constitutional order might be one way to better understand how rules can become laws, returning to R2P as an example of how this might function.

Rules

Rules are purposefully created guidelines for the behaviour of individuals within a specific group. Rules can be of two types, formal or informal (Lang et al. 2006a). This distinction does not correspond exactly to any specific philosophical or legal theory; rather, it reveals itself through an examination of the force of rules in international politics over the past few centuries. Informal rules provide a means of conducting international politics by emphasizing prudence or attention to the particulars of political interactions. These rules assume that guidelines cannot be formulated in advance for every situation and that appeals to written texts cannot resolve every conflict. Formal rules make concrete the assumptions and norms of a community in texts and treaties that aspire to permanence and to which appeal can be made when there is disagreement; that is, formal rules are closer to laws, although there are certain kinds of formal regulations that are rules rather than laws.

One way to see the difference between formal and informal rules is to look at how international politics sometimes produces rules that guide the behaviour of states in their interactions but which are not codified into laws. The debate about the R2P speaks directly to this idea. For some, the R2P rules are informal guidelines for how states should behave. For others, the rules are more formal and actually oblige states to respond to humanitarian emergencies. Louise Arbour (2008), a former UN High Commissioner for Human Rights, argued that R2P is grounded in international law and, as such, is a formal rule that creates obligations for states. In response, Stephanie Carvin (2010) argued that this is clearly not a legal obligation, for it misunderstands the nature of law. William Bain (2010) also critiques Arbour, arguing that she conflates natural law ideas with existing international law. This debate suggests that what some consider to be formal rules, or laws, are perhaps better understood as a species of informal rules.

This is not to dismiss informal rules as vacuous, however. In some cases, an informal rule will lead to the creation of more formal rules and may even bind powerful actors. For instance, the ideological and geopolitical conflict between the US and the Soviet Union created its own set of rules, in large part a throwback to the more prudential assumptions that governed the early practice of the European states system. After the Korean War and Cuban Missile Crisis, leaders in both states came to realize that a modus operandi was needed for their survival and for the good of international order. The policy of détente provided a broadly understood, albeit informal, set of rules that allowed the great powers to interact at the level of summits and the management of certain conflicts. In an interesting evolution, however, what were seen as informal rules of interaction led to the strengthening of a formal set of rules. Human rights provisions, in agreements like the Helsinki agreement of 1975, were initially seen as window-dressing by some and yet came to have a powerful impact on the ability of the Soviet Union to control its empire. When Soviet leaders signed the Helsinki Accords in 1975 – with which they wanted to secure the borders of East European states – the rules concerning the protection of human rights became an important part of the dialogue. Western governments and NGOs, as well as opposition groups and individuals such as

Andrei Sakharov within the Soviet empire, continued to press upon these provisions, increasing the importance of rules that were once seen merely as pieces of paper but were slowly gaining not only in legitimacy but also actual influence (Gaddis 1992: 61).

After the end of the Cold War, it seemed as if the character of rules in the international system was increasingly of the formal sort. In addition to an increase in the rules on peacekeeping and peace enforcement that came with a succession of crises in the late 1980s and early 1990s, NGOs worked to revise and strengthen the rules on global civil society. These groups – Amnesty International, Human Rights Watch and others – sought to expose governments that failed to act upon the increasingly well-known rules about how to treat citizens. This 'diplomacy of conscience' practised especially through the media had important effects on governments as they forced violators to change behaviours and also convinced more powerful states to take up their case in more 'ethical' foreign policies (Clark 2001).

This ethical foreign policy agenda, however, led to an important strain on the rules. International law only allows the use of force if authorized by the Security Council (or in self-defence), which is a collective political institution that nevertheless gives particular member states scope for promoting their own interests. When Serb forces continued their aggressive policies in the primarily Albanian district of Kosovo, violating the human rights and self-determination aspirations of the majority population, North American and European states argued for the use of force to protect the Kosovars and punish the Serbs. But the refusal of the Chinese and Russians to authorize the use of force meant this was an 'illegal' but (possibly) 'ethical' intervention. This led many to ask whether or not the rules governing the use of force, especially the provision that any use of force must come from the Security Council, were in need of revision. Others, however, argued that overriding those rules would lead to more long-term chaos, even if it meant allowing violations of human rights to go unpunished. In a sense, Kosovo provides one of the starkest instances of a clash between the informal and formal rules. As noted above, the R2P doctrine, a set of rules designed to structure intervention, arose from this failure to act. The rules and laws, as they existed at that moment, failed to prompt any action and, as a result, a new set of rules was proposed.

One critique of using rules as a way to think about political life rather than law is the question of enforcement. Breaking the rules usually leads to sanctions being imposed, especially by the strong on the weak. Some argue that only in a legal system can any sort of punishment or enforcement take place. In domestic legal systems, punishments are imposed on those who do not follow the rules after a procedure that determines that the rules have been violated. The international realm is different because it lacks a clearly defined central authority to determine violations and impose sanctions. In the current international system, sanctions and punishments are not imposed by clearly defined authorities but by quasi-authoritative structures composed of the agents themselves (often the most powerful agents). Can agents not only interpret but also enforce rules that they themselves should be obeying? Does an 'international society' attain, by its very nature, rights and capacities to develop, interpret and enforce rules (Lang 2008)?

According to the compliance or constructivist approach, violations of the rules might lead to questions being raised about the identity of the agent as a member of a particular group. In international politics, the discourse of 'civilized' states is sometimes employed in this way. That is, when some states engage in policies that violate the core principles of the society, they are castigated as being outside the boundaries of normal states. American discourse about 'rogue' states is one example of this. But do judgements such as these lead to the enforcement of rules? Or, rather, are they examples of a moralistic discourse that does not create conformity with rules but enemies?

If there is no sanctioning authority, does the violation of rules have any consequences? Indeed, have rules any reality if their violation has no consequence? An internal consequence could be guilt or bad conscience. While for individual persons, such reactions might not lead to changes in the future, for states this may or may not be the case. Because states are composed of various individuals and corporate bodies (civic groups, legislatures, bureaucracies) that might react differently to the state's violation of the rules, the reactions of those component parts of the state might lead to changes in behaviour. In other words, a guilty conscience among members of one part of the state might be the most important consequence of violating the rules.

Finally, the consequences of rule violation for the entire system or society must be considered. The violation of some rules, perhaps not constitutive ones, will force changes in societal and political relations among agents. When core rules or constitutive rules are violated, however, this may cause the entire system to collapse. Such collapse would, undoubtedly, be the worst possible outcome for a rule-governed system. One might ask, however, whether or not the need to live in rule-governed systems means that the collapse of one system will lead to near automatic creation of a new system of rules, one that either reflects the interests of the most powerful, or, hopefully, a more fair and just set of rules. This said, history tells us that such collapses do occur, and that they are often followed by determined efforts to develop new and 'better' rules and rule-bearing institutions. The 20th-century's great wars and subsequent efforts to reconstitute the international order provide telling examples. They also beg the question whether profound changes in rules and institutions can only be instigated after upheavals, or whether they can be achieved gradually and peaceably.

As the preceding discussion suggests, rules are essential to political life. But simply asserting the need for rules does not necessarily result in a more peaceful or orderly society. One of the ways in which rules translate themselves into international affairs is through international law, as has been hinted at above. But the way in which international law is made means it is very different from domestic law. The next sections turn to two different traditions of legal theory, both of which are found in international legal debates. The natural law tradition and positivist law are key ways in which rules become more binding and legitimate. In these sections, the benefits of IPT become evident, for only through understanding the moral and political foundations of these traditions do they make sense.

Natural law

Natural law refers to the idea of law that exists prior to any formal law-making process. It is meant to be the source or foundation of laws that are made by people. It is an immutable moral code that is universal for all peoples across all times and places. It is not particular to any religious or moral tradition, but many traditions integrate it into their teachings.

Baldly stated as such, one can immediately imagine criticisms of this idea. How do we know such a law? How can such a law encompass the plurality of moral and religious traditions that constitute the human condition? Does this law derive from a shared human nature? Or, is it divinely inspired? Clearly, natural law is not as simple as it seems. Yet it continues to provide an important source for thinking about not only domestic legal traditions but also transnational and international law.

Natural law finds its origins in the classical world of Greece and Rome. The Ancient Greek playwright Sophocles provides one of the most famous examples of natural law in his play *Antigone*. The story takes place in the city of Thebes and revolves around the conflict between Antigone, a young princess, and her father King Creon. Antigone's brother has died after seeking to foment rebellion against the king, and so, according to the laws of the land, he does not deserve to be buried with the proper religious rites but is to be left out in the plains to rot and be eaten by animals. As such, he will not be allowed to enter the afterworld and will become a ghost who can never rest. Antigone, however, argues that every person deserves a decent burial so that they may die in peace. Antigone buries her brother herself and is then arrested. She openly challenges Creon, but is executed at the end of the play for her refusal to follow the law of the land. Antigone's complaint against Creon is a classic example of the conflict between law and morality. According to the law as promulgated in Thebes, Antigone has no case; her brother was a traitor and thus does not deserve a burial. But Antigone appeals to a 'higher law', a law that she argues is true for all peoples.

Many religious traditions present instances of this same conflict. In the Judeo-Christian scriptures, the prophets insist that the kings of Ancient Israel obey the laws of God rather than their own dictates. In the story of King David, the prophet Nathan forces David to realize the error of his ways on more than one occasion, perhaps most famously in the scene in which the king sends one of his generals to the front line in order to take his wife for himself. Nathan asks: 'Why have you despised the word of the Lord to do what is evil in his sight?' (2 Samuel 12: 9). This prophetic role reminds even the anointed king of his duty to God.

Another key figure in the natural law tradition is the Greek philosopher Aristotle. I explore Aristotle and his ideas of nature in more detail in Chapter 6, but for now it is important to note that Aristotle's natural law is not the same as other versions. In *Politics*, for instance, Aristotle (1996: 13) says that 'the state is a creation of nature and man is by nature a political animal'. This is not a statement about law but that politics is something we do by our very nature. In fact, much of Aristotle's philosophy derives from the idea that the human condition can be understood through what is natural. Aristotle's biological and metaphysical works provide the foundations on which he develops his theories of ethics and politics. Importantly, however, most of us would not agree with his natural arguments – for instance, he argued that some people are slaves by nature and that women are less human than men by nature. As a result, he justifies slavery and also the exclusion of women from the public realm.

Founding politics and ethics in nature in this way is one important aspect of natural law, but it is not a fully developed idea of natural law. Cicero, the Roman orator and political philosopher, argued that the law must reflect the order of the universe, something similar to what Aristotle had argued, but more cosmic in scope. While not exactly a divine source for law, he famously presented an ordered universe in *The Republic*. This text, which was only uncovered in a relatively full version in the 19th century, is a fictitious dialogue between Scipio, a Roman general, and various individuals in the Roman aristocracy. Their discussion centres on the best political order and includes an extensive discussion of law. In the final scene, often called Scipio's Dream, Scipio describes to his interlocutors a dream in which he ascends to the heavens to see the ordered progress of the stars around him. This orderly structure of the universe is one that Cicero (1998), and many after him, believed was a model for human law. Just as the stars follow the same path across the skies, orderly and in perfect alignment with each other, so human laws ought to be similarly structured. The laws of nature should govern the entire world, both physical and human. C.S. Lewis (1994), the author and Christian apologist, argued in a series of lectures on Renaissance literature that Scipio's Dream presents the ordered universe that captured the natural law idea in the classical and medieval world.

Of course, human behaviour is not so easily ordered, a point Cicero well recognized. The tradition of natural law develops from this dilemma, one that sees how a perfect order ought to exist but recognizes how human beings, in pursuing their own interests, come into conflict with each other and with any kind of overarching order. Thomas Aquinas (1225–74), the Christian theologian and philosopher, sought to refine these classical ideas in his treatment of law. Aquinas drew heavily on Aristotle, seeking to combine him with the Christian scriptures. Aquinas's method of writing is not easy for us to access today, for he wrote in a question and answer form called a 'disputation'. This method means that it is sometimes difficult to appreciate Aquinas's actual views, for he presents a series of problems first, then a set of responses to those problems that rely on some authoritative sources, and finally a definitive answer to the problems. Aquinas also does not write on discrete topics such as law, politics and morality. Instead, his thought is integrated into a whole, one that begins with the existence of God and proceeds through the human world (and includes extensive discussions of angels and devils).

The most important part of Aquinas for our purposes comes from his master work, the *Summa Theologica*, where he discusses the idea of law. In Question 94, which includes a series of subquestions, Aquinas establishes a four-part division of law: divine, eternal, natural and civil:

1. *Divine law:* comes from specific commands in the biblical texts, such as the size of the temple that Solomon was to build or the provisions concerning diet.
2. *Eternal law:* something akin to modern physics or the ordered universe in Cicero's account; it is the set of laws that govern the operation of the universe, from movement to biological growth to human desire. These laws are also divinely inspired, for in Aquinas's world, everything emanates from the mind of God. But, they are not specifically stated in the Bible or any other text but can be observed and understood through the exercise of 'right reason'. This is not the same as logic, so Aquinas

is careful to state that the eternal law is not the same as mathematics; rather, it is the law that governs created things rather than ideas.

3. *Natural law:* or the eternal law as it is applied to individual people in the political and social realm. The natural law is thus a part of the eternal law, but it differs in that it is only that which applies to human interactions.

4. *Civil law:* the body of laws that are passed by individual communities in their own governance. This law should, of course, correspond with the natural law, but Aquinas is quite aware that often it does not.

Importantly, for Aquinas, natural law is also something that improves the human person. While natural law should be something that is simply found in nature, it is also the case that Aquinas (2002) recognizes 'unjust laws', meaning that not all law is natural law, and that the idea of natural law can be used to discipline unjust laws. This means that natural law can serve the heuristic device of 'teaching' people what it means to be good.

Natural law flourished in medieval Europe. Medieval theology became ever more specialized, resulting in what came to be called the Scholastic movement. These thinkers focused on the technical details of not only natural law but the wider theology within which it was embedded. In the late medieval and early Renaissance periods, though, some of those theorists made advances on Aquinas's thinking about law that remain important today, particularly in terms of international affairs. For instance, Francisco de Vitoria (1492–1546), the Spanish Renaissance theologian, drew on the natural law tradition but used it to help understand the discovery of the New World. Ideas about the human person that were central to Aquinas's formulations were called into question with the discovery of new peoples. In debates about whether or not to use force to convert the natives of the New World, Vitoria argued that while there was an obligation to spread the Christian faith, it was also necessary, according to natural law, to only use force in self-defence or to punish wrongdoing. These ideas continue to be important in the just war tradition, a body of thought that seeks to explore the moral foundations for using military force, which is covered more extensively in Chapter 5. The tradition is closely tied to natural law, with many early thinkers drawing heavily on the idea that there is a shared body of moral knowledge that all persons can access in deciding whether or not to use force in pursuit of their policies in the international order (Vitoria 1991).

Following from Aquinas, perhaps one of the most important theorists of the natural law is Hugo de Groot, or Grotius (1583–1645), the Early Modern Dutch lawyer, theologian and political theorist. Grotius's contribution to the natural law tradition and the just war tradition are found in his book, *The Rights of War and Peace* (sometimes translated as *The Laws of*

War and Peace), written in 1625. Divided into three books, the text begins in Book I with an effort to redefine natural law. Famously, Grotius argued that natural law can be found through different sources, including the rationality of the human person, divinely inspired guidance of religion, and evidence from history and current events. All these sources provide insight into the proper behaviour of not just states but individual persons.

Grotius's work as it relates to war and peace will be explored in more depth in Chapter 5. For now, though, it is important to locate his role in the transformation of the natural law tradition. In *The Rights of War and Peace*, Grotius became famous, or infamous at the time, for what came to be known as the 'impious hypothesis'. Grotius stated that natural law would still be true even if there was no God. The very next sentence goes on to say that, of course, this is not true. At the same time, Grotius became known as the 'secularizer' of international law and the just war tradition with this one phrase. Many have argued that this misrepresents Grotius's strong Christian beliefs, and a simple reading of the text of *The Rights of War and Peace* demonstrates that he draws heavily on the Christian tradition (Jeffrey 2006). But because of this phrase and the way in which he expanded the foundations of natural law beyond the largely Christian context of the medieval natural law thinkers, he did play an important role in shifting our understanding of natural law.

As recent evidence suggests, Grotius's (2005 [1609]) understanding of law as deriving from the Christian faith and contemporary practice arose in his earlier defence of the freedom of the seas. This account of Grotius in international law has been borrowed by theorists of international society, who find in Grotius's middle way between realism and idealism a fruitful source of insight (Bull et al. 1990). Recent literature has sought to reconsider Grotius, however, highlighting the centrality of religion to his understanding of the international (Jeffrey 2006), the imperialist heritage Grotius bequeathed to IR and ILT (Grovugui 1995; Keene 2002) or questioning the statism that constitutes such an important part of the international society account of his ideas (Lang 2009b).

Grotius was followed in this effort by Samuel Pufendorf (1632–94), a German philosopher and jurist. Pufendorf (2003 [1691]) drew from Grotius and Hobbes in constructing a theory of society and law that was universal and did not rely on any single state for its foundations. In so doing, he furthered Grotius's interpretation of natural law by giving a rational foundation to it, one that emphasized the importance of the human desire to protect oneself.

After the early modern period, natural law went into abeyance, kept alive mainly in the Catholic Church. In the mid-20th century, natural law theorizing, while still undertaken within a Christian framework, began to appear in theories about international law, human rights and the just war tradition. In part, the effort to create a sounder foundation for international law and especially human rights relied on natural law ideas, sometimes in an unacknowledged way. For instance, the creation of the Universal Declaration of Human Rights emerged from a UNESCO-organized commission chaired by Jacques Maritain, the Catholic moral and political philosopher (UNESCO 1949; see Glendon 2001). The commission brought together philosophers and theologians from a wide range of traditions and asked them to develop a shared sense of what rights were universal. Such an approach reflects a natural law idea, one in which the very existence of shared moral ideas demonstrates the truth of natural law.

Natural law can provide a foundation for international law, although it is rare that people refer to it today (O'Connell 2008). Some who draw more from a theological perspective have made the argument that natural law can serve as a foundation for human rights, international humanitarian law, and even broader customary law. Such arguments, however, founder at times on the questions noted above, specifically those about how we know what natural law is. Moreover, even among those who cite natural law, there is often disagreement about what laws we can actually derive from it. For instance, Grotius argues that a right to property is an important part of the natural law tradition, while Pufendorf argues that it is not central. Those who want to argue that the larger capitalist economic order is based on natural law must then make a case for which position to take.

Positive law

An important alternative to natural law is positivism. Legal positivism is the doctrine that law is defined by what the sovereign commands. This means that there is a possibility that a law passed by a sovereign may not be in conformity with morality, the assumption underlying natural law. As such, positivist legal philosophy articulates a theory of law that gives more power to the sovereign in a domestic context than does the natural law tradition. Because it relies primarily on the sovereign, positivism thus avoids the problems of epistemology that bedevil natural law; if law is defined by what the sovereign says it is, we can easily see what constitutes law.

An immediate problem at the international level, however, is that there is no sovereign. Although I suggested in Chapter 1 that authority may well exist at the global level, most legal positivists rely on the notion of sovereignty rather than authority as the defining feature of positivist law. This means that without a sovereign, it becomes more difficult to identify the law. Positivists, however, do not deny that international law exists. Instead, they argue that positivist law is the result of agreements among sovereigns, meaning that the most important source of international law is the treaty. Treaties, as agreements among sovereigns in an anarchic order, construct a law that is identifiable and reflects the interests and powers of those sovereign agents.

Based on this premise, international law can then extend outward from the treaties that states make. Because international organizations arise from treaties, they can be potential sources of international law. Naturally, this becomes complicated in cases when organizations take on agendas and purposes of their own. Perhaps the clearest example of this is the UNSC. Created as an executive agent of the UN, the UNSC has, in recent years, begun to engage in what looks to some like law making. For instance, when it passed Resolution 1373 on 28 September 2001, it criminalized terrorism and imposed sanctions on individuals who supported terrorism through financial means. In so doing, the UNSC did not simply create a short-term effort to resolve a threat to security, but instead created a law that would have effect long after the specific incidents that might have prompted it – the 11 September attacks in the US. In terms of positivism, one might ask whether or not this type of 'law making' is coming from a 'sovereign', for the UNSC is not usually defined as such. It is important consider, though, whether or not the idea of an 'authority' would suffice for a positivist to consider such resolutions to be law.

One of the first statements of positivism comes from Thomas Hobbes, the 17th-century political theorist. In Chapter 1, I compared Locke to Hobbes, pointing to how Hobbes' *Leviathan* established a particular understanding of what it means to be an authority. In this text, Hobbes (1968 [1651]: 312) also defines law in the following: 'Law in general, is not Counsell [or a suggestion] but Command; nor a Command of any man to any man; but only of him, whose Command is addressed to one formerly obliged to obey him.' In other words, law is what the sovereign commands the citizen to do, nothing more and nothing less. In a separate but related work, *Dialogue between a Philosopher and a Student of the Common Law in England* (1971 [1681]), Hobbes reinforces this idea by critiquing the idea of the common law. This work, a later piece from Hobbes and only published posthumously in 1681, presents an argument that law does not derive from a mystical rationality but only from the command of the sovereign. In so doing, it reinforces the arguments in *Leviathan*.

Perhaps because of its association with Hobbes, positivism is sometimes seen as a conservative and illiberal legal philosophy. This view is faulty, however, both because it misunderstands Hobbes but also because of its failure to see the progressive dimensions of positivist thinkers who followed from Hobbes. The two most important figures during the 18th and 19th centuries were Jeremy Bentham and John Austin. Both wrote from within a broadly utilitarian tradition, an approach to political philosophy I explore in more detail in Chapter 3, when I turn to John Stuart Mill and his ideas about rights. Mill attended lectures by Austin and his father, James Mill, was a secretary for Bentham. Utilitarianism is a consequentialist theory, which evaluates moral and political action in terms of its consequences. Utilitarianism, more specifically, proposes a means by which to calculate the utility or overall goodness of an action in terms of a standard of measurement. Generally, this measure is the greatest amount of good for the greatest number of people.

Bentham believed that in order to create a more utilitarian society, it was necessary to revise the law. This led him to criticize the 'common law' tradition that constitutes so much of the English legal tradition. He responded specifically to William Blackstone's *Commentaries on the Laws of England* (1979 [1769]). Blackstone did not attempt to provide an overview of all law, for England did not have a single legal code but a set of common laws derived from a mix of philosophy, theology, judicial decisions and parliamentary statutes. In his critique of Blackstone and the wider common law tradition, Bentham (2008) proposed a more rational and justifiable code of laws in an effort to achieve this utilitarian end.

A student of Bentham's and an even more important figure in the creation of positivist legal theory is John Austin. Austin wrote very little and even the text in which he developed his conception of positivism – *The Province of Jurisprudence Determined* – is actually a set of lecture notes. Austin (1995 [1832]: 10) continued with Hobbes' point in the first sentence of these lectures: 'Laws proper, or properly so called, are commands; laws which are not commands are laws improper, or improperly so called.' Moreover, the command must come from a 'political superior', which Austin takes to be the sovereign (ibid.: 16). Finally, attached to those laws should be sanctions, for it is only by sanctioning or punishing that a law becomes effective.

Austin does not, however, sever law from morality, or even from religion. He divides law into three types: divine law, positive law, and positive morality. The first is that set of laws that comes directly from God. The second is law from a sovereign to those beneath the sovereign. The third is composed of a slightly wider range of laws than the others, laws that are near to natural law. According to Austin (1995 [1832]: 109), the second set is the most directly relevant for governing the political community, although the first and third are important as well. For instance, the third set of laws include those

> which are set by men to men, but not by men as political superiors, nor by men, as private persons, in pursuance of legal rights [and] laws which are closely analogous to laws proper [positive laws], but are merely opinions or sentiments held or felt by men in regard to human conduct. These laws of positive morality, combined with some positive laws, create the constitution. (Austin 1995 [1832]: 215)

This can sound confusing to some, for to say that something is constitutional is to say that it is legal. But recall that Austin was responding, as was Bentham, to the dominant English common law tradition, articulated by William Blackstone (1979 [1769]), in which the structure and institutions and even laws of the government arise from traditions and actions that have evolved over centuries and that reflect a broader political and perhaps even cultural consensus. This idea of an 'ancient constitution' was drawn upon by those who revolted against the sovereign, in the specifics of the English Civil War of the mid-17th century and later (Pocock 1987). What they were drawing upon when rejecting the sovereignty of the king were these positive moral laws, not the laws of the sovereign. As a result, Austin (1995 [1832]: 216) states: 'although an act of the sovereign which violates constitutional law, may be styled with the propriety unconstitutional, it is not an infringement of law simply and strictly so called, and cannot be styled with propriety illegal'.

Austin's heritage is central for those wishing to develop a positivist legal philosophy. The two most influential positivist legal theorists of the 20th century were H.L.A. Hart and Hans Kelsen. Hart, a British legal philosopher, wrote widely on legal philosophy, including commentary on and edited collections of Jeremy Bentham's works (Bentham 2008; Hart 1982). But his most important work was *The Concept of Law* (Hart 1994). This work is a sort of critique of Austin, although inspired by his positivist heritage. Hart believed that to say law is merely a command by a sovereign is to make law a coercive tool; his famous example is that of a mugger commanding one to hand over his money, something we would certainly not call law but which might be said to fit into Austin's definition. Instead, Hart sought to determine what it was that made a command or, more specifically, a rule into a law. To do so, Hart introduced the idea of law being composed of two sets of rules, primary and secondary. The primary rules are those which we think of as actual law; that is, the rules and regulations that guide us through our social lives. The secondary rules are those rules which create the possibility for the primary rules; that is, they are the enabling or structuring rules that create the conditions in which something can be considered a law at all. One might call the secondary rules 'constitutional', in that they lay out the conditions for which a rule gets turned into a law, that is, a primary rule. This also differs from Austin's notion in that both constitutional and regulatory rules are laws, but Hart's distinction between them allows for greater clarity in understanding what it means to talk about law in both senses.

The second positivist legal theorist who has played an important role in international legal theory is Hans Kelsen. For a short period, he served on the Austrian constitutional court, until he was forced to resign because of his affiliation with a more liberal political party. He moved to Germany, but then was forced to leave in 1934 because he was Jewish. After spending time in Geneva, he eventually made his way to the US, where he lived out the remainder of his life. Kelsen's most important work of legal theory is *Pure Theory of the Law* (1960 [1934]). While Hart focused on the idea of a rule, Kelsen used the concept of a 'norm' to orient his work. Legal norms are what constitute the law, and they rely on a basic norm for a society, what in German is called a *Grundnorm*. This basic norm is the overriding and ultimate source of all other norms, although Kelsen was careful not to identify this norm with any metaphysical idea as a natural law theorist would. From this basic norm, a hierarchy of norms emerges, which structures the legal order. This hierarchy is usually understood as a constitution; in fact, Kelsen helped to write the Austrian constitution of 1920, which continues to influence Austrian law to this day.

Kelsen, unlike Hart and other positivists, turned directly to international law. After moving to the US, he wrote numerous works on the international legal order. His book, *Peace through Law* (Kelsen 1944), argues that the international legal system could be better served by a strong international judiciary that could understand and interpret the reigning *Grundnorm* of the international order. This was written in response to proposals for the new UN in which much effort was being put into the creation of a powerful international executive, what eventually became the Security Council. As a positivist, Kelsen understood the arguments that a powerful executive is important for law implementation and sanctioning, but his belief in a pre-existing *Grundnorm* meant that a judiciary that could interpret the law was more important than an executive body that might eventually violate those norms if it became too strong.

Positivism is an influential idea within international law. It has been subject to a number of criticisms, from natural law theorists and other theoretical traditions, but supporters continue to defend it (D'Aspremont 2011). Because it presents law as separate from morality, there are some who have argued that it denudes law of what they would regard as its inherently normative content. But, to be more accurate, legal positivism is not a theory of law without any normative element. Rather, it is a theory of law that argues law must be coherent and justifiable on its own terms rather than through an appeal to alternative foundations. This means that law can be normative but it must be normative on its own terms rather than through an appeal to foundations outside itself (Nardin 1998, 2008). In international law, for instance, this normative element means respecting the fact that all states are equal and there is a rule of law that all agents in the international order should obey.

Both natural law and positivist law provide foundations for international law. There are areas of the law that correspond better to each framework; so, for instance, human rights law might rest more comfortably in a natural law approach, while the rules governing economic law seem to arise more clearly from positivist approaches. In any case, both approaches are important and worth considering when trying to evaluate international rules and laws.

International law

While the distinction between natural law and positivist law can shape our understanding of some global issues, international law has its own normative and theoretical bases that arise from its historical evolution. As briefly mentioned in the Introduction, international legal theory has long been a location for normative debates at the global level. Indeed, one might argue that international law has existed ever since communities have engaged each other. The notion that there are codes in war, for instance, reaches back to the ancient world, with some shared overlaps in Ancient Greece, Rome and Israel (these sources and codes are discussed at more length in Chapter 5). But war is not the only place where we can find evidence of codes governing the interaction of ancient communities. One of the most important is diplomacy. In certain ancient communities, diplomats were considered to be sacred, a status that allowed them to travel between and among warring communities in order to bring about peace (Hamilton and Langhorne 1995). Naturally, diplomacy as a practice has evolved since this time, for diplomats are no longer considered sacred, although their protected status echoes this sacred heritage. At the same time, diplomacy has become, for many, including realists such as Hans Morgenthau (1948), a means to promote a kind of peaceful order (see also Lang 2013a). Of course, diplomacy is not rule governed in the sense that diplomats follow rules; one of the virtues of diplomacy is the ability to make political choices when international legal structures do not allow for movement forward. But in fact, it is diplomats who play a crucial role in creating international legal structures, and there are rules governing how diplomats need to be treated. The point to make here is that diplomacy is one of the original spaces in which international law emerged.

The historical evolution of international law can be told as a story about the shift from natural law through positivist law. Three figures constitute this transition: Francisco de Vitoria, Hugo Grotius and Emerich de Vattel. For some, the evolution through all three constitutes the progressive development of international law into a non-religious universal law. For others, however, the transition reveals hidden practices of imperialism and exclusion that suggest international law is founded on something less morally attractive than progress.

Francisco de Vitoria, the 16th-century Spanish Scholastic thinker, developed the first modern account of law and war in the midst of the European encounter with the New World (Scott 1934). Vitoria (1991) made a case for treating the inhabitants of the Americas as persons who could be understood in relation to natural law (Box 2.1). Importantly, however, he argued that natural law rather than papal pronouncements should be the source of insight into how to treat the Amerindians. This encounter with the Other has shaped the way in which European thought and international law developed, through overt political conflicts and more general intellectual developments (Anghie 2003; Pagden 1995; Todorov 1999).

BOX 2.1   The Valladolid debate (1550–1)

Vitoria wrote his works in the context of the European encounter with the New World. Soon after he died, a famous debate took place between Bartolomé de las Casas (1484–1566) and Juan Ginés Sepúlveda (1489–1573), which focused on the moral and legal agency of the native tribes. One of the moral arguments made for conquering the Americas was the need to convert the natives to Christianity, which was connected to the argument that they needed to be converted from their heathen ways, which included human sacrifice. As a result of controversy surrounding the treatment of the natives, King Charles V of Spain called for an official debate on what status they had and how they should be treated as a result, which was held in the Colegio de San Gregorio in the Spanish city of Valladolid. Las Casas argued that the natives were fully human and according to natural law should not be forcefully converted. Sepúlveda, relying on Aristotle, argued that the natives were 'natural slaves' who were not worthy of any kind of legal protection. The outcome of the debate is not clear, although by making public these issues, it raised awareness of the treatment of the native populations and resulted in efforts to protect them.

See: http://en.wikipedia.org/wiki/Valladolid_debate.

The previous section discussed Grotius, and his ideas are explored in more depth in Chapter 5, so I will leave him for now. The last figure in this trajectory is Emerich de Vattel (1714–67), the Swiss diplomat who argued for an international order in which states were the primary members who could regulate their affairs on the basis of treaty relations they formulated, rather than a broader natural law heritage. Building on the philosophy of Christian Wolff, Vattel (2008 [1758]) argued that there is a 'civitas maxima' or a 'great republic' that constituted Europe, making him one of the founders of modern republican thought. He also argued that this republic functioned by keeping in place a balance of power, a concept that has continued to be central to IR theorists, although not ILT theorists. Vattel has not been subject to much scrutiny by theorists of IR, other than through the work of Nicholas Onuf. Onuf, first in collaboration with his brother Peter Onuf and then in his own work, has argued that Vattel is central to the 'republican legacy' that has shaped the modern world (Onuf 1998; Onuf and Onuf 1993). This legacy results from the way in which Vattel combined the ancient republican thinking of Aristotle with the contemporary problems (of the 18th and 19th centuries) in European diplomacy.

The transition from natural law to positivist law took place in the 19th century, when international law became a specialized field of inquiry. Martii Koskenniemi (2001) has explored how the 19th- and early 20th-century evolution of international law, while resulting in the triumph of positivism, included a commitment to certain political projects, especially the liberalization of politics in Europe. Antony Anghie (2004: 32–114) has argued that the emergence of positivism is not simply about the politics of Europe but about the imposition of colonialism. Gerry Simpson (2003) has argued that the construction of an international legal order in which 'sovereign equality' was the central principle ignores the role the great powers played in the 19th-century construction of that order and the resulting creation of 'outlaw states'. A range of other theorists have explored the hidden tensions in international law, although not necessarily with a historical focus (Bowring 2007; Carty 2007; Orford 2006; Simpson 2007).

International legal theory has developed important accounts of the rules that structure the international order. Some international lawyers see their role as reinforcing those rules, such as those engaged in the World Order Models Project led by Richard Falk and others (Falk and Black 1969). Falk (1983) has made important contributions to international law by focusing on the normative dimensions of the wider legal and political order and, more recently, by focusing on religion and international order (Falk 2001). Some scholars have tried to link international law to IR theory, primarily through the constructivist theoretical agenda that focuses on rules (Reus-Smit 2004).

International law arises from sources that have different normative foundations, ones that parallel to some extent the differences between natural and positivist law. The primary source of international law is the treaties that states make with each other; this source parallels the positivist idea that the sovereigns in the system are the ones from who law emanates. There is, however, another source, known as 'customary international law'. This is the idea that, over time, state practices and normative beliefs can eventually become a form of law, one that has the same status as treaty-based law. The normative importance of this law can be traced back to the idea of *jus gentium*, the Latin term for the laws shared by all communities and differentiated from the *jus civile*, the positive laws of states (Box 2.2). *Jus gentium* was considered to be part of the natural law, and was drawn on by thinkers such as Grotius as evidence for the applicability of the natural law to all peoples.

Built into international law, though, is a tension, one identified by Koskenniemi (2011), who has described how international law sits between power politics and ethics. He highlights something that is a problem for many who study international law, which is that the law is made by powerful agents, which serves their interests, yet it also serves as a vehicle for the hopes and aspirations of many in the world. Koskenniemi suggests that international law, and especially international lawyers, need to be wary of falling into either trap, for law must remain distinct from both the vagaries of power politics and the idealism of global ethics. The idea that there is an overlap between law and ethics has been argued through traditions such as natural law. Yet, there is one other important effort to link law, ethics and politics. It is to the work of the thinker who undertook that effort, and much else besides, that the chapter now turns.

BOX 2.2 Customary law

A number of terms often appear in reference to what is broadly understood as customary law. *Jus gentium* is the older notion, one drawn from Roman law, which describes the laws that are shared by all states in their relations with each other. *Jus cogens* law, which are sometimes called 'peremptory norms', are the basic principles from which no derogation is allowed in the international legal order. These are widely accepted norms such as slavery, genocide or torture. Of course, even in suggesting these as examples, we still see evidence of communities violating these norms, perhaps the most glaring example in recent years being the violation of the norm against torture by the US and its allies in the war against terror.

See: Beyers 1999 for more on the status and importance of customary law in international affairs.

Kant and law

Immanuel Kant (1724–1804) is one of the most important and influential philosophers of the Western tradition. Kant spent his entire life in the city of Königsberg in what was Prussia, but is today Kaliningrad, which is part of Russia (although physically cut off from the rest of Russia). His personal life was rather dull, spending his time interacting with university colleagues and merchants in the city. However, his intellectual output was significant, and it helped to shape the trajectory of modern philosophy in important ways. Politically, he did not live through the tumultuous times that affected Locke and Hobbes, although he was censured by the Prussian King Frederick William II for his writings on religion and he was a witness (albeit distantly) to the events of the French Revolution (Kant 1991: 2).

Kant is best known for his work on metaphysics and moral philosophy. Kant (1998 [1781]) proposed the idea that all reality exists by means of two constructs – time and space – in his work, *Critique of Pure Reason*. These basic ideas structure the reality of the world around us and how we access that world. In proposing these constructs, Kant was reacting in part to the empiricism that Locke had proposed, that is, the idea that all our knowledge comes through sense perceptions. Instead, Kant argued that there are certain basic constructs that allow us to know the world around us. Without time and space, we could not take in any ideas at all.

In terms of morality, Kant is best known for his idea of the 'categorical imperative'. As Kant (1993 [1785]: 30) states in the *Groundwork for the Metaphysics of Morals*: 'Act only according to that maxim whereby you can, at the same time, will that it should become a universal law.' The imperative is categorical in the sense that it applies to every person in all situations. This is opposed to the idea of an imperative that is hypothetical, or one that depends on particular circumstances. For Kant, this imperative is the basis of morality; it means that for an action to be considered morally acceptable, it should conform to this imperative. More precisely, one should act in such a way that one's will is in conformity with this imperative, a distinction that is sometimes missed when Kant is seen as a theorist of 'rule following'. To follow a rule is not simply to do what one is told, but to act autonomously in such a way that one's will reflects the spirit of the categorical imperative.

Kant's political writings were not traditionally considered to be as important as his metaphysical and moral writings. For some, this was because these works tended to be more accommodating to the 'realities' of the world, unlike his more rigorous metaphysical and especially moral writings. For others, since they came towards the end of his life and seemed more like reactions to events than well-worked-out theoretical arguments, they did not have the same resonance as his more developed writings. Some even argued that his political writings were hampered by the dementia that Kant increasingly suffered towards the end of his life (Kant 1991).

Despite these concerns, there has been something of a resurgence of interest in Kant's political writings. As noted in the Introduction, for some IR theorists, his essay on *Perpetual Peace* presents an account of how peaceful relations among nations can be possible if states are republican and adhere to international law (Doyle 1986). Others have taken this essay, along with Kant's writings on political right, as proposals for how to construct a cosmopolitan global order (Brown 2009; Franceschet 2002). Political theorists have also drawn on Kant more in recent years. John Rawls' (1971: 11) political philosophy of liberalism relies heavily on Kant, although he noted that he wanted a 'Kantian conception of justice' detached from certain background elements of Kant's thought. At the same time, Rawls' (1999) international political thought is less indebted to Kant and seems more inspired by John Stuart Mill's concerns about intervention than Kant's advocacy of republican governments adhering to a global rule of law.

Jürgen Habermas has been a central advocate of Kant's international political thought, particularly in his recent work on international law and Europe. For Habermas (2006), Kant presents a template for how to understand not only the benefits of adhering to international law, but how doing so can reinforce democratic tendencies at home and move the international order towards a cosmopolitan one. Habermas sees in Kant a means by which the international order can become more constitutional, something that is normally the province of a domestic polity rather than an international one.

What, then, does Kant have to say about international affairs? Not much directly, other than in the *Perpetual Peace* essay. But, we can extrapolate from his political and ethical writings a means by which to understand and critically assess international affairs. The contribution Kant makes to understanding international politics (and, indeed, domestic politics) is his idea of law and its role in political life. Kant is not a legal theorist, per se, but law and legislation constitute the most important elements of his political writings. In order to understand his ideas about law and specifically his ideas about international law, three concepts require greater attention: liberty, publicity and republicanism.

The first and most essential part of not only Kant's political philosophy but his moral philosophy is freedom, an idea he develops in the *Groundwork for the Metaphysics of Morals* (Kant 1993 [1785]). The moral law is something we know through reason. This law differs from natural law described above, for Kant was not a natural law theorist. Rather, he believed that the proper use of the faculty of reason would allow individuals to understand the necessity of morally correct behaviour. Connected to reason in Kant's philosophy is the will and it is through the use of our reason that the will's role in moral life can be understood. The will is central to Kant's moral philosophy; morality only makes sense for Kant if we are able to act through a will that has not been coerced. Indeed, to understand this point does not require fully assimilating Kant's philosophy, for it is a rather commonsense idea. If I am to be judged as acting rightly or wrongly, it is necessary that my actions be seen as emanating freely from something internal to me. If my actions can be explained away as the result of some force outside me, whether it be God or nature, then it is difficult to see how I might be responsible for my own actions. For Kant, this internal element by which I can be judged to have acted morally or not is the will.

The will should not, however, be understood here as simply my desires. In fact, for Kant, a good will is one that acts in accordance with duty rather than desire (Kant 1991: 18). This results from the fact that I live in community with others and for me to act in a way that allows me and others to have the same freedom means my actions must be constrained. This constraint, again, is not from an external authority. Because we live with others, our internal freedom must correspond to our external freedom. This external freedom means acting in accordance with the rule of law. So, to be truly free in Kant's philosophy does not mean doing what we desire, but acting so that our wills conform to our duty, which creates a world of law-abiding individuals.

The second principle of Kant's philosophy is publicity. This means that politics should not be hidden from the citizenry in the name of some mythical national interest or security. For Kant, this is connected to his idea of enlightenment, which is in the background of much of his political writing. In his famous essay, 'An Answer to the Question: What is Enlightenment?', Kant (1991 [1784]) develops this idea in connection to the idea of freedom. To be enlightened, for Kant, means that one's public use of reason is not subject to restrictive or paternalistic authority, especially governments and churches in Kant's day. For us today, that might mean thinking about matters in such a way as we are not unduly influenced by the media, friends or family. In other words, for Kant, to be enlightened means to 'think for oneself'. But it also means that we must be able to think in public, something he describes in the following:

> For enlightenment ... all that is needed is *freedom*. And the freedom in question is the most innocuous form of all – freedom to make *public use* of one's reasons in all matters ... The *public* use of man's reason must always be free, and it alone can bring about enlightenment among men; the *private use* of reason may quite often be very narrowly restricted, however, without undue hindrance to the progress of enlightenment. But by the public use one's own reason I mean that use which anyone may make of it *as a man of learning* addressing the entire *reading public*. What I term the private use of reason is that which a person may make of it in a particular *civil* post or office with which he is entrusted. (Kant 1991 [1784]: 55)

Kant is arguing that freedom is the most important foundation for enlightenment, but it should be freedom that is made use of in public. The 'public' space here is somewhat confusing, though. As Elisabeth Ellis (2005: 20) has argued, this space is one which does not involve one's roles in civil society; so, for instance, a member of the clergy is acting in 'private' when they make official statements about church doctrine, but is acting in the public sphere when they are stating how those doctrines relate to public life shared among citizens in a community. Ellis develops this idea of publicity in Kant further, arguing that it provides us with a conception of civil society in which individuals can make their voices heard in an intelligent manner, one which will help the society and humanity overall evolve towards greater peace, justice and harmony.

The third idea that requires some clarification is Kant's conception of law and legislation. Kant's political theory is very much a republican one, or one that emphasizes the creation of political space that allows for the maximum amount of liberty with a balance for political order. Importantly, this means it is not only about ensuring rights for citizens, but ensuring that the state is organized such that no single agent within the state can dominate it. Today, this is called a 'separation of powers', or a state in which the three primary elements – legislative, executive and judicial – are kept separate. Kant's political system establishes such a separation, although not in the full sense in which this concept is understood today. Kant lays out this idea in the first part of his work, *The Metaphysics of Morals* (1991 [1797]). This work comprises two parts, the first focused on right and the second focused on virtue. This first section is sometimes referred to by its German name, *Rechtslehre*, which means something like the 'science of right'. Note that this is not about 'rights' in the sense of human rights as we understand them. Rather, this section of Kant's work is about the idea of right as an organizing principle of politics, specifically how to organize the political system so that everyone's freedom can be respected, or as Kant puts it: 'Right is therefore the sum total of those conditions within which the will of one person can be reconciled with the will of another in accordance with the universal law of freedom' (ibid.: 133).

In this work, Kant separates the three institutions of governance analogously to the way in which individuals act. The legislator is like the operation of reason, the executive like the will, and the judge is the actual outcome of the decision-making process in specific cases (1991 [1797]: 138). Of course, this analogy is not exact, nor is it helpful if one is not fully conversant with Kant's works. Nevertheless, it does give one the idea of how Kant understood law, that is, as a reflection of morality.

Moreover, the legislative power is the most important one in Kant's conception, in the same way that reason is the most important faculty in the human person. This legislative power constitutes the sovereignty of the people, for it is through participating in the legislative process that people unite into the general will. As Kant (1991 [1797]: 139) states: 'The legislative power can belong only to the united will of the people.' Further, it is in so acting as the legislative power that the people become citizens: 'The members of such a society (*societas civilis*) or state who unite for the purpose of legislating are known as *citizens* (*cives*).' The power of legislation, then, is not simply about creating good laws; it is the fundamental element of political life for the ordinary human person. Of course, this does not mean that all people are directly part of the law-making process, for this happens through various configurations such as parliaments. But, it is important to note that Kant distinguishes this legislative action from other kinds of rules, such as regulations, by the fact that it comes from a unified will of the people. When the executive makes commands, these are not instances of law but of ordinances or regulations. When the executive seeks to make laws, this is when government becomes despotic (ibid.: 141), for it conflates the role of the sovereign (reason) with that of the agent who enacts the law (will).

These three ideas of freedom, publicity and law are central for understanding Kant's international political thought. As noted above, for many IR scholars, Kant's international political thought is reduced to his 1795 essay *Perpetual Peace: A Philosophical Sketch*. Some scholars, such as Michael Doyle (1983a, 1983b), have argued that Kant's essay demonstrates why democracies do not go to war. This emphasis on democracy captures only one part of Kant's essay, however. Kant's essay is divided into two sections, the first laying out six 'preliminary' articles concerning peace and the second laying out three 'definitive' articles to achieve peace. The first section suggests advances that European states during Kant's day should seek to achieve; so, for instance, the second preliminary article states that 'no independently existing state, whether it be large or small, may be acquired by another state by inheritance, exchange, purchase, or gift' (Kant 1991 [1795]: 94). Such a suggestion means less today as it is unlikely that any state could be bought, sold or inherited. But, in his day, small European principalities were transferred in such ways. Kant argues that such practices violate the idea that individuals living in those states have a special relationship with each other and their ruler through something like a social contract (although Kant is not the same kind of social contract theorist as Locke). More importantly, these preliminary articles are ones that were achievable in Kant's day and reflected, one might argue, a more realistic understanding of the international order in which he was living. In other words, rather than an idealist cosmopolitan, these preliminary articles demonstrate that Kant understands that some practices can be changed simply by treaty and do not require more radical shifts.

The more radical elements of his argument in this essay, however, are the definitive articles. Moreover, these articles reflect more closely his ideas about law that I described above. The three articles are related to each other, and have a kind of progressive nature to them, that is, they seem to build on one another. But, at the same time, they can also be seen as either being achievable simultaneously or not in sequence at all. The first article is the one that theorists like Doyle have emphasized, that all states must be republican. Crucially, though, Doyle (1986) uses the term 'democracy', highlighting the representative nature of these republics. While this is one of the reasons why Kant argues that republics will be more peaceful – individuals will not submit themselves to war if they have a say in the matter – perhaps the more important point about republics is that they have a separation of powers. This separation of powers ensures that the law-making function in a state is not conflated with an executive function, so that a monarch can send individuals off to war without some deliberative element of debating that war. This slowing down of war making makes the separation of powers element of this article perhaps even more important than the representative one.

The second article is that states should seek to form federations in order to work together. If one reads the articles as necessarily building on each other, this would mean that only republics or democracies can make these federations. But, importantly, Kant does not presume that only republics can form federations. His argument here is simply that the fact of federating and creating a union of sorts will lead to more peace. This reflects the assumptions underlying the UN more than, say the European Union (EU). As such, it is important to note that Kant sees peace in more realist terms here. Kant also notes here that a federation is to be preferred to a world state, which he says is 'contradictory', for it violates the idea of a political order in which individuals are represented in a legislature (although he does not acknowledge that there could be such a thing as a global parliament).

The final article is one that has led to many seeing Kant as a cosmopolitan theorist. He argues that rather than a political structure, cosmopolitanism might be achieved through the promotion of the virtue of hospitality. If enacted, this idea would lead to freer movement of peoples across borders and, importantly, treating foreigners less as 'foreign' and more as 'human'. Such a change might contribute to a long-term shift in attitudes that would undermine nationalism and the conflicts it generates. Again, we have an example of this in the current world with the 1985 Schengen Agreement in the EU, which allows for the movement of individuals across borders in a way that is not possible in other regions. For Kant, the virtue of hospitality will embody and reinforce greater respect for individuals as ends and not means, which connects back to his moral philosophy.

Kant's *Perpetual Peace* essay is more complex than is sometimes presented in IR scholarship. Rather than simply the fact that democracies do not go to war with each other, Kant is arguing that a greater appreciation of law and law making in a republican system with a separation of powers will reinforce the moral principle of the categorical imperative and will help contribute to peace by ensuring that laws are respected even in the realm of war.

Responsibility to protect

As noted in the Introduction, R2P sits uneasily in the international legal and political order. It arose from a normative agenda, one that seeks to protect civilians by emphasizing the responsibilities of leaders for their citizens, and when they fail to live up to that responsibility, places that responsibility on the international community. The concept was then affirmed in the summary document that arose from the 2005 World Summit. Yet, there has been no treaty that establishes R2P, nor does it constitute a customary international law or *jus cogens* principle. As such, it seems to fit neither a natural law nor positivist law framework.

Yet not all agree that it lacks international legal status. As noted above, Louise Arbour (2008) has argued that the legal principles on which R2P are based reflect a wide consensus concerning the protection of civilians and the importance of states as guarantors of the rights of their citizens. When the UN Security Council used the phrase 'responsibility to protect' in Resolution 1973, which authorized the use of force in Libya, many saw this as the moment when the idea came into force as a principle of the international legal order. In addition, UN Secretary-General Ban Ki-moon has created the position of Special Adviser on the Responsibility to Protect. This position, linked with the Special Adviser on the Prevention of Genocide, is designed to advance the R2P agenda in the UN system and more widely. Anne Orford (2011) argues that R2P is part of the UN becoming more authoritative in the international order, especially in the way the concept has located the international community's responsibility in the UN system.

Orford's suggestion that the R2P has reinforced the authority of the UN points us back to Kant and the intersection of law, politics and ethics. For if we critically examine exactly how R2P functions in the UN, we can get a better grasp of whether or not it is part of international law, and, more importantly, whether or not we should care if it is. In July 2013, Secretary-General Ban Ki-moon appointed Jennifer Welsh, an academic from Oxford University, to the post of special adviser. Welsh, who has written on a wide range of topics relating to international affairs, including one about Edmund Burke, the 18th-century conservative thinker and parliamentarian (1995), published a short article on R2P in 2011 (Welsh 2011). In it, she highlights one element of R2P that many have forgotten. In the World Summit statement of 2005, the drafters emphasized that the UNSC and the UN General Assembly (UNGA) have a role to play in the implantation of R2P:

> the Outcome Document specifically identifies the General Assembly as the organ that will continue discussion of the R2P – a nod to dissenters, who wished to ensure that the concerns of developing countries would be fully taken on board. (More cynically, one might argue that giving the General Assembly the mantle for advancing R2P was one sure way of guaranteeing slow progress.) After 2005 it was therefore the General Assembly, and not the Security Council, which became the focal point for discussions – some of them heated – about R2P's implementation. (Welsh 2011: 256)

These debates about R2P within the UNGA have indeed been contentious, including arguments that it is colonial in nature and will simply advance the interests of the most powerful. As Welsh points out, when the UNSC did invoke it in the case of Libya, this moved control of the R2P agenda away from the UNGA to the UNSC.

How does this relate to Kant's point? The UNGA is not a legislative body in the sense that Kant requested, for its resolutions are not binding in the way that the UNSC's resolutions are. And, there is some evidence that the Security Council is engaged in forms of legislation, a task it was not designed to undertake (Lang 2014). So, the General Assembly does not pass laws in any traditional sense. But it might be better at capturing some elements of Kant's ideas of the moral value of legislation than the Security Council. The General Assembly undertakes forms of public deliberation that the Security Council avoids. For instance, concerning R2P, the General Assembly held a series of hearings in July 2009 that included testimony from strong critics of the idea such as Noam Chomsky (UNGA 2009). This kind of public disagreement and effort to work out the problems of R2P reflects the deliberative model that Kant argued was so important for the legislature to undertake. Further, what Welsh notes in an aside, that giving the R2P to the General Assembly was a way to slow down its adoption, is something that Kant may well have welcomed. One of the points about legislation is that it slows down decision making, which is essential when it comes to the use of force.

It may be that R2P will eventually be adopted as a formal legal principle; indeed, its sceptics (Hehir 2012) and its supporters (Bellamy 2011) agree this is necessary. And the current structure of the international legal order does not allow the General Assembly to legislate. The point of this brief discussion is to highlight that the UNGA does at least embody some elements of the legislative process, even if the outcome of its deliberations is not the creation of binding laws. Rather, the importance of the UNGA is precisely in its deliberations, for it is this process that better reflects the idea of a law being the result of a debate about reasons and interests. The fact that no international law results from the formal, legislative process that exists in the domestic realm is, of course, a problem as well. But if we see how at least one international norm is making its way through different elements of the international political and legal order, we can see intimations of how it might function in a more Kantian legal sense.

Conclusion

This chapter has undertaken an exploration of rules and laws. It explored the different philosophies of law, such as natural law and positivism. The final discussion of R2P and legislation leaves more questions than answers, and it should certainly not be seen as the last word on the subject. Rather, by using R2P as an example of a norm that has some rule-like characteristics, and the difficulty of seeing it as a law, we can see some of the ways these elements relate with each other.

International law is not domestic law, so using the Kantian principle of legislation as a normative standard to evaluate principles such as R2P is problematic. Yet, it suggests a standard that can be refined and developed further in evaluating international politics and law. As noted above, some have argued (including me; see Lang 2013a) that there is an emerging global constitutional order. If such a thing exists, and the rule of law and international law are part of that order, we need to consider how theorists of different kinds of constitutions, such as Kant, can contribute to our normative assessment of that order. Chapter 3 will continue this kind of exploration as it turns to another important principle that combines law, politics and ethics – the nature of rights. But, rather than rights alone, it will also explore the nature of responsibilities, and how these two concepts relate to each other and help structure our international order.

Further reading

C. Fred Alford. 2010. *Narrative, Nature and the Natural Law: From Aquinas to International Human Rights*. Basingstoke: Palgrave Macmillan.
Historical overview that connects modern human rights to the natural law tradition. Rather than a focus on natural rights, it locates these issues in the context of natural law, and gives it a proper context for understanding how it works.

David Armstrong, Theo Farrell and Helene Lambert. 2012. *International Law and International Relations*. Cambridge: Cambridge University Press.
Provides an excellent overview of how IR theories speak to international legal issues. Focuses on the question of sources of law and enforcement issues, key disputes among scholars from the two fields. Designed to introduce students of IR to ILT and students of ILT to IR.

Jürgen Habermas. 2006. *The Divided West*. Cambridge: Polity Press.
Habermas is one of the leading political theorists in the world today. His effort to link Kant to international law and the EU represents a nuanced approach to Kant's relevance for today. Includes previously published essays and interviews with him, all of which circle around the importance of international law and how to defend it from a normative, largely Kantian perspective.

Martti Koskenniemi. 2011. *The Politics of International Law*. Oxford: Hart.
Excellent introduction to the relationship of law and politics at the global level. Koskenniemi, a well-versed theorist, also served as a diplomat to the Finnish foreign ministry, and so provides an experienced perspective on the role of law in IR. His overall argument is that law is positioned between ethics and politics, but should not be reduced to either. The essays touch on a wide range of topics.

Anthony F. Lang, Jr and Amanda Beattie, eds. 2009. *War, Torture and Terrorism: Rethinking the Rules of International Security*. London: Routledge.
A response from a range of authors to the challenges posed to international law from the events of 9/11 and the response by the US in its launching of a war on terror. Substantive topics include preventive war, torture and the impact of technology on international law. Explicitly focused on rules rather than laws alone, giving it a wider theoretical purchase than other texts.

Chapter 3

Rights and Responsibilities

On 11 January 2011, the United Nations Human Rights Council (UNHRC) issued a Report of the Working Group on the Universal Periodic Review: United States of America (UNHRC 2011). The report results from the UNHRC's mandate to review each country in the international system every four years to examine its record on human rights. Each country is assessed by a troika of other member countries from the UNHRC. They are tasked with examining the extent to which countries conform to their obligations under the various human rights treaties in the international order. The US government provided the UNHRC with a detailed report in advance, which resulted in part from extensive consultations with members of the public (US Department of State 2010).

The report on the US reflects the strengths and weaknesses of the UNHRC's efforts to review all countries' adherence to human rights norms. While the report emphasized many of the positive contributions the US has made to human rights over the years, it also highlighted a number of areas where the US has failed to implement its human rights obligations. These include the continued use of the death penalty, racial discrimination, violation of the rights of Native Americans, the use of torture, and the continued use of illegal forms of detainment in the war on terror. The report concludes with a series of recommendations, including ratification of a number of treaties and changes to many of the US's internal legal institutions, such as the creation of a national human rights body that would ensure the protection of human rights across all local, state and national levels. These recommendations come from two sources: the state parties that constitute the UNHRC and a number of NGOs, known in the UN system as 'stakeholders'. These groups submitted reports and played a role in the determination of those topics on which the US government was failing to uphold human rights.

Unsurprisingly, the report generated controversy in the US. The Republican administration of George W. Bush had refused to join the UNHRC when it was first created in 2006. When the Democratic administration of Barak Obama joined the UNHRC in 2009, it meant that the US would be subject to a periodic review for the first time in its history. The administration argued that by subjecting itself to periodic review, it was strengthening human rights around the world and admitting that its own efforts to conform to human rights standards was part of a process. Quoting US Secretary of State Hilary Clinton, the report notes that: 'democracies demonstrate their greatness not by insisting they are perfect, but by using their institutions and their principles to make themselves ... more perfect' (US Department of State 2010: 3).

In a comment written for the Fox News website, a conservative news source in the US, George Russell argued that the Obama administration's decision to be subject to review demonstrated its failure to resist encroachments on US sovereignty. He also highlighted the role of the stakeholders in the process, pointing out that one NGO in particular – the UN Human Rights Network (UNHRN) – had contributed the bulk of recommendations to the review committee. Some of the NGOs, including those in the UNHRN, are not US based, a point Russell argued gives them less legitimacy than US-based commentators. Russell (2010) lambasted this coalition, composed of a wide array of groups within the US, as promoting a 'militant vision of the US as a malignant force'.

While Russell's article can be dismissed as a political critique of the Obama administration or even a nativist American response to international institutions, underlying it are some important questions about human rights and international politics. The process of the review raises questions about how human rights should be understood and enforced in the global order. Should states be subject to the scrutiny of other states – some with questionable human rights records – and NGOs that are not necessarily representative of the states they are critiquing? Would the creation of a national human rights institution in the US actually ensure the protection of human rights? Does this recommendation misunderstand the role the various levels of governance play in the US?

This chapter provides some ways of thinking about these questions and will return to the UNHRC in its concluding sections. But, in line with the overall purpose of this book, I explore these questions through an engagement with political theorists. The next section examines a range of theories about rights. I then turn to the topic of responsibilities as a corollary to rights, arguing that rights without responsibilities result in more rhetoric than action. I then explore the UN system, which includes not only the UNHRC but other institutions as well, as an institutional framework within which human rights issues can be addressed. Finally, the chapter uses the thoughts of John Stuart Mill as a theorist of rights and utility, whose reflections on international affairs point to some of the tensions in articulating a liberal theory of human rights in a global political order.

Rights

One definition of rights is that they are justified demands we make on others. This definition condenses a wide range of legal and political theories, but owes its formulation to the work of the early 20th-century legal philosopher Wesley Hohfeld. Hohfeld was an American law professor who taught at Yale and Stanford universities but published very little. His overarching goal was to provide conceptual clarity for terms such as 'right', 'duty' and 'obligation'. These concepts were, and are to this day, used in a variety of ways. As part of the legal positivist movement, Hohfeld believed that to clarify the meaning of terms would help sharpen and clarify the legal arguments being made in domestic American law.

His arguments along these lines were published in two journal articles in 1913 and 1917, which were then combined into a book and edited by others after his untimely death in 1918. *Fundamental Legal Conceptions as Applied in Legal Reasoning* (Hohfeld 1946 [1919]) focuses on eight terms that he argued were central to clarifying the meaning of law: right, duty, privilege, power, immunity, disability, liability and no-right. These concepts are related to each other by Hohfeld in a structure that linked some terms as opposites and others as correlatives. For the purpose of understanding human rights in the legal order today, however, it is only the concepts of right and duty that deserve attention.

For Hohfeld (1946 [1919]: 38), a right is simply a claim made, but it only makes sense if it is correlated to a duty since one cannot make a claim against no one. He went on to clarify two concepts of rights in the common law tradition – rights *in rem* and rights *in personam*. For those against whom Hohfeld was arguing, this distinction had traditionally meant rights relating to people and rights relating to things, using a literal translation of the Latin terms. Hohfeld (1946 [1919]: 72), however, redefined the words so as to clarify the scope of the claim being made, that is, to whom the duty applies. Rights *in rem* are those rights that create duties for all persons, while rights *in personam* are rights designed to create duties for particular persons.

These distinctions and clarifications are rarely used in international human rights discourse, as they are specific to the context in which Hohfeld was writing. Yet, they provide an important entry into thinking about rights. First, they clarify the idea that rights are part of a relationship rather than things or concepts that somehow exist without other people. Put differently, one might say that Robinson Crusoe stranded on his desert island would have no rights until the arrival of another person.

Second, rights are to be understood as something stronger than requests or suggestions; they are justified claims made against one or more people, claims that create correlative duties for those against whom they are made. Hohfeld used the word 'duty' to correspond to rights; in this chapter, I use the term 'responsibility'. These are not the same word, of course, although their meanings do overlap in important ways. Hohfeld helps us to see that when we talk about rights, these are not simply in existence by themselves; they create responsibilities, or duties, towards others. The idea of responsibility is just as complicated as the idea of rights, a point I will explore later in the chapter. For now, though, it is important to emphasize that a right creates a responsibility.

These clarifications from Hohfeld cannot be the final definition of rights, however, For one thing, Hohfeld's expertise was in property and corporate law, and so much of the analysis on which he draws explores how rights and duties relate to the ownership of property. This link between the concept of rights and a foundational element of capitalism could be seen to reinforce the critique that Marx and others made of rights; they are simply part of a complex set of socioeconomic relations that only reinforces the capitalist order.

A second critique of Hohfeld's formulation is that it is a domestic rather than international or global understanding. Because he was writing in the context of domestic American law, his concern wasn't really a global one. The idea that there is something called 'human rights', a body of rights that exists outside the boundaries of liberal states, would be a strange concept to many of Hohfeld's contemporaries. Clearly, things have changed since then, so that now rights are understood just as much in global terms as they are in domestic terms. That is, rather than simply being something that arises in particular domestic contexts, rights arise from wider dynamics in the international realm, as demonstrated by the existence of an international human rights regime.

Connected to the previous point, a third critique of Hohfeld's idea of rights is that it does not really capture the history of human rights. Analytic philosophy often assumes that its claims are universal in scope, across time and place, which includes Hohfeld's understanding of rights. For thinkers such as him and others in the analytical philosophy tradition, once we define rights and clarify their conceptual meaning, we can apply them to all cases and across all time. But this ignores the point raised above; the idea of rights as global or as 'human' has a historical trajectory and did not exist prior to the 20th century. As such, before pursuing questions about the conceptual foundations of human rights or how they function in the international order, it is worthwhile briefly exploring what it means to say that human rights have a history.

The history of human rights

Simply stating that human rights have a history needs further clarification. There are three ways in which we can talk about the history of a concept:

1. *Evolutionary:* Human rights have evolved from early versions that were not quite clearly defined to the more robust version we have today.
2. *Pluralist:* Human rights have existed in various times and places in a wide variety of manifestations. All these manifestations play a part in creating what we have today as modern human rights.
3. *Genealogical:* Human rights might have a history, but it is not the progressive evolutionary one. Rather, human rights have developed in fits and starts and arisen from unexpected political and legal changes in different times and places. Uncovering this history is more complicated and might highlight how human rights are imbricated in a wider set of practices that are not necessarily liberal ones.

The evolutionary idea of human rights is one that reflects the progressive development of the human person over time. It assumes a dark past in which there may have been glimmers of something like rights, which have evolved and developed into the idea we have today. Generally, these approaches locate human rights within a Western or European tradition of thought. Some begin with the ancient world, particularly the Greek and Roman context. These accounts highlight the contributions of Plato, Aristotle and Cicero, all of whom are seen as contributing to the idea of the person as a rights-bearing individual (Box 3.1). These accounts tend to focus on natural law rather than rights, concluding that an idea of rights can be found more easily in the Roman tradition of law than in the Greek conceptions of the polity and virtue.

Another version of the evolutionary idea locates human rights in Europe (Vincent 2010: 37–68). One argument places human rights in early medieval contexts, especially the way in which natural law turned into natural right, particularly surrounding the right to property in relation to the monarch (Tierney 2001). Others have argued that our understanding of rights only arises in the 17th century or early modern period in Europe. For some, the central figure in this development is Grotius (Tuck 1979), while for others it is Hobbes (Strauss 1953). Even more important than these two in the context of liberal conceptions of human rights is Locke (Zuckert 2002), whose influence stretched from his own English context across the Atlantic to the early American context, especially in its founding moment.

Micheline Ishay provides an example of this approach in her work on the history of human rights. Ishay (2004: 360–2) argues that human rights are

> ### BOX 3.1 Greeks and Romans on citizenship and rights
>
> Aristotle (1996: 81), the Ancient Greek political theorist, argued that to be a good citizen meant being able to rule and be ruled. This suggests that citizenship is not only about a set of rights that individuals use to protect themselves, but, more crucially, rights must be linked to responsibilities in governance. In opposition to this view, the Roman conception of citizenship was primarily about protection against abuses by those who governed. One famous instance of this conception of citizenship can be found in the Christian scriptures, when the Apostle Paul invokes his rights as a Roman citizen to protect himself from arrest in Jerusalem (Acts 22: 27–9). These two different versions of citizenship relate to different conceptions of rights and how they relate to the wider society. The 'Greek' model emphasizes responsibility for governance and the 'Roman' model emphasizes the protections provided by rights. Although these models do not make their way precisely into modern politics, they at least point to different ideas of how rights, responsibilities and citizenship relate to each other.
>
> *For a full development of this idea, see:* Pocock 1994.

very much the product of the West, although it is somewhat unclear what she means by this concept. She locates ethical formulations that approach human rights in ancient religious traditions, but argues that only those that contributed to the Enlightenment can be seen in this progressive story. Indeed, she argues that it is the Enlightenment, which included a rejection of religious traditions as having any authority (Israel 1994), which truly constitutes the birth of the modern human rights regime (Ishay 2004).

Some evolutionary stories begin even after the Enlightenment period. The 20th century is when human rights began to be used as a meaningful term, especially in the postwar era. The rise of UN institutions created a new world in which human rights could be meaningfully deployed by people around the world (Mertus 2009). Samuel Moyn (2010) has argued that human rights did not become a meaningful concept until even later, in the decade following the uprisings of the 1960s in Europe, the US and Latin America. Moyn claims that human rights became part of a more active and progressive political agenda after the failure of rights to have an impact in the early 20th century.

The second conception of history that shapes our ideas of human rights is the pluralist one. This story of human rights is generally progressive, as the evolutionary one is, although it does not locate human rights in a single path, moment or geographical context. These arguments find intimations of human rights in a broad range of contexts. For instance, Cyrus the Great, the ruler of Persia in the 7th century BC, allowed religious groups to worship as they wished, and he was celebrated by some as the founder of modern human rights. Others have argued that human rights can be found in Confucianism (de Bary 1998). Those engaged in comparative political theory have explored not only rights but a wide variety of different political concepts as they appear in diverse contexts around the world. Fred Dall-mayr (2002: 51–70) has explored how different traditions and thinkers from around the world can speak to each other in a way that reveals alternative conceptions of concepts such as rights.

The story of human rights in Islam can be located in this pluralist account. Islam was in dialogue with Western, that is, Jewish and Christian, philosophy and theology from its foundations through the medieval period, especially through such figures as Avicenna (or more accurately Ibn Sina), who synthesized Aristotelian thought with Islamic theology. In the history of Islam, stories of Muhammad promulgating respect for the rights of combatants (Kelsay 2007) or in the creation of a constitution in the accord reached with various tribes in Medina (Lecker 2004) provide instances of how rights can be found in this tradition. Other theorists of Islam have argued that interpretations of the sacred writings and the theological core of Islam provide strong protections of human rights. One of the leading theorists of this position is Abdullahi An-Na'im (2008), a Sudanese thinker who works in the US. He argues that for Islam to truly encompass human rights, its interpretative strategies must evolve further. Others have explored the possibilities and tensions found in an Islamic human rights approach (Sachedina 2010).

The pluralist understanding of human rights can be seen in the background to the drafting of the UN Universal Declaration on Human Rights (UDHR). Theologians, philosophers and political actors from a wide range of perspectives contributed to the drafting of the UDHR. Jacques Maritain edited a collection of their contributions, under the auspices of the United Nations Scientific, Educational and Cultural Organization (UNESCO 1949). Figures such as the philosopher Charles Malik, whose Catholic background and Lebanese nationality embodied the pluralist idea, played a key role in framing the UDHR. These contributors sought to find a basis for human rights on which they could all agree (Glendon 2001). Susan Waltz (2004) has argued that Islamic states played an important role not simply in deliberations about the UDHR, but also in the drafting of the two key human rights instruments on civil and political rights and economic and social rights.

One final approach to the history of human rights is what I call the genealogical. Genealogy as an approach to political theory and ethics can be traced back to the philosophy of Friedrich Nietzsche. Nietzsche (2007 [1887]) argued that what we see as moral is in fact the result of the weak trying to limit the powerful. He makes this argument by reversing the positive, progressive story of ethics and, relatedly, rights that existed in 19th-century Europe and highlighting the ways in which Christianity and humanism more generally can be understood as part of a bland bourgeois set of practices and ideas. Michel Foucault, the French social and political philosopher, built on Nietzsche's approach to propose alternative histories of social institutions such as the hospital and prison, and practices such as sexuality and psychoanalysis. Foucault did not address rights directly in many of his works, although his recently published lectures on politics and society argue that the liberal constitutional state is undergirded by a Clausewitzian conflict among various agents in modern society (Foucault 2004).

One quasi-genealogical account of human rights comes in David Boucher's (2009) recent critical treatment of the evolution of natural rights to human rights. While providing great detail on the move from natural law to natural right and the key thinkers from the medieval through the early modern period who contributed to these ideas, Boucher concludes by criticizing the idea that human rights can be seen as a progression from natural rights. Instead, he argues that the largely religious dimensions of natural rights were taken by the British idealist philosophers and translated into a secular conception of rights that fit better into the modern state. For Boucher, efforts to ground human rights at the global level on natural rights cannot ignore their largely religious and specifically Christian foundations. Boucher does not draw directly on Nietzsche and Foucault, but he does employ something like a genealogy in his efforts to disrupt a traditional narrative and provide evidence for how unintended outcomes arise at key moments in history.

These different approaches demonstrate how human rights can be seen to arise from a historical context, either in an evolutionary, pluralist or genealogical way. These historical accounts can sometimes be conflated with the foundations of human rights. But, as is evident especially in the genealogical account, to assess the history of a concept does not necessarily give it a foundation. It is to the question of foundations that the next section turns.

Foundations of human rights

There are three kinds of foundational arguments about human rights: divine, natural or consensus-based foundations. There are also non-foundational arguments, which can be divided into two types: pragmatic and political. These categories do not coincide precisely with others that have been proposed, but they certainly overlap with them.

Divine origins

Perhaps the least common today, but one that was most common in the past, is the view that human rights have a foundation in the divine. Within the monotheistic traditions – primarily Judaism, Christianity and Islam – this foundation is sometimes located in the idea of a creator God. The argument here is that because God created humans in his likeness, the human person – body and soul – is sacred. As such, it is worth protecting, and human rights discourse and practice provide that protection.

This foundation can be described as an example of the divine command ethic, one in which moral rules arise from specific commands given by God. It is not a perfect version of this kind of ethical view, for there is nothing in any of the holy books from these traditions that points directly to a list of human rights. But, there are injunctions, as in the Ten Commandments, that point towards some version of rights, such as the core injunction 'thou shall not commit murder'. This is a moral rule that incorporates some conception of the right to physical safety and even, by using the Hebrew word for murder rather than simply killing, assumes a sort of legal code surrounding the decision to take a life.

But this is a difficult position to sustain today, even if one is a believer. John Carlson (2006: 5), in the first edition of the journal *Religion and Human Rights*, asks the pointed question: 'Does God believe in human rights?' Writing from a Christian theological perspective, Carlson notes that to place human rights at the centre of politics and ethics displaces God, something that does not conform to standard accounts of the Christian tradition. Carlson seeks to elide this difficulty by arguing that God would care enough about humans to ensure their dignity and lives are protected, perhaps by something like human rights.

This foundational claim is rarely invoked in the literature on human rights. For instance, Charles Beitz (2009) leaves out divine origins completely. As noted above, Boucher's (2009) account of natural law dismisses it largely because it has links to the religious traditions of medieval Christianity. While some have argued that secularism should not be the predominant language of human rights discourse, they tend not to turn to the divine command idea as their foundation.

Natural right

A second foundational claim relates to the religious one, especially the Christian tradition. The idea of natural law, as explained previously, grew out of the classical and medieval Christian context. Natural law is the belief that the rules governing our collective lives arise not from human activity, such as legislation, but from a combination of divine and natural sources. Natural right is the idea that there is a set of claims that arise not from any stipulated relationship in the Hohfeldian sense but from elements inherent in the human condition. Natural law does not create any kind of claim on others. Rather, natural law constructs a system in which all persons must obey the rules and, in so doing, create a more peaceful order. Natural right is linked to the creation of a specific kind of person, one who requires protection from the rest of the human race. In one sense, natural right assumes a much more conflictual world, one where, because others do not obey the natural law, there is a need for an articulation of some conception of rights.

The evolution from natural law to natural rights was helped by the fact that the Latin word *ius* can be translated as either law or right. As such, the early modern theorists who wrote in Latin and English were central in eliding the distinction between the two concepts. For Grotius, whose work was addressed briefly in Chapter 2 and who will be explored in more depth in Chapter 5, the first natural right is that of self-defence. He does not look for this right in scriptures or Christian tradition alone, but finds it in the behaviour of animals, who, he notes, will fight to protect themselves at all costs. Rather than seeing this as a base form of behaviour, Grotius argues that this is natural, and hence creates a natural right to self-defence.

Locke and Hobbes articulated a similar set of rights. As noted in Chapter 1, both were writing in the context of civil unrest in England. As such, they needed some foundation on which to make an argument for what justified resistance to authority. Locke explicitly grounds his ideas about natural rights in the Christian tradition, which he combines with appeals to the natural world. Jeremy Waldron (2002), for instance, has made the strongest argument for this position, claiming that Locke's entire political philosophy relies on a divine presence, especially in the ways in which the equality of all persons grounds his conception of human rights.

The thinking of Locke in particular made its way into the justifications of the American colonists for their resistance to the British Parliament and king. Their resistance was articulated by Thomas Jefferson in the *Declaration of Independence* in 1776, which is primarily an enumeration of rights violations by the king of Great Britain. And, when the French Revolution broke out, it culminated in the famous statement of the *Declaration of the Rights of Man* in 1789, all of which built on the natural rights tradition. Thomas Paine (1984 [1791]), who played a role in the American and French Revolutions, presents the clearest articulation of these Enlightenment notions of rights in his famous work, *The Rights of Man*.

By the time of the American and French Revolutions, however, the link between natural law and natural rights, including the former's foundations in the Christian tradition, had been weakened (Boucher 2009). While Boucher has made a strong case for the failure of the natural rights tradition to provide foundations for human rights today, others continue to look to natural rights for this foundation. One of the leading natural rights and natural theorists today is John Finnis (1980), who developed one account of the distinction between natural law and natural rights in an early work, but has argued that natural rights can continue to provide a foundation for human rights. Jack Donnelly (1982) proposed a version of natural rights as a possible foundation for human rights in an early article, but moved away from this argument in later publications. Alford (2010) has also argued that natural rights provide a valuable foundation for human rights today, noting that the transition from Aquinas to Locke provides evidence for how rights can be grounded in a foundation that stretches beyond the specifics of the medieval era.

An alternative, but related set of foundations for human rights comes from the capabilities approach proposed by Martha Nussbaum and Amartya Sen (1993). Nussbaum (2000), drawing on Aristotle, has argued that there are certain capabilities that all people require to be fully human. In her book on women and development, Nussbaum explores what it means to provide civil and social rights simply because having such rights is what defines the human person. Nussbaum's argument is not based on the Christian natural rights tradition of the early modern period, but she does draw on a concept of 'natural' in her use of Aristotle.

This foundation also has tensions built into it, however. C.B. MacPherson (1962) argued that Hobbes and Locke helped create the idea of natural rights by constructing a person that 'owns' himself. This means that natural rights are really part of a political-economic structure in which individuals defend themselves for the same reasons they defend their property – because they 'own' it. Grotius and Locke in particular made the defence of property one of the core natural rights. This suggests that the natural law tradition may be fatally linked to a particular type of economic structure that privileges ownership and does not allow space for social and economic rights. Another critique of the Grotian/Lockean conception of natural rights comes from Anthony Pagden (2003), who argues that the link between natural rights and human rights produces a kind of universalism that is linked to the colonial efforts of Europeans in the early modern period. This inherently imperialistic dimension of the natural law tradition continues to bedevil human rights to this day.

One of the most important critiques of natural rights and natural law more broadly, however, is that our idea of nature was radically changed in the 19th century. Andrew Vincent highlights the fundamental role played by Charles Darwin and the idea of evolution in undermining the logic of looking to nature for anything like a coherent foundation for political or moral practices. Darwin's theories were, of course, used by some to create the idea of social evolution, a politicized conception of development and race, which is discussed in Chapter 6. The longer term shift in ideas, however, was the undermining of nature as a foundation for what it means to be a good person. As Vincent (2010: 78–81) notes, there was no longer a rational and benign natural world, but one in which contingency, danger and possibility are the new norms. This fundamental shift in our understanding of nature, explored more fully in Chapter 6, has made appeals to the natural world as a basis for human rights increasingly difficult.

Consensus-based foundations

A third foundation is consensus. If most of the world agrees upon a set of rights, this means they must be somehow true or have a basis that can be accepted by all. This idea can be found in the classical Roman conception through their idea of the *jus gentium*, or the law of nations. This idea is sometimes conflated with natural law, but there is a conceptual distinction here. The idea is that if all communities share a conception of what is right and wrong, it must have some truth to it. This notion has made its way into modern debates about customary international law, where the premise is that some laws are accepted by all and, as a result, should be seen to have clear foundations.

Human rights are sometimes seen to have this foundation, especially as they were constructed in the postwar world. As noted above, UNESCO put together a group of philosophers and theologians to determine what human rights means across different cultures. Rather than demonstrating that all agree on the foundations of rights, however, that dialogue was summed by Maritain, who famously said: 'We agree about the rights but on the condition that no one asks us why' (quoted in Moyn 2010: 67). In other words, the foundations of rights are not to be found in shared divine sources of philosophical arguments, but simply in the fact that everyone agrees that rights exist.

However, this does not seem like the kind of foundation found in divine or natural rights accounts. But, it is a powerful claim to a shared sense of human rights. Beitz (2009: 74–95), while critical of this position, explains it carefully. He notes that there are three versions of this idea: the common core, the overlapping consensus, and the progressive convergence:

1. The *common core* is that all traditions and cultures agree on a set of basic rights. This closely reflects the naturalism of Nussbaum's account, although it need not be based in nature.

2. The *overlapping consensus* is drawn from John Rawls, who suggested that through the political use of reason, we may come to an agreed upon consensus. It may not meet everyone's ideas of what counts as basic rights, but the consensus that develops will contribute to a shared idea of rights.
3. *Progressive convergence* is the idea that over time a consensus will develop. This reflects a liberal progressive conception of rights and governance that underlies a great deal of discourse surrounding rights.

These three versions of the consensus idea can be found in popular ideas about rights, ones that reflect the kind of nonjudgemental attitude often found in liberal politics. As Betiz and others demonstrate, however, such assumptions can be faulted for their failure to provide a moral reason for accepting human rights. More importantly, there are some issues on which there is a serious lack of agreement. The idea of religious freedom, for instance, has long been a difficult issue for a consensus-based approach to human rights. Perhaps more accurately, the idea that someone can change their religion goes against certain interpretations of Islam; to convert from Islam to another religious belief system or none at all means one can be labelled an 'apostate' and be subject to punishment in certain political systems. Another challenge concerns LGBT rights. Because a non-heterosexual approach to sexuality stands counter to many religious traditions, there is little ground for seeing a convergence towards respecting these rights more broadly. While there may be a long-term trend towards acceptance of these rights, it is unlikely that convergence around this set of rights will be forthcoming any time soon.

Politics and human rights

As opposed to a foundational approach, some theorists of rights have taken a more pragmatic approach to the question of human rights. I have labelled these approaches 'political', not because they share any single idea of what politics is, but more because their pragmatic and practice-based approach tends to reinforce the idea that human rights are part and parcel of a political process rather than a divinely inspired or naturally based foundation.

Michael Ignatieff's Tanner Lecture in 2000 argued that human rights had become a form of 'idolatry', that is, a false idol that has replaced God in the world. He does not, however, argue that we need to return to God but rather uses this idea to argue that human rights activists need to scale back their utopian aspirations. Ignatieff (2001) suggests that human rights have become a sort of 'trump' that can win every political argument, resulting in a narrow and idealistic conception of political life. Instead, he argues that we need to place human rights in their political context and appreciate the complexities that face us in modern life when we draw on human rights.

Ignatieff's argument is directed towards those who agitate for human rights, primarily activists. William Schultz, the former director of Amnesty International USA, made a similar point, but one directed at Americans. He begins *In Our Own Best Interests* by asking why someone from East Tennessee should care about human rights abuses abroad (Schultz 2002). Schultz goes on to develop a practical and pragmatic argument about how protecting human rights can benefit Americans in areas such as economics, the environment and even security. In the one quasi-theoretical chapter, Schultz places to one side natural or religious arguments, appealing to something like human sentiment as a possible reason for respecting human rights.

Ignatieff's lectures and Schulz's book are less well developed theoretically in their understanding of the political, posing a kind of 'realism versus idealism' framework within which to position human rights. Other conceptions of a political approach to human rights are more theoretically developed. One way to understand the idea of a practice is to turn to the philosophical idea of pragmatism. Pragmatism as a philosophical position can be traced to the late 19th and early 20th-century theories of thinkers like C.S. Peirce and John Dewey. The basic idea of pragmatism is that rather than beginning from a theoretical foundation and then analysing or critiquing specific practices, we should begin with the practices of what people are doing and develop our understandings and theories of the world on the basis of those practices. Moreover, these understandings and theories should be focused on changing the world for the better rather than simply understanding it. Naturally, social scientists might claim this is what they do in gathering data and developing theories to explain that data. Pragmatism, however, differs from this approach in that it does not seek to develop traditional theoretical models that offer explanations. Instead, a dynamic develops in the interplay of practice and theory that grounds knowledge in a more accessible and programmatic direction. As such, pragmatism has a built-in normative dimension, that is, it is designed to provide the means by which individuals, societies and groups can progress in addressing issues that confront them.

An important pragmatist theorist is Richard Rorty (1989), whose writings drew on Dewey but who developed a more critical perspective on a broad set of philosophical issues. While his wider philosophy is too complex to summarize here, when it comes to the topic of human rights, Rorty explored how concrete practices such as education and politics can construct greater respect for the human person. Rorty argued that rather than focus on what humans are, we should focus on how we can help humans evolve so as to achieve their fullest potential. For Rorty, this entails not simply providing rational reasons to respect human rights, but educating people in some deeper way. He drew on not only pragmatism but also 18th-century philosophers such as David Hume to argue that if we want to convince people to change their views on human rights, we need to appeal to their 'moral sentiments', a term used by Hume and Adam Smith (Smith's ideas are explored in more detail in Chapter 4). This sentiment-based approach, which Schultz also deploys, focuses on how we can see others as like ourselves and how that understanding leads to a greater appreciation of what we share with others. This appeal to sentiment, through educational practices, will have a far stronger impact than an appeal to rationally grounded reasons for respecting human rights (Rorty 1998).

Other political approaches to human rights focus on activism and citizenship, such as Vincent (2010). Interestingly, Vincent does not conclude that rights can only be protected within the state, nor does he argue for cosmopolitan citizenship. Instead, he critically assesses the idea of the state, arguing that it remains indebted to a 19th-century Hegelianism that reified a kind of quasi-natural community. This idealization of the state resulted in extreme attempts to 'purify' the state, culminating in abuses of individual rights and even genocide. Opposed to this, Vincent argues that the idea of a vigorous state-based citizenship needs to be recovered, one that will best protect the rights of individuals within it and globally.

Beitz (2009) also argues for a political conception of rights, but one that is grounded in the international as opposed to the state. Beitz critically reviews naturalist and consent-based approaches to foundations, but concludes that neither of these provides the firm foundations that they propose. Instead, he argues that human rights can only be understood, globally or internationally, as a set of practices that resulted from 20th-century events and the responses to those events undertaken by state leaders and activists. The triumph of human rights is an international or global one and should be understood as such. Beitz emphasizes the evolution of the UN human rights system as evidence for how rights should be understood globally rather than domestically.

One effort to combine the domestic and the global comes from the constitutive theory of Mervyn Frost. As noted in the Introduction, Frost (2002) has drawn on a Hegelian-inspired notion of the state to argue that if states developed in such a way as to perfect their practices, they can be the foundations for a world in which human rights can be protected. This overlaps with Vincent's idea, although he differs from Vincent in finding

Hegel a valuable source for understanding the state. Frost proposes how states play a role in 'constituting human rights' by constituting the state as an entity that can protect them, a democratic state. He parallels Beitz's claim by exploring how global practices create our modern notions of rights, but he diverges from Beitz by emphasizing how human rights must be reconnected to the domestic state in order to have real effect. In Chapter 7, I briefly return to Frost when I describe Hegel's ideas of politics and international life.

As is evident from this section, there are multiple ways to understand human rights through the lens of the political. They range from the pragmatism of Rorty to the constitutive theories of Frost. All these arguments see politics as a kind of active citizenship, either in the global or cosmopolitan sense or the domestic and liberal sense. One way to further explore the idea of human rights as politics is to turn to the corresponding idea of responsibility. Returning to the opening discussion of rights as only making sense within the context of a relationship, what is it that those who are tasked with protecting rights should do? What responsibilities do they have for the protection of those rights?

Responsibilities

Responsibility is the idea that certain kinds of actions can be attributed to certain agents, which they should or must perform. We think of responsibility primarily in terms of individual people, but agents, particularly in the political realm, can also be corporate, ranging from states to businesses to NGOs. Understanding these kinds of corporate agents as responsible is complex, but a number of thinkers have tried to develop this idea in some detail over the past few years (Erskine 2003).

Responsibility can be prospective or retrospective. Prospective responsibility means an individual has certain roles assigned to them, which should guide their actions in the future. We assume that for a person to be prospectively responsible, they have freely chosen the role that generates those responsibilities. So, for instance, the decision to run for office means that one freely chooses to become a politician, with the responsibilities that go along with that role. Prospective responsibility is sometimes referred to in terms of obligations and duties, although these terms all have slightly different valences. The roles that accompany prospective responsibility can be freely chosen, but they can also be imposed or even result from a mix of choice and coercion. Marion Smiley (1992) describes how such roles construct a range of responsibilities, which we may not necessarily appreciate until they appear in the political realm. For instance, if one chooses to be a mother, certain responsibilities accompany this role. Smiley points out, however, that when debates about child rearing in the wider society become politicized, the role of 'mother' can take on responsibilities that arise from political assumptions about education, working mothers and a host of other issues.

A different way to understand responsibility comes from seeing it on moral, legal and political levels. Moral responsibility is the idea that one is responsible for actions an individual has freely chosen. These are not actions that rely on specific social or political roles, but on the very nature of what it means to be a human being, particularly when it comes to retrospective responsibility. Such accounts often focus on the link between free will and responsibility (Fisher and Ravizza 1993). Legal responsibility is the idea that individuals are prospectively and retrospectively responsible for their actions as they relate to the laws of a particular polity. This is related to moral responsibility, and has been treated as such by those who write within legal philosophy (Hart and Honore 1959).

Political responsibility is a slightly different conception. It is similar to moral responsibility, in that it relies on our ability to formulate and undertake plans that can be attributed to us. It is linked to legal responsibility, in that it is linked to the rules that govern a polity. But, unlike moral and legal responsibility, political responsibility does not have their same underlying causal logic. Instead, political responsibility constructs a role for an individual as a result simply of being in a community. This is not tied to obeying specific laws and being held responsible if one violates those laws. Rather, it is being connected to the decisions made by that community and undertaken in its name. Arendt (2003) provides one version of this notion of responsibility, when she argues that belonging to a community, such as a nation-state, means that one is responsible in some way for the actions undertaken by that community. This form of responsibility, again, is not about linking individuals to specific actions; rather, it is about linking individuals to communities and forcing them to understand how their actions, or more commonly lack of actions, construct them as responsible for outcomes. John Williams (2013) uses this notion of responsibility to critique those who protest against war, suggesting that even if one protests against it, living in a community from which one benefits makes one responsible for it in some way.

A third way to understand responsibility is in terms of either individual or corporate responsibility. Individual responsibility is our default understanding of all these different categories, especially since it is easiest to locate some conception of free will in and attribute roles to people. The complicated notion is corporate responsibility, or the idea of holding groups of people responsible. To be responsible, such groups must be more than random groupings, for they must be able to undertake actions with intentionality. Various efforts have been made to understand how groups can be held responsible, drawing on business corporations and states as models (French 1984; Isaacs 2011). IR scholars have also tried to explore how corporations, ranging from states to international organizations, can be understood as being responsible (Erskine 2003; Isaacs and Vernon 2011). International law has recently developed a set of standards by which states can be understood as responsible agents, although attributing responsibility to agents of such disparate and complicated political structures raises a host of difficulties (Crawford 2013; Erskine 2003; Lang 1999).

Responsibility can be paired with rights, especially if we build on the initial section of this chapter, in which rights are understood as part of a relationship. To claim a right means it must be claimed from someone or some institution, which creates a set of responsibilities for those who must ensure that the rights of the claimant are respected. In some cases, this might be nothing more than the responsibility not to interfere with others, as with rights to free speech or the practice of religion. In other cases, it means something different, particularly when the right to education or healthcare is claimed. In both cases, it is probably more accurate to say that institutions have responsibilities that correspond to the rights claims of individuals. When it comes to rights, for instance, states are the agents most commonly responsible for ensuring the protection and enforcement of rights. At the same time, businesses might also be responsible for the protection or rights, particularly where the state might be weak and the corporate agent strong (Karp 2009). We might also hold international organizations responsible for the failure to protect individuals in certain situations (Lang 2003).

Responsibility, then, can help in understanding human rights by locating the agent to whom we should look for enforcement and protection of those rights. But the discourse of responsibility is not as widely accepted as the discourse of rights. Moreover, we tend to see human rights as something that exists outside any relationship with any specific agent. There is one area where responsibility has emerged as an important discourse, one directly connected with human rights – the responsibility to protect, addressed in Chapter 2. Locating this responsibility to protect is complicated, but it seems important to relate it to the UN system, because it is there, perhaps more than anywhere else in the current order, where a truly international discourse surrounding rights and responsibilities is taking place.

The United Nations, rights and responsibilities

The UN was designed to create a more peaceful and secure world after the end of the Second World War. The protection and advancement of human rights is part of this mandate. The Charter of the United Nations, which mentions human rights seven times (Morsink 1999: 4), does not specify any specific rights, but it does help create structures through which rights can be protected. It tasks the Economic and Social Council (ECOSOC) with making recommendations to advance rights (Article 62) and to create a commission to promote human rights (Article 68). The then Commission on Human Rights undertook the drafting of the Universal Declaration of Human Rights (UDHR) in fulfilment of these articles. The UDHR took two years to write, a process that included a wide range of individuals from different states, philosophical backgrounds and political experiences (Morsink 1999). The UDHR, however, was only a declaration at its adoption in 1948, and thus was not seen to imply legal obligations. A number of related treaties, which had the force of law, were soon passed, covering such issues as genocide, refugees and slavery (Forsythe 2006: 29–56). More directly addressing human rights, the Commission on Human Rights drafted two documents that, along with the UDHR, form what some call the 'international bill of human rights' – the International Covenant on Civil and Political Rights and the International Covenant on Economic and Social Rights. These documents, completed in 1966, entered into force in 1976 when two-thirds of the signing states had ratified them.

Almost every constitutive part of the UN system has some role to play in advancing or protecting human rights, although human rights is only a part of their larger institutional roles. So, for instance, the UN Security Council, tasked with promoting peace and security in the international system, has also been involved in the promotion of human rights. In its early years, some states did bring human rights concerns to the UNSC in light of the fact that 'threats to peace could arise from violations of human rights' (Forsythe 2006: 59). But it was not until the end of the Cold War, when the UNSC was no longer paralysed by the conflict between the US and USSR, that it was able to play a more prominent role in the promotion and protection of human rights, primarily through the creation of peacekeeping forces and even the promotion of rights and democracy in wartorn societies such as Cambodia in 1993. Other parts of the UN system, such as the Secretary-General and General Assembly, have also been involved in promoting human rights, by promoting the normative idea and the creation of bureaucratic institutions that help advance human rights.

Two parts of the UN system are directly connected to the advancement of rights. Julie Mertus (2009) argues that the Office of the High Commissioner for Human Rights (OHCHR) is the most important constitutive element of the UN. The OHCHR was created as a result of the Vienna Conference on Human Rights held in 1993, although the idea of a single administrative officer within the UN system responsible for human rights had been proposed at the very outset (Mertus 2009: 9). The office came into being in December 1993 with passage of General Assembly Resolution 48/141 and has, since then, enabled a single institution to be a focal point within the UN system for the advancement of human rights. The mandate of the OHCHR was greatly expanded in 2002 when Secretary-General Kofi Annan requested that the High Commissioner integrate human rights across all activities of the UN (Mertus 2009: 8).

The OHCHR has become an important part of the UN system, with an extensive reach throughout the organization and across the international community. It provides technical support to states as they seek to create more robust and effective forms of human rights protection. But, one might argue that by placing the promotion and advancement of human rights in the hands of an administrative office within the UN system, state leaders and citizens around the world may believe that they have done all they need to do for human rights. The fact that the High Commissioner is part of the UN bureaucratic structure rather than an elected official makes them less a political figure than an administrative officer. While this might be necessary to promote human rights in contested areas, it can also depoliticize rights to the extent that they are no longer understood as part of a wider international political order, but as part of a technical 'package' of changes that are required to promote democratic and liberal political systems. In other words, one might argue that by creating this office, the UN system removed human rights from any one person or agency's responsibility for ensuring those rights are protected and promoted.

The other primary institution for human rights in the UN system is the UNHRC. This body, created in 2006, replaced the Commission on Human Rights. As noted above, the Commission was created by ECOSOC and played a key role in creating human rights obligations through its drafting of the International Bill of Human Rights. But by the late 20th century, the Commission was subject to a great deal of criticism for its failure to promote human rights; instead, many argued it had become an institution where states with poor human rights records were able to hide their records by using the Commission as a platform to critique other states. Over the years, for instance, the Commission consistently targeted Israel in its condemnations, seemingly more than any other state. This focus on one state to the exclusion of others that had far worse human rights records rendered the Commission a body with no real ability to promote or protect human rights.

Partly as a result of these criticisms, the UN General Assembly created the UNHRC in 2006. Bertrand Ramcharan (2011) describes how it emerged in 2004 and 2005 as a result of advocacy by then Secretary-General Kofi Annan and disillusionment with the Commission. Ramcharan, who worked in the UN bureaucracy, argues that the UNHRC remains a political body, in that its members are states that will continue to promote politics and declarations in the interests of their own constituencies, as they did with the Commission. At the time, he argues that the UNHRC is a great improvement over the Commission, especially in the creation of the universal periodic review structure noted in the introduction to this chapter. In contrast to the High Commissioner, one might note that precisely because it is a political body, it creates a different kind of responsibility. While it may still engage in politically motivated activities, perhaps because of its political nature, the UNHRC can be a more effective actor in highlighting how human rights are not simply claims outside a political system, but inherently part of the political order, one in which responsibility for their promotion is part and parcel of a wider set of political practices.

The idea that human rights might be best protected and promoted by a political body such as the UNHRC rather than an administrative body such as the OHCHR goes against the grain of most human rights theorizing. Often, human rights are seen as something that should be promoted by neutral and impartial actors who stand above the fray of political interests and conflict. But perhaps it is only by injecting human rights and their related responsibilities into the political realm more directly that they can best be promoted and protected. One political theorist, John Stuart Mill, gives us a way to understand this essentially political dimension of human rights.

John Stuart Mill and rights

John Stuart Mill (1806–73) was a British philosopher and political actor of the Victorian era. He was the son of the utilitarian philosopher James Mill, who subjected him to a rigorous upbringing that included learning classical languages at the tender age of five, although Mill went through something of a nervous breakdown in his twenties, partly as a result of the pressures put on him by his father. Mill was greatly influenced by his father's philosophical views along with those of his father's friend and collaborator, Jeremy Bentham, at whose house the young Mill would sometimes holiday with his family. While he worked his whole life at the East India Company, it was as a public intellectual and political actor, including serving time as a Member of Parliament, that Mill had his greatest influence. He published a series of highly influential books, as well as a wide range of essays that established his influence as a radical reformer. When he died in 1873, Mill's reputation as a thinker and political activist was firmly established, leading one recent biographer to suggest that: 'he is unquestionably the greatest public intellectual in the history of Britain – and perhaps even the world' (Reeves 2007: 486).

Mill is not the usual theorist to whom we might look for insights into human rights. In fact, Jeremy Bentham, one of his mentors, famously described rights as 'nonsense on stilts', although he was not critiquing all rights but those derived from natural law (Waldron 1987). Moreover, Mill's utilitarian philosophical background is sometimes posed in opposition to the deontological, or duty-based, political philosophy of theorists such as Kant. Here, I want to suggest that Mill is an important theorist of rights for two reasons. First, his wider philosophical ideas locate rights in the context of how the human person can become a more responsible and active member of political life. As such, his theories usefully combine the ideas of rights and responsibilities in the sense I have developed them in this chapter. Second, and more critically, Mill's thinking on rights does not extend beyond certain kinds of states and was not conceptualized globally. For instance, he wrote briefly on intervention, arguing that it was only justified in a few instances and in certain kinds of states, particularly in those communities that Mill describes as 'barbaric'. So, Mill is worth exploring not only because he provides an interesting way to understand the relationship of rights to responsibilities, but also because he failed to go beyond a European framework for where such rights were relevant.

Mill's most famous political work, *On Liberty*, was published in 1859. More of a pamphlet than a systematic philosophical argument, *On Liberty* argues that the primary principle of any political system should be the protection and promotion of the maximum amount of liberty, primarily in the area of thought and speech. Unlike most human rights theory today, though, Mill believed that the greatest threat to liberty was not the state but public opinion. He argued that because public opinion was becoming more influential in governance today, the threat from widespread social norms would be more and more yoked to political power, making the protection of freedom essential. Also, because government policy arises not only from principles of good governance but also from traditions of social and religious origin, protecting freedom of thought and speech becomes even more important in a liberal political order. For Mill in his time, threats from the established Church of England were central; he has long passages arguing that anyone should be free to think about religious and moral matters as he sees fit (Mill 2008 [1859]: 22–8, 56–9). In passages that echo more recent debates in the Islamic world concerning rights and religious belief, Mill argues that

Christianity creates a passive acceptance of social norms that are not conducive to human flourishing, and that, as such, Christianity should not be seen as the only source for moral behaviour (ibid.: 46). Mill continued to insist on rights in his other works, one of which became a key text in advancing the rights of women. Published in 1869, *On the Subjection of Women* pushed for women's suffrage, greater rights in divorce and inheritance, and rights in the workplace. This book begins from the same premise as *On Liberty*; that the oppression of women results from longstanding assumptions, often reinforced in religious traditions that are socially widespread (Mill 2008 [1869]: 475). In this work, Mill expresses his underlying utilitarian philosophy more clearly when he argues that giving women more rights is not simply a good principle but will benefit the wider society.

Mill's justification for rights, then, has a strong utilitarian dimension to it. Moreover, he also links the rights of individuals to their responsibilities, or, more accurately, to their ability to be active members of society and politics. In *Considerations on Representative Government* (Mill 2008 [1861]), he sought to improve the British form of government by making it more representative and better able to serve the people. In the 19th century, Great Britain was a parliamentary democracy, but its electoral system was severely flawed. For instance, rotten boroughs were electoral districts with a tiny number of constituents designed to ensure the continued dominance of Parliament by wealthy landowners. The Reform Act of 1832 eliminated many of these boroughs, a legislative act that Mill fully supported (Reeves 2007: 87–8). In fact, Mill was eventually elected to parliament, serving as an MP in the House of Commons from 1865 to 1869. In the text of *Considerations on Representative Government* and his speeches in Parliament, Mill argued for the creation of citizens who were informed, active and educated. This meant proposing electoral reforms that were not purely democratic, however. For instance, he argued for increasing the number of votes available to more educated members of the public. While this is certainly not democratic, it was designed to improve governance and, importantly, to ensure that majorities would not violate the rights of minorities and even of themselves. In other words, Mill's focus in designing a constitutional system, even one that was more representative, was less about ensuring that all had equal votes and more about ensuring that the system protected the rights and interests of all.

Mill's ideas about politics, then, allow us to see how responsible citizenship can lead to the protection of rights and good governance. His international theory, on the other hand, reveals how those ideas were bound (at least in his mind) to certain kinds of states. In *On Liberty*, Mill argues that the benefits of free speech and freedom of thought accrue only to those in the fullness of their faculties. So, for instance, giving children the right to freedom of expression is perhaps not as beneficial as giving it to adults. More controversially (at least for us today), Mill (2008 [1859]: 14–15) extends that logic to the developing world:

> For the same reason [as not giving rights to children] we may leave out of consideration those backward states of society in which the race itself may be considered in its nonage ... Despotism is a legitimate mode of government in dealing with barbarians, provided the end may be their improvement, and the means justified by actually effecting that end.

These ideas were more widespread at the time, especially the use of terms like 'barbarians'. Mill worked for much of his professional life as a clerk in the East India Company, which was, in effect, a quasi-state business entity operating in India. It cooperated with the British government in ensuring the use of resources from India, although Mill was also actively involved with improving (as he understood it) the governance of India by introducing British forms of governance there.

Mill also addressed the question of whether or not a state should be subject to intervention if there are violations of rights, or in his framing a civil conflict, taking place. In *A Few Words on Non-Intervention*, Mill (1859) critiques the claim that intervention should only be undertaken for national self-interest, engaging in a debate in Britain at the time about intervening in Greece where civil conflict was generating demands to support minorities. One might therefore assume that he supported something like humanitarian intervention. Instead, he argued that intervention is only allowed if it is in response to an already ongoing intervention by a more powerful entity, that is, when a state was subject to 'foreign' intervention. Mill was writing at a moment when the idea of 'foreign' and 'domestic' had solidified in the minds of European intellectuals and political actors. To intervene in this context meant undermining the normative structure of the European order, making the idea of humanitarian intervention largely irrelevant here. Instead, there was only intervention, which violated the norms of the European society of states.

Yet, this was not the only context within which intervention took place during the time of Mill's writing. Although he concludes that interventions should not take place among 'Christian' nations, Mill is quite clear that intervention is allowed and even necessary between imperial powers and their dominions. Allowing intervention in this imperial context while forbidding it in the European context resulted from the different international societies in existence at this time, a difference defined in large part by assumptions about moral progress and race, as Mill (1859) describes it:

> To suppose that the same international customs, and the same international rules of morality, can obtain between one civilized nation and another and between civilized nations and barbarians, is a grave error into which no statesman can fall into ... [Barbarians] cannot be depended on for observing any rules. Their minds are not capable of so great an effort.

Again, we see here Mill's assumptions about the difference between societies and how some rules apply in one context but not another.

So, what can we draw from Mill's insights? First, Mill allows us to see that rights cannot be extracted from wider ideas about citizenship, governance and political life. For Mill, his support for liberty of conscience and speech is not a naked right outside particular forms of government. Rather, he understood rights to be part of a framework of political life, one that was designed to improve the political system for all. As such, he links rights and responsibilities in an important way, one undergirded by his wider utilitarian philosophy. But, at the same time, Mill's ideas about governance were limited by his understanding that certain kinds of political systems were more advanced than others. He did not see rights as a global practice, or as principles that all relate to all peoples.

Even more importantly, Mill's failure in this area may continue to be a failure in the way we think about rights at the global level. That is, there is a broad consensus that human rights apply to all peoples. But, there is sometimes a sense that some peoples need to be 'taught' rights; that is, some peoples are not capable of governing themselves, so Western powers need to step in and ensure that a political order is put in place which will allow them to function as successful liberal citizens. It is, I would argue, from the same kind of paternalistic impulse that motivated Mill that we wish to help others; that is, we see problems in the world, and so we might well advance arguments for intervention to resolve those problems. Yet, in so doing, we undermine the agency and legitimacy of political actors in many places, ignoring local dynamics and political practices that we may well see as 'barbaric' because they do not correspond with out notions of proper political activity. In drawing on and criticizing Mill, we engage in a critical analysis of his political theory, and our political practices, something this book is designed to enable you to do.

Conclusion

This chapter introduced you to the idea of rights as part of IPT. It has explored the basic idea of rights and linked this with the idea of responsibility. In so doing, I emphasized that rights need to be linked to responsibilities in a political system, concluding with Mill's ideas about how rights are part of wider debates about constitutional and representative government.

At the same time, because this is a book about IPT, I suggested that rights are no longer just about domestic political life. Rather, they are now instruments of the international political order, one that has institutions such as the UN at the core of promoting and protecting those rights. Mill's failure to appreciate the global scope of rights suggests how many ideas about rights need to be reframed in light of the practices and institutions in place today.

These two insights – rights are linked to responsibilities and rights are global – can help in understanding the debate introduced at the outset of this chapter. When individuals in countries like the US object to having an international institution such as the UNHRC monitor their domestic politics, this reflects the views of theorists such as Mill who did not believe that certain countries should be assessing rights practices in democratic states. The idea that only democracies can speak to the practices of other democracies assumes that rights are only understood in certain contexts, contexts that are structured by ideas such as 'developed' and 'developing'. Some countries do indeed have poor human rights records, but this may not mean that their diplomats or NGOs from those states are not in a relationship with the UN in which all members have responsibilities to monitor and explore problems of human rights together. If we see the international or global political system as a space in which rights and responsibilities interact and work together, all members should play a role in monitoring human rights practices, nor matter where they speak from or where they are speaking to.

This chapter does not answer the problems of human rights practice and protection that have been raised throughout. Rather, it suggests that in exploring these issues, rights should not be seen as simple claims that have no connection to wider political dynamics. Instead, we need to locate rights in the context of a complicated international order in which overlapping claims of rights and responsibilities are constantly shifting and evolving. Chapter 4 points to how debates about justice, wealth and economics also provide that context, one that is no less easy to understand than the practices of rights.

Further reading

Charles Beitz. 2009. *The Politics of Human Rights*. Oxford: Oxford University Press.
Excellent treatment of the nature of human rights from a leading international political theorist. Presents a range of arguments about the foundations of rights, and argues that most foundational and consensus-based accounts are problematic. Instead, posits that locating human rights in their global political role provides more insight into what they are and how they work.

David Boucher. 2009. *The Limits of Ethics in International Relations: Natural Law, Natural Rights, and Human Rights in Transition*. Oxford: Oxford University Press.
Written by a leading figure in the field of IPT, it argues that human rights, while indebted in their emergence to natural law and natural rights, can no longer rely on these ideas to found them. Highlights the continuing link with religious belief that structures the natural law/natural rights tradition, making it problematic as a universal guide and foundation for the human rights regime today.

Gregory Claeys. 2013. *Mill and Paternalism*. Cambridge: Cambridge University Press.
Well-grounded historical study of John Stuart Mill, providing insights into the paternalistic dimension of his political views. The argument is made in relation to his ideas about domestic and international affairs. Also argues that Mill's ideas were decisively shaped by his wife's feminist ideas.

Toni Erskine, ed. 2003. *Can Institutions Have Responsibilities? Collective Moral Agency and International Relations*. Basingstoke: Palgrave Macmillan.
Brings together scholars seeking to rethink the idea of responsibility at the global level. Opens up the debate about responsibility to include a range of institutions, from states to non-state actors to international organizations. Critically analyses whether or not such institutions can truly be held responsible and the consequences of so doing in the current international order.

David Forsythe. 2006. *Human Rights in International Politics*, 2nd edn. Cambridge: Cambridge University Press.
Clear, concise overview of the history and function of human rights in the international order. Focuses on legal texts and international institutions. Mixes realist-inspired scepticism about rights with a strong moral push for greater awareness of and attention to the possibilities of rights.

Micheline Ishay. 2004. *The History of Human Rights: From an Ancient Times to the Globalization Era*. Berkeley: University of California Press. Excellent historical overview locates human rights in the ancient world, although does not fall victim to the idea that such rights have remained the same over time. Rather, critically argues that such rights only became what they are today as a result of the Enlightenment.

Andrew Vincent. 2010. *The Politics of Human Rights*. Oxford: Oxford University Press. Argues that the natural rights foundations of human rights collapsed in the 19th century as a result of Darwin's ideas about evolution. This change gave more power to the state as the only meaningful agent in people's lives, which Vincent suggests culminated in the genocides of the mid-20th century. This event more than any other, in his view, explains the rise of human rights in the 20th century.

Chapter 4

Wealth

In 2011, the head of one bank in the US received a total compensation package of over $20 million. In the same year, an average farmer in Ethiopia earned around $200 a year. Their respective roles undoubtedly require different amounts of time and different levels of education, and the cost of living in their respective locations is not the same. Yet, do these differences truly justify such a vast inequality in income levels?

Domestic governments seek to moderate inequalities through tax policies, welfare and the provision of social services. The political theorist Ronald Dworkin (2000: 1) has argued that equality is a 'sovereign virtue', or one that is the responsibility of government to ensure, and if they fail to ensure that equality, the government is tyrannical. Without some level of equality, there will be tensions within a civil society, which can result in conflict and perhaps even violence, as evidenced by the riots that broke out in London and elsewhere in the UK in 2011. The response of the British government to those riots suggests that when levels of inequality result in violence to persons and property, governments see it as their obligation to respond – even if their responses do not resolve the problem.

But is there a similar responsibility to resolve inequality at the global level? Dworkin famously 'ducked the issue' and did not provide a way to translate his arguments to the global level (Brown 2009). There is clearly a problem of inequality at the global level and it has become a central concern for many theorists (Moellendorf 2009). The numbers alone are staggering. If poverty is defined as living on less than $1.25 per day (the standard international definition), then around 1–1.5 billion people live in poverty worldwide, or roughly one-fourth of the world's overall population. According to one estimate, almost 25,000 people die from starvation-related problems every day (Thurow and Kilman 2009).

At the same time, some studies have indicated that global inequality is actually decreasing. While this is true in the aggregate, a closer examination of the figures suggests that this conclusion results from the increased income levels in China and India over the past 20 years. Branko Milanovic (2012), a leading economist at the World Bank, suggests that this means one's 'location' rather than one's 'class' is a more important indicator of whether or not one will be poor or rich. That is, a determining factor of one's wealth and, crucially, one's ability to increase that wealth may be determined more by one's country of birth and employment than more traditional notions such as class or upbringing. Milanovic (2011) also argues that making such claims is complicated, since measuring inequality can be done across countries, within countries, or across individuals. Moreover, the difficulty of gathering data on these questions when countries employ a wide range of survey and data collection techniques makes it even more difficult to draw any clear conclusions on such matters.

If it is the case that being born in one country rather than another is an important determining factor in levels of wealth or income equality, the international political order has created a system that is, in some deep way, unfair. Individuals cannot choose where they are born, so this factor becomes a matter of luck or chance that stands counter to most theories of equality. And, because we lack a global authority that can redistribute wealth through mechanisms such as taxation, we are left with something of a problem. What the problem is, however, and how to resolve it are not clear. When confronted with these facts, we may feel a desire to help change this situation. But doing so requires not simply compassion, but clear thinking about the politics and economics of the global order. In the field of IPT, many have addressed this dilemma, largely through the lens of the rights of the poor and the responsibilities of the wealthy. In this chapter, some of this literature is reviewed, but placed alongside some more traditional works in political theory, which highlight the deeper tensions in trying to address wealth distribution in any society. The chapter also brings our attention back to themes that are not often invoked in discussions of global wealth issues, those of rules and authority. In so doing, this chapter seeks to demonstrate how IPT should not be limited to a focus on rights and responsibilities; rather, it will more broadly explore the political theory of global wealth.

The chapter begins with a brief discussion of the idea of justice as one core theoretical principle that relates wealth to politics, especially in terms of equality, and connects these ideas to the core themes of this book. I then turn to two of the most important theorists of political economy, Adam Smith and Karl Marx. I compare their ideas about justice and wealth at the global level, suggesting the benefits and drawbacks of their solutions. I then turn to two more recent approaches to global distributive justice that come from a broadly liberal perspective: John Rawls and the works inspired by his approach, and Peter Singer and his utilitarian response. In the former case, the work of Rawls and others draws primarily on the concept of rights, while Singer and other utilitarian approaches employ the concept of responsibility. I suggest that while the approaches offered by these thinkers are helpful in responding to global poverty, they remain disconnected from the wider sphere of the global economic order. As a corrective, I suggest that a focus on authority and rules is also necessary. I conclude by briefly discussing the work of Susan Strange, who sought to link authority to the problem of global finance. I propose that Strange's work on authority and global affairs helps us to understand not only some of the issues addressed surrounding global poverty but also how those issues arise from wider practices in the international realm.

Justice and equality

Issues of wealth distribution are often understood through the lens of justice, which is a central term for many who write about international political theory. Its basic meaning is one of fairness; a just society is one that distributes resources or opportunities across all peoples in a way that is agreed upon by that community and results in a roughly equal set of outcomes. Naturally, justice is not so simple a concept. Plato (428–348 BC), the Ancient Greek philosopher whose ideas about metaphysics, ethics and politics have been and continue to be central to philosophy, developed a theory of justice in his famous dialogue, *The Republic,* written around 380 BC. In that text, Socrates, Plato's protagonist (and teacher), argues against some of the conventional conceptions of justice of his interlocutors in order to promote a version that finds in the order of the soul a way to understand the order of the city. For Plato, a soul is composed of reason, spirit and appetite; reason directs and structures the soul, spirit moves the soul to act, and appetite is the desire for material goods (food, sexuality and so on). Together, these three elements must be combined in the individual so that each plays its proper role and does not interfere with the others. Plato uses this concept as a metaphor for the city, or political community. He argues that a just society is one in which the different parts contribute to the proper functioning of the city. The parts in Plato's city are the philosophers, the warriors and the labourers. Just as in the soul, the philosopher (reason) rules, the warrior (spirit) drives the city forward and the labourer (appetite) provides for the material goods for all. This division among roles is not a class-based one, that is, economic status, but a functional one, based on the roles of each group in the ideal society (Plato 1991).

It is unlikely that we would adopt Plato's configuration for either a domestic or global political society in constructing a just system. At the same time, a core element of Plato's vision is one that still animates some discussions of justice – the idea that an order arises from specifying roles for different persons, groups or even nations to play in a system. This conception differs in important ways from one of the other core principles that arises when considering the problems of wealth – equality. Plato's idea of the city and justice is distinctly unequal, with individuals located in specific groups related to their capacities, which are either inborn or the result of training by the city. Labourers are not expected to rule, and warriors are not expected to farm in *The Republic*. This stands in direct contrast to most liberal (and other modern) theories, which are premised on the claim that all persons are equal. This basic fact of equality provides a foundation for many modern discussions of justice.

But clarifying what it means to be equal in either a domestic or global civil society is not as easy as it sounds. Plato's vision highlights the fact that people (and peoples) have different skills and abilities, not all of which are the same. So, not everyone can paint like Michelangelo or compose music like Bach. These people deserve to be rewarded for their abilities in a way that perhaps an academic writing a textbook does not deserve to be. How to integrate those differences into a just system is one of the dilemmas of modern politics. This dilemma is even more complicated at the global level. In terms of people, some individuals certainly seem more talented than others in certain realms, and perhaps they deserve to be rewarded for this talent. This issue becomes even more complicated when it comes to peoples or states. Are some states wealthier because of some skills they have cultivated in their society? Are they simply wealthier by the chance of having certain natural resources in their territory? Are they wealthier as a result of adopting a particular political or economic system?

It is important to add that justice is not only relevant to questions of wealth. For instance, we talk about criminal justice, an idea that has important implications when it comes to global affairs, with the creation of international criminal tribunals and the International Criminal Court. Justice is relevant here in terms of different ways of responding to crime, such as through punitive measures (some of these themes will appear in Chapter 5 when I turn to questions of violence).

This chapter focuses on wealth, though, and the idea of justice will be central to that discussion. In recent years, justice has become a more important theme in the study of politics, especially through the work of John Rawls. Rawls reinvigorated the study of justice in his famous work, *A Theory of Justice*, published in 1971. Based on this book, a number of scholars sought to make an argument for justice that addressed the global realm. Before turning to these works, however, I want to explore the question of wealth by comparing two of the most important figures to write about political economy in the past 250 years: Adam Smith and Karl Marx.

Adam Smith and the invisible spectator

Adam Smith (1723–90) was a Scottish natural philosopher (Ross 2010). He taught at Glasgow University and served as a public intellectual at a time of great intellectual ferment in his native Scotland and more broadly throughout Europe. He was good friends with some of the leading intellectuals of his day, particularly David Hume. Smith is best known for his 1776 ground-breaking work, *The Wealth of Nations*, in which he argued that the market is the best means to distribute domestic and international wealth. As such, he has become one of the leading lights in the pantheon of capitalist political economy (see Box 4.1).

But Smith did not write solely on economic matters. His first book, *A Theory of Moral Sentiments*, was published in 1759 and was hugely influential. In fact, he republished it a number of times, responding to criticisms and developing his arguments more carefully, with a final edition appearing in 1790 (Smith 1986). Ultimately, Smith argues that morality results from sentiments that arise from within us and not from a natural or divine law that we must intuit from observing nature. Smith's moral theory arose from what he saw to be common sense and, as such, 'functioned without transcendent truths supplied by religion or philosophy, which were always deeply contentious' (Forman-Barzilai 2010: 14). Smith translated this feeling of morality into what he called the 'invisible spectator'

BOX 4.1   Neoliberal theory

Adam Smith is seen as a hero of neoliberal theory. Neoliberalism is an economic and political theory that promotes the market as the best means by which to distribute goods in a society. It begins with the theories of Smith, but draws more heavily on the ideas of the Austrian theorist Friedrich Hayek (1899–1992) and the American economist Milton Friedman (1912–2006). Neoliberal theorists argue that by eliminating government intervention in society, in a range of areas, freedom and justice can best be protected. Their ideas have been influential in many countries, leading to the deregulation of markets in a number of different realms. At the global level, neoliberalism has been promoted as a way to advance economic development and create wealth outside governmental controls, just as Smith advocated. But, deregulation has been blamed for the collapse of the global financial markets in 2008. As a result of an unregulated market in securities, banks and financial investors created financial instruments out of mortgages that had little real value. Without any regulation, these instruments contributed to a global economic crisis. For some, neoliberal theory discouraged governments from playing a more active role in these markets. Smith seems far removed from this extreme form of neoliberal theory. He did not seek to eliminate government from a regulatory role but to prevent it from collecting all the wealth of society, as in mercantilist theory.

For more on neoliberalism, see: Crouch 2011; Harvey 2007. *For neoliberalism and the 2008 economic crisis, see:* Gamble 2009.

who provides a kind of check on our actions. In developing this concept, Smith was arguing against thinkers such as Thomas Hobbes or Bernard Mandeville, who believed that politics resulted from an enlightened form of self-interest. For Smith, while sentiments arose in the individual, they were not the same as self-interested behaviour; instead, they were part of a dialogue with the conventions of society within which one lived:

> Indeed, the *Moral Sentiments* in its entirety might be profitably read as Smith's empirical description of the very process through which people learn actively to balance their social and unsocial passions, actively to put them into harmony. (Forman-Barzilai 2010: 49)

Smith's theory of moral sentiments also went beyond the problems found in Hume's account of moral sympathy. Some have noted that Hume's moral arguments lead to a form of conventionalism, in which the specifics of a particular context can limit that moral sympathy. This leads to tensions in Hume's idea of justice for it fails to provide fairness and equality outside very limited domains; in fact, when reading him as a theorist of global ethics, Hume becomes even more problematic because of this conventionalism. Smith, drawing on the same foundations as Hume, moves towards a greater understanding of justice by emphasizing the individual reactions to injustice. Ironically, Smith argues that by highlighting the strong feelings we have when witnessing injustice, we can more clearly avoid the self-interest that can easily arise from a theory of moral sentiments. This focus on the individual and the impartial spectator in Smith makes him a liberal theorist as opposed to Hume's more conservative theory (Frazer 2010: 111).

The invisible spectator makes its way into Smith's ideas of capitalism. In his framework, the market distributes wealth and does not simply enrich a few. This is because the market operates in accordance with an 'invisible hand', a concept for which he has become famous, although he uses the term only once in the text (Smith 1986: 265). This idea reflects the fact that, for Smith, when we pursue our self-interest in the marketplace, trading and acting to enrich ourselves, the entire community benefits because the market redistributes wealth to all. For Smith, this fundamental construct means that a capitalist approach to wealth distribution is to be preferred to the prevailing mercantilist approach of his day. Mercantilism was the assumption that all trade and commerce was to be directed towards the enrichment of the state or government, which would then distribute it to the people. This meant high taxes, specifically import and export duties, which would direct wealth from productive activity to the coffers of the state. In contrast to this, Smith argued that a capitalist economy would mean wealth went to individuals and thus enriched all. Rather than the government controlling the distribution of wealth, in a capitalist society individuals would be able to channel those funds through their own activities. The government's responsibility was simply to create the legal and political conditions in which the market could function properly.

While an invisible presence of some sort seems to function in Smith's moral and economic theories, they do not connect well. The impartial spectator in the breast of each person results in moral norms arising as that spectator engages with the conventions of society. Yet, the invisible hand of the market has no connection to the societal norms or conventions and is the result of simple self-interest. How do these concepts fit together? One argument can be found when Smith is read through the lens of the international. Fonna Forman-Barzilai argues that Smith's moral theory alone leads to a domestic and particular perspective. Because the moral sentiments arise from the individual living in their own social context, such views will be bound by the cultural norms in which that person lives, which results in a Humean conservatism. While sympathy can indeed stretch beyond borders, it weakens as it expands beyond immediate circles. But Forman-Barzilai (2010) argues that the economic theory found in *The Wealth of Nations* actually creates a 'commercial cosmopolis'. Rather than a jealousy of other nations because of wealth, a global capitalist economic system would mean encouraging the wealth of other nations so that trade can enrich all:

> Smith observed that free, self-interested commercial intercourse among nations might mitigate aggression and cultivate international peace without goodwill or coercion, produce cosmopolitan ends without cosmopolitan intentions, balance national wealth with global 'virtue'. (Forman-Barzilai 2010: 212)

In other words, rather than simply being a way to enrich individuals in a domestic society, a capitalist system can bring about a more cosmopolitan order by turning particular moral sentiments into a global mode of behaviour.

While this reading of Smith presents him as a cosmopolitan theorist of a sort, there is another dimension to his cosmopolitan theory that is less progressive. Book V of *The Wealth of Nations* is where Smith develops his ideas about the proper role of government. He is explicit here, perhaps even more than Locke was, that government is established to protect private property. Moreover, the particular concern of government is the property of the wealthiest, for theirs is most subject to attack by others: 'Civil government, so far as it is institute for the security of property, is in reality institute for the defence of the rich against the poor, or those who have some property against those who have none at all' (Smith 1986: 297). Clearly, this is not a picture of government designed to engage in redistribution; rather, it is a form of government designed to protect those who have attained property.

Smith does acknowledge that government must create the infrastructure necessary for political and social life to flourish, which is a kind of redistribution of income. In terms of international commerce, he also argues that there is a role for government in supporting joint stock companies and entrepreneurial efforts to trade with other, particularly if those efforts might be threatened by attacks from other states. Smith is clear here that the primary duty of government is protection, and it is again protection of those who have the means to trade overseas. There is very little discussion of the role of government in making rules or governing in accordance with a logic that might mitigate extremes of wealth.

Overall, then, Smith first and foremost supports the liberty of individuals to pursue their economic welfare. He is also concerned with ensuring that others in society respect those rights. This focus on rights is what locates Smith in the liberal tradition. His conception of authority as a means to protect the rights of those who have found wealth through trade suggests that his picture of domestic and international economic order is limited to ensuring wealth creation and protection rather than distribution.

Karl Marx and the liberation of the human person

Adam Smith's cosmopolitanism relied on a theory of moral sentiments supplemented by the invisible hand of the marketplace. Karl Marx argued for a different kind of cosmopolitanism, one that did not derive from the moral sentiments of individuals but sought to liberate individuals from a false consciousness about their interests. Marx (1818–83) lived through a period of rapid political and economic change in Europe. He was born in Trier, Prussia, but because of his political activities, he was forced to move at various stages in his life to Brussels, Paris and, eventually, London. As a young man, Marx studied philosophy and was greatly influenced by what has come to be called German idealist philosophy. The philosophical ideas of G.W.F. Hegel (1770–1831) were the most important for his early development. Marx was among a group of German-speaking scholars who called themselves the Young Hegelians, although he soon distanced himself from many of these individuals as his own ideas developed further. Marx drew from Hegel a conception of history, particularly the idea of dialectical history. According to this idea, history progresses by means of an interaction between opposing forces, which is then resolved by means of a revolutionary change (Boucher 2012). For Hegel, this dialectic operated primarily in the world of ideas, with clashing philosophical and theological ideas creating new outcomes as they interacted. Marx borrowed this idea but also famously inverted the Hegelian concept by arguing that it was not a clash of ideas that produced this dialectical process but a clash of material forces.

Marx was critical of another important element of Hegel's thought, which related to the idea of the state. Hegel argued that the state was the perfection of human freedom and that man's identity as a citizen was the culmination of what it meant to be a person. Marx was critical of this idea of the state, because it undermined the importance of civil society and the material relations that constituted the idea of the state. So, rather than rights, citizenship and political institutions, Marx believed that the more important aspect of human life to understand was the modes of production, or the ways in which a society organized itself to sustain its material existence.

This critique of Hegel is scattered throughout Marx's writings but it finds expression, if indirectly, in *On the Jewish Question* (1978 [1843]). This essay was a response to efforts by one of the Young Hegelians, Bruno Bauer, who had suggested that Jews would never achieve political rights in Germany because of the essentially Christian nature of German political culture. Marx seems to agree with this point in the first part of his essay, but then goes on to provide a more radical critique of any conception of civil rights, including the right to freedom of religion. He argues that Jews are seeking a form of political emancipation, but in so doing, they are failing to see that they need to seek human emancipation. This means, for Marx, a much deeper change, one that would lead to the abandonment of religious beliefs such as those of Jews (and Christians and any other believer) and instead turn towards efforts to emancipate the human person:

> Political emancipation certainly represents a great progress. It is not, indeed, the final form of human emancipation, but it is the final form of human emancipation within the framework of the prevailing social order. It goes without saying that we are speaking here of real, practical emancipation. (Marx 1978 [1843]: 35)

He goes on to critique the ideas of rights, such as private property, that are part of this political emancipation. Such rights only reinforce the egoism of the individual, separating him not only from the community but also his true nature, what Marx calls the 'species-being' of the human person.

To understand the idea of species-being means focusing on the work of another Young Hegelian against whom Marx developed his ideas, the theologian Ludwig Feuerbach (1804–72). In his work *The Essence of*

Christianity, Feuerbach used Hegel's ideas to propose a radical account of Christianity, in which the person of Christ is not divine but a perfected ideal of the human condition, or the idealized 'species-being' of humanity. The human person needs this idealized picture because he is alienated from himself; he is an incomplete person that cannot understand his place in the world. Feuerbach developed this idea through an engagement with early theories of anthropology and sociology, highlighting the material dimensions of the human person rather than Hegel's idealism. This reinforced Marx's ideas of the importance of focusing on material elements as opposed to idealized ones.

Marx objected to Feuerbach because he believed that the latter had created a static, ahistorical picture of humanity in his idea of Christ as the species-being. In contrast, Marx argued for a more historical, evolutionary conception of the human person, which manifests itself in different modes of production; as Boucher (2012: 19–20) notes:

> as the implements and methods of labour vary, human beings alter the expression of their essence. The consequence is that labour is both generated by human species being and in turn forms that species being as a historical product.

Marx lays out his critique in the *Theses on Feuerbach*, a series of short notes he wrote as an outline to a longer manuscript, *The German Ideology*; neither the notes nor the full text were ever published in Marx's lifetime, but have become important in understanding Marx's ideas. Marx (1978 [1845]: 143) claimed that Feuerbach had failed to grasp the 'significance of the "revolutionary", of practical-critical, activity'. Because his species-being is an idealized individual whom the human person can only understand through contemplation, Feuerbach fails to appreciate the necessity of practical political activity. Marx states this critique, not only of Feuerbach but of much of idealist philosophy, in the 11th thesis, which has come to be one of his most well-known quotes: 'Philosophers have only interpreted the world, in various ways; the point is to change it' (ibid.: 145).

It is through his engagement with Hegel and Feuerbach that Marx developed his core ideas of the human person, a being that is alienated but who can achieve liberation of sorts in order to attain the fulfilment of the species-being of humanity. In order to do this, Marx turns to the study of economic modes of production, for it is through man's labour and how that labour shapes the human person and society that liberation can be achieved. In his masterwork, *Capital*, Marx argued that economic systems have evolved over time, moving through phases such as proto-communism, feudalism, capitalism, socialism and communism. The world at the time of his writing was moving into the capitalist stage, which Marx believed was necessary for all societies. But in order to achieve full emancipation, humanity had to progress through to the stage of socialism and then eventually communism, which would allow for new forms of social interaction and, crucially, a new human person. Marx famously did not define carefully what this final stage would look like, either in the specifics of how society would work or what the human person would become.

Before turning to some more recent works in international political economy, it is important to say something about the work for which Marx and his collaborator Friedrich Engels are perhaps most famous, *The Communist Manifesto*. This revolutionary pamphlet, issued in 1848, was commissioned by the trans-European political party, the Communist League. It begins with the famous sentence: 'A spectre is haunting Europe – the spectre of Communism' (Marx and Engels 1978 [1848]: 473). Here, Marx focuses on another key element of his thought, the primacy of class relations (Box 4.2). As they describe it in this pamphlet, all history is that of the class struggle, with the bourgeoisie being the dominant class that has sought to oppress the workers. In opposition to this class, the pamphlet calls to the proletarian class to take up the charge to change the world. Importantly, as a pamphlet written for all Europe, it states that the revolution of the proletariat will not be confined to one nation, although they do need to start in the local contexts. While 'the working men have no country' (ibid.: 488), Marx does believe that they must first take control of the social and political order in their own states before moving on to international order. No matter where this happens, Marx is clear in this pamphlet that the primary goal is the elimination of private property, for it is this structure that prevents the working classes, and indeed all people, from ever achieving their true emancipation from oppression.

Marx presents, then, a theoretical framework not just designed to change the economic order into one without private property. Rather, the goal of eliminating private property is ultimately designed to liberate the human person from his alienation from himself and his true nature. Marx's ideas are truly revolutionary, in that if they were adopted, they would lead not simply to minor adjustments in the international political and economic order, but to the creation of an entirely new political reality. As such, they are profoundly political and radical. But, they assume a great deal about what it means to be a person and how persons relate to each other in political life. I will return to Marx in the final section of this chapter when I address the problems of global wealth. But, before doing that, I look to a more recent political theorist of justice, one who revived liberal political theory in the 20th century and whose works have been a source of inspiration to a number of individuals working in IPT.

BOX 4.2   Marx and Marxism

When the Berlin Wall came down in 1989 and the Soviet Union imploded in 1991, some argued that Marxism and communism had been proved false and should be consigned to the dustbin of history. Francis Fukuyama (1989), the American intellectual and diplomat, famously argued that the international system had reached the 'end of history' because of the failure of communism to provide a legitimate alternative. But this misunderstands Marxism as a theory rather than as a political programme. Terry Eagleton (2011), the cultural theorist, recently published a work with the provocative title, *Why Marx Was Right*. Eagleton (2011: 126) points to the continuing truths of some of Marx's arguments, such as the idea that capitalism may increase wealth, but it increases wealth in such a way that individuals must continue to work perhaps even harder than they did under pre-capitalist society; as such, capitalism is a 'self-thwarting system', a fact Marx identified long ago. The financial crisis of 2008 strengthens Marx's idea that capitalism will need to evolve into something different (Gamble 2009). Marx's ideas are also being used not only in the field of economics, but in other areas of international life; for instance, there is a well-developed tradition of Marxist international law (Marks 2008; Mieville 2005). In the field of IR, critical theorists have explored the ways in which states construct the political order such that it benefits particular classes, a structure that reinforces the position of some states at the core and others at the periphery (Wallerstein 1976). Critical theorist Robert Cox (1981) has argued that Marxism provides a way to see certain kinds of theories as simply reinforcing the status quo (problem-solving theory), while others seek the type of liberation that Marx advocates (critical theory). In other words, as a set of ideas, Marxism still has much to tell us.

For more on Marx and Marxism, see: Boucher 2012.

Rawls and global justice

Probably the most influential liberal political theorist of recent years is John Rawls (1921–2002). Much of Rawls' work focuses on domestic political theory, but towards the end of his life he turned his attention to international affairs. Rawls does not engage directly with Smith or Marx in his work, but rather proposes a political order that would ensure justice. His account is, moreover, not only focused on economic issues, but also is an effort to draw on the liberal tradition in such a way that it can take into account the principle of equality and fairness.

Rawls' *A Theory of Justice* (1971) has been one of the most influential works of 20th-century political philosophy. At its basis, the book makes two main points. First, Rawls proposed that in order to determine the institutional arrangements that would be most just, we should envision ourselves in an 'original position' that is posited behind a 'veil of ignorance', in which we do not know what kinds of attributes, benefits or deficiencies we may have as individuals. This will mean that even if acting self-interestedly, we will choose to arrange society in such a way that it will be to the benefit of the worst off since we might well find ourselves in that position. Second, as a result of this starting point, Rawls proposes that we will choose to organize the political realm in such a way that it will guarantee that:

1. Each person has an equal right to the most extensive liberty compatible with a like liberty for all.
2. Social and economic inequalities can only be justified if they are to the benefit of the least advantaged, and all offices and positions should be open to all members of society in accordance with the idea of equal opportunity.

The first part of the second principle, sometimes called the 'difference principle', distinguishes Rawls from previous conceptions of liberalism, which tended to prioritize liberty above all else. This basic idea has generated a huge amount of secondary literature, testament to the intuitive insight that Rawls provided in his work.

Rawls' second major work, *Political Liberalism* (1993), responded mainly to communitarian critics, who argued that his argument does not take into account how various kinds of deeply felt moral and cultural claims on our identity will be behind any choices we make. Rawls argued that his theory of justice was primarily political, allowing individuals to keep their deeply held identities. In 1993, Rawls addressed the international sphere directly in a lecture titled the Law of Peoples, which was later published as *The Law of Peoples* (1999). Here, Rawls applied his account of justice to international relations, focusing on whether or not liberal societies should tolerate the existence of non-liberal societies in the global realm. His answer was a conditional yes, assuming that those non-liberal societies, what he called 'decent societies', do not violate the most basic human rights norms and do not engage in aggressive activities in the international society writ large.

A large amount of critical commentary arose in response to *The Law of Peoples*. Many commentators were disappointed with this text, seeing it as mainly a justification for modern international law, with its emphasis on state sovereignty and toleration of differences. In a sense, it was a very liberal argument, one grounded in the classical liberalism of Locke and Mill. One overarching critique of *The Law of Peoples* has been that it assumes what Allen Buchanan (2000) calls a 'vanished Westphalian world'. That is, Rawls' theory assumes a world of nation-states that pursue interests and foreign policies without being subject to a lack of agency as a result of serious deprivation or lack of natural resources (Beitz 2000; Meckled-Garcia 2008). This critique reveals that Rawls is much more of a statist than modern cosmopolitans would like him to be (Caney 2002). Some theorists, particularly Thomas Nagel (2005), take Rawls' position in *The Law of Peoples* even further, concluding that global justice is not possible except through the institutional structure of the nation-state.

Prior to Rawls' lecture on the society of states, however, a number of thinkers, frustrated that such an impressive theoretical apparatus did not address global issues, sought to push Rawls' agenda further. The primary problem for these theorists was that *A Theory of Justice* assumed its focus was on a particular political community, one bounded by borders and able to determine its own particular political, economic and social structure. One of the first to challenge Rawls' statist account was Charles Beitz, whose work on human rights was discussed in Chapter 3. Arguing against the view that a state is a self-contained entity that can provide justice for its people without any outside interactions, Beitz drew on Rawls' difference principle to argue for greater distribution of resources around the world. Beitz argued that an international order constituted by state autonomy 'lacks a coherent moral foundation' (1999 [1979]: 121; see also Beitz 1975). Beitz claims that such a picture of the world is empirically incorrect and then combines this with the Rawlsian difference principle to develop an argument for a principle of international distributive justice. In an afterward published in 1999, Beitz suggests that his cosmopolitan liberalism is a theoretical way forward for understanding global justice.

Thomas Pogge (2012), who has been the most influential theorist in internationalizing Rawls' ideas, suggested in an interview that Rawls wished to address justice primarily in the US rather than internationally. While Rawls does provide one answer to how to address international affairs in *The Law of Peoples*, Pogge and others have argued that it does not fully confront the very nature of an international order in which domestic and global economic processes are interlinked. In his book, *Realizing Rawls*, Pogge (1989) argues that Rawls failed to appreciate that his theory, when applied to the global level, does not distinguish between individuals qua individuals and individuals qua representatives of states. Pogge argues that the international economic reality is such that distributive issues cannot be confined to a single nation-state. Hence, Rawls' attempt to keep such issues confined to a single community fails to appreciate the modern world. His critique, though, is even deeper than a simple failure to understand the world. Pogge argues that Rawls is essentially conservative on this point, for he fails to understand the dilemmas generated by global wealth distribution. Pogge also believes that Rawls assumes that the current international order based on the sovereign state system is the preferred way to organize the world, a claim that is certainly reflected in Rawls' *Law of Peoples*.

Pogge (2002) develops his argument about global poverty by teasing out the idea of negative and positive duties. For many, providing welfare and poverty relief sounds like a positive duty, something related to the idea of positive rights examined in Chapter 3. That is, positive duties are those that arise from positive rights; we are obligated to provide certain things to others in light of their positive rights. So, I have a positive duty to ensure that others have adequate healthcare, or, more accurately, an institution in which I am a part has that duty. The opposite is the idea of negative duties, related to negative rights. This is the idea that we are responsible for not violating the rights of others; so, for instance, I am obligated not to interfere with the rights of someone else's freedom of speech. Pogge argues that while we might assume poverty alleviation is a form of positive duty, it is in fact a negative duty. He bases this argument on the fact that the global economic order is set up such that it benefits some of us much more than others. More importantly, the benefits we might derive from the global economy are in fact harming the economic welfare of others. So, it is not that we owe a positive duty to others; it is that we have a negative duty to stop harming others through the ways in which the global economy works.

Pogge (1994) made some of his ideas more concrete in proposing a 'global resource dividend' (GRD). The idea here is that if Rawls' conception of justice is to be realized on a global scale, we must also imagine that no community should be specially privileged by being founded on valuable natural resources. In order to account for the accidents of geography, the GRD mandates that whenever a natural resource is drawn upon by a community, they are to contribute a small dividend to a fund that would then be used to alleviate poverty. This idea reflects Rawls' ideas, in that it constructs a world in which no one agent (states in this version) are privileged over others and, if there is any benefit to one agent over others, it should be to the benefit of all. So, if a state is lucky enough to have natural resources that are valuable to all, that luck should be translated into the creation of a fund that will be used to benefit all.

These Rawlsian-inspired efforts to deal with global justice focus on the institutions of international society. In this way, they rely on a broadly liberal tradition, one that assumes a system of states and a capitalist world order. Rather than trying to replace these institutions, theorists such as Pogge have sought to work within them to construct ways to alleviate global poverty. This global liberalism differs from Smith's capitalist idea; it may share the assumption that the invisible hand creates wealth, but it does not share the assumption that the market will efficiently distribute that wealth. Rather, as Rawls' difference principle articulates, there are reasons to alter political and economic arrangements in order to create a more just distribution of resources. Pogge's suggestion of the GRD translates this idea into an international context by creating a 'tax' that will enable the distribution of wealth. These approaches fall within a broadly liberal effort to create a globally just distribution of wealth.

Peter Singer and global utilitarianism

There is another strand within liberal political theory that has also generated important insights on global wealth distribution. The utilitarian approach of John Stuart Mill was explored in Chapter 3. As we discovered, though, Mill's ideas about international affairs remained tied to the sovereign state system, especially in his strong defence of non-intervention. But some modern utilitarian thinkers have made an argument for distributing wealth in the global realm, relying on a notion of personal responsibility to animate new forms of distributive justice.

This approach is perhaps best captured in the work of the utilitarian philosopher Peter Singer (1972), who first approached this issue in a well-known essay on obligations to the poor who have suffered from humanitarian disasters. To make this point, he uses the following hypothetical example: if one came across a child drowning in a pond and it took very little effort to save the child, one would have a responsibility to help them. The idea that one might choose not to help the child because it would muddy up your trousers or ruin your nice shoes seems horrific to us. Rather, our common sense suggests that the minor harm to ourselves would be balanced by the great good we would provide in saving the life of the individual child. Singer argues that this simple thought experiment can be extrapolated away from the local case to the global one. If each individual gave a small percentage of their income to a global fund, it could easily contribute to the alleviation of global poverty. This simple idea has been the focal point of his efforts to deal with global poverty, with a book, *The Life You Can Save* (Singer 2009), and website (www.thelifeyoucansave.org) dedicated to the idea. When this idea is applied globally, proposals like Singer's make good sense. To return to the example at the start of the chapter, if the wealthy banker gave up 1 per cent of their overall compensation for 2011, it would generate $23,000,000. This would probably not make a dent in their lifestyle, but would provide a huge amount of money to a great number of people.

Singer does explore the wider economic order in some of his works. For instance, in *One World*, Singer (2002) critiques the World Trade Organization (WTO) for failing to advance a reduction in global poverty. He highlights the ways in which decisions about the global economy are made in the context of powerful states setting the agenda rather than taking into account a wide set of concerns, particularly those related to global poverty reduction. Interestingly, Singer (2002: 84) argues that we should be less focused on global inequality and more on simply reducing absolute poverty, in part as a result of his utilitarian approach.

One might point out that Singer's utilitarianism, while generating this important push to act in order to alleviate poverty, remains disconnected from the wider political context within which such funds, once collected, would need to be distributed. The simple utilitarian logic can be a useful means for seeing one's responsibility to act, but it fails to provide an institutionalized context within which such action can take place (Barry and Overland 2009). So, Singer's utilitarian logic may prompt in us a feeling of responsibility and may even generate income for the purpose of alleviating global wealth problems. In the same way, Pogge's ideas about the GRD provide ways to raise funds, but they do not tackle the problem of how to distribute those funds. Moreover, neither of them can help to promote a more equal distribution, in that they do not provide resources for how we might address the problems of the global financial system, both in its generation of vast disparities of wealth and in its collapse. That is, they do not provide us with concrete ways to think about global wealth in its fullest sense.

Perhaps one of the reasons for the failure of Pogge's and Singer's proposals to advance solutions to global wealth problems is that they do not conceptualize their approaches in explicitly political terms. They focus on rights and responsibilities in their formulations, so they give us one way to see these issues. But, they do not address their solutions through the lens of rules and authority, the other two key conceptual frameworks for understanding the global political order. In the final section of this chapter, I will turn to these concepts as a way to consider the problems of global wealth, concepts that lead us to some possible alternative ways to understand the dilemmas of global wealth distribution.

Rules and authority in the global political economy

Rawls' theory of justice, as part of a liberal tradition, privileges rights. His first principle of justice states this clearly, and any derivations from that first principle can only be undertaken on the basis of advancing the overall conditions of justice in the system. Pogge furthers this idea with his attempt to make Rawls more global. The idea of poverty alleviation as arising from a negative duty further connects this approach to a focus on rights, yet it also combines those rights with responsibilities. The work of Singer makes the link to responsibilities even more central. The utilitarian tradition does not focus explicitly on rights, and it is in fact sometimes seen as antithetical to rights (even though I deployed the work of one utilitarian philosopher, John Stuart Mill, to make an argument about rights in Chapter 3). Singer's work demonstrates how a utilitarian effort to alleviate poverty relies on a conception of responsibilities that might be disconnected from wider concerns about the international economic order. As noted above, he does highlight the power of institutions such as the WTO, but his suggestions take us primarily back to what individuals can do to alleviate poverty, that is, what are the responsibilities of individuals in the global political order. This maps onto Singer's broader cosmopolitan orientation expressed in the title of his 2002 book, *One World*.

So the Rawlsian and utilitarian approaches link justice to rights and responsibilities, two of the terms I have proposed as central to IPT. In the remainder of this chapter, I want to suggest that what might be lacking from these approaches is a focus on authority and rules, the other two elements of IPT I have highlighted in the previous chapters. This is not to say that every theorist writing about IPT needs to deploy all four concepts simultaneously; rather, I would suggest that theorists who highlight the importance of these four terms in their approaches can better conceptualize the wider set of issues confronting the global order.

What would it mean to address questions of authority in terms of global wealth? To turn back to Adam Smith, authority sits uneasily with the individualist account that he developed. By this, I mean that Smith's idea of moral sentiment, or something that arises from within individuals and prompts them to act in certain ways, is not linked to any conception of authority. Authority of a sort arises from the moral sentiments, for, as Smith argued, these sentiments will eventually translate into a kind of common sense, one that will shape societal norms. And, as argued above, the practice of global economic relations will ensure that our sentiments are not confined to a single society but stretch beyond them to encompass our interactions with diverse groups and individuals around the world. At the same time, in his arguments about the practice of capitalism, Smith does leave some room for authority, for he recognizes that a market cannot function without a structure of law that governs it. But, in part because he was arguing against the dominant role of the state in the mercantilist tradition, Smith did try to move economic ideas away from the formal authority of the state. So, his liberal capitalism leaves less room for authority structures and their rule-making abilities than other traditions.

Marx has perhaps less to tell us about authority and rules other than that they rely on the mode of production a society has adopted. That is, for Marx, questions of authority and rules are largely derivative of other factors. At one level, this is an important point to make, for it reveals how the 'mystical' nature of authority that Arendt (2006 [1963]) identified is not that mystical at all; rather, it is the result of social practices and institutions that benefit some more than others. This may seem odd if one considers the history of communist states, in which the state and its authority becomes central to all political life. But, these states largely distorted Marx's ideas and failed to grasp his emphasis on the human person. That is, they simply adopted the structures and institutional frameworks of the modern state system in order to manage economic relations internally and among themselves. Marx argued for a utopian outcome, in which there would be less need for formal authority and rule making, although it is not entirely clear what a truly communist society would look like in Marx's thought.

In any case, both Smith and Marx leave little room for formal authority and the rule-making power that authorities have. And yet, one of the dilemmas of the global financial crisis was that there was little to no structural authority in the international order that could make rules or regulations to govern interactions among the different players involved. Does this mean that we can only talk about rights and responsibilities when it comes to the global economic realm? Should we simply put to one side the problems of authority and rule making in this realm of the international system? One IR theorist who did focus on authority in understanding the global economic order was Susan Strange (1923–98), a political economist whose work was fundamental in creating the field of IR in the UK. She was a journalist early in her career and then moved to the academic realm with a focus on global finance. Strange (2002) famously argued that there is no field of international political economy separate from IR, but that IR is in fact constituted by the authority and rules that arise from the intersection of the economic and political realms.

In her book, *The Retreat of the State*, Strange (1996: ix) prophetically identified some of the same key problems that contributed to the current international financial crisis. She begins the book by noting that a trader in Japan is able to move money around the world with little or no limits or regulations stopping them. In that work, which brought to a culmination many of her previous ideas about the global economic order, she argues that this ability to move money and make decisions needs to be regulated. She explores the reasons why states can no longer control these practices even as they claim to be the primary sovereign entities in the international order. She argues that we need to expand our conception of authority away from sovereign states to encompass a wider range of actors. For instance, while multinational firms or banks may not be sovereign in the formal sense of the word, they have a good deal of authority. Strange also identifies specific fields of expertise as providing a kind of authority that states accept, such as accountancy (Strange 1996: 93). As such, scholars interested in international affairs need to pay greater attention to these multiple authority structures, especially in an area of the world that is so important.

Strange can be faulted for failing to differentiate power from authority in places, which renders some of her analyses somewhat problematic. But Strange is important for not simply identifying the fact of alternative authorities; she also critiques the study of IR more generally. She believed that too many scholars were fixated on the idea of the sovereign state as the only authority. She also did not argue that we should abandon the sovereign state, and emphasized that the authority of the state was crucial for dealing with the distribution of wealth internally and for playing a key role in rule making at the global level. She also explored the increasingly important role of organizations like the EU in governing financial transactions in the international order, a role that was less developed when she was writing than it is today. Again, her insights were both provocative and prophetic in this realm.

Finally, related to the point that Strange made about multiple authorities playing a role in creating the rules governing the international economic order, some authors have argued in recent years that there is an emerging global set of rules that are almost constitutional-like in their functions, but which lack some of the moral foundations of a truly constitutional system. David Schneiderman (2008) has proposed the idea that a global economic constitution has been created to govern global financial transactions, a structure that includes not only rules and regulations but also judicial-like authorities interpreting the rules. Yet, these rules and structures have been made by and are controlled by those who are being governed, that is, the firms and banks moving money around. As such, Schneiderman feels these institutions are failing to live up to a morally acceptable constitutional structure, especially as these institutions failed to provide any form of governance for the collapse of the current order. So, in one way, the constitutional order that Schneiderman describes is related to the structure that Strange describes, although she does not use the idea of constitutionalism to describe her ideas. Others have looked at constitutional-like structures in the functions of the WTO, especially its appellate panels, which provide judgements that, over time, become authoritative, just as judicial decisions do in a constitutional structure (Dunoff and Trachtman 2009).

Conclusion

Authority, then, is important for the distribution of international wealth. Whether authority is understood through the critical work of scholars like Strange or the quasi-constitutional work of others is less important than highlighting the role of various authority structures in the global political economy. This takes us back to the points raised in Chapter 1 about the centrality of authority. At the same, as the work of Singer, Pogge and others emphasizes, the practice of rights and responsibilities is also crucial for a full grasp of the international politics of wealth distribution. This chapter has demonstrated how IPT can bring together these very different approaches to the study of wealth in the global system.

Further reading

Terry Eagleton. 2011. *Why Marx Was Right*. New Haven: Yale University Press.
  Provocative book by a leading literary and cultural theorist, it defends Marx's continuing relevance, especially in light of the global economic crisis that began in 2008 (and was preceded by others). Organized around responses to a series of criticisms of Marx and Marxism, resulting in a vigorous defence of Marxism today, written in an accessible and witty style.
Thomas Pogge. 2008. *World Poverty and Human Rights: Cosmopolitan Responsibilities and Reforms,* 2nd edn. Cambridge: Polity Press.
  Careful, powerful account of world poverty and the ways in which a cosmopolitan sensibility would respond to this problem. Builds on Pogge's Rawlsian approach, developed over the years in engagements with different theorists and issues.
John Rawls. 1999. *The Law of Peoples, with The Idea of Public Reason, Revisited*. Cambridge, MA: Harvard University Press.
  Extended version of a lecture Rawls gave in 1993 in which he tried to make his ideas international. While the responses from some were critical of his efforts, it demonstrates how Rawls remained a liberal even in his international thinking, in that he greatly respected the importance of non-intervention.
Peter Singer. 2009. *The Life You Can Save: Acting Now to End World Poverty*. London: Picador.
  Brings together Singer's arguments about the responsibility of individuals to bring about an end to poverty. The simplicity and power of the argument are persuasive, and are linked to a website he created to give people the chance to donate in support of ending poverty.
Susan Strange. 1996. *The Retreat of the State*. Cambridge: Cambridge University Press.
  Excellent analysis of the evolution of the global economic order from a leading theorist of international political economy. Its empirical evidence remains relevant as it focuses on deeper questions of political authority and justice. Easily accessible style, reflecting her years as a journalist before turning to academic life.

Chapter 5

Violence

On 24 January 2013, Ben Emmerson, the UN Special Rapporteur on the promotion and protection of human rights and fundamental freedoms while countering terrorism, launched a formal inquiry into the use of drones and other forms of targeted killing in counterterrorism operations. In his statement launching the inquiry, Emmerson (2013: 2) stated that the investigation was the result of requests by states in the UNHRC as well as 'increasing international concern surrounding the issue of remote targeted killing through the use of UAVs [unmanned aerial vehicles]'. Emmerson's investigation focused primarily on establishing whether or not drone strikes conform to international humanitarian law, or what was once called the 'laws of war'. His efforts focus on 25 cases of drone strikes drawn from Pakistan, Yemen, Somalia, Afghanistan and Palestine. The states using drone strikes in these areas that are the focus of the investigation are not named in his statement, but evidence suggests they will be focused primarily on the US and the UK, with the possible inclusion of Israel.

On his commission of inquiry, Emmerson included individuals who had recently authored a report on drone strikes. The report, *Living Under Drones* (International Human Rights and Conflict Resolution Clinic 2012), criticizes the US for its attacks in Pakistan and elsewhere. It begins with the US claim that drone strikes are more precise and in conformity with international law, which the authors argue is manifestly false. They go on to demonstrate:

- how drone strikes have undermined the daily lives of those living in the border regions between Pakistan and Afghanistan because they are unable to meet in public open spaces, which might attract the attention of drone operators
- how more innocent civilians are being killed than the US admits, as it depends on how one defines innocent
- how the US is failing to conduct its strikes in an open, democratic and accountable way, vis-à-vis its own citizens, since it will not acknowledge publicly what it is doing or release information about how it determines targeting.

In other words, the report highlights that the use of drones is not simply a precise and targeted way to kill potential terrorists (which it may be in part); rather, the point of this report, and the UN Special Rapporteur, is that this particular use of violence has an impact on the ability of small communities in the border region to function and the ability of democracy to work in the US. That is, using violence is not just about harming or killing people, although it is indeed about that; but when violence is used by international actors across borders, it raises problems of authority, rights, rules and responsibilities, along with a host of other political issues.

I return to this issue at the end of the chapter, as there are now some attempts to address the ethical and political dimensions of drone war, which overlap with the themes of this book (Brunstetter and Braun 2011; Kennedy and Rengger 2012). Before turning to this theme, however, the chapter provides an overview of different ways of understanding violence and war. It then goes on to explore some historical traditions concerning the use of force, ranging from the religious to philosophical. The chapter turns to the just war tradition as a means to frame a number of different issues surrounding the use of military force. It then provides a more detailed study of one figure in the history of thought about war and peace, Hugo Grotius, the 17th-century religious, moral, political and legal theorist. Grotius is a significant figure for many reasons, including his ability to straddle the moral and legal ideas about war, but also because of his deep political insights into sovereignty and violence. He was briefly discussed in Chapter 2 in terms of his contribution to the natural law tradition; in this chapter, I address more directly his writings on war. The chapter concludes by returning to the problem of drones in warfare, with some ideas about how a focus on authority, rights, rules and responsibilities might give us new insights into the changing nature of warfare.

The politics of war and violence

This chapter is about violence, but violence is not a simple concept. Violence is the exertion of force by people so as to injure or abuse other people. In the modern world, most ethical frameworks propose that violence is wrong and should be limited if at all possible; the extreme form of this point would be pacifism. Violence on its own is not necessarily political, for it can be between two individuals or within an apolitical context, for example a family. War, however, is the traditional way in which violence has appeared in the international realm. War can be defined as the use of violence by one political community in its relations with another political community. According to this definition, war makes violence political. This point was most famously made by Karl von Clausewitz (1989 [1832]), the Prussian philosopher and general, who argued that war is 'politics by other means'. Von Clausewitz, who served in the militaries of Prussia and Russia during the Napoleonic Wars, developed an abstract notion of war, one that relied on a set of philosophical categories that linked war to the state as the manifestation of its political nature; that is, calling war political meant that war is only something states do. Von Clausewitz was less interested in the normative or evaluative dimensions of war, although his arguments resonate with certain forms of moral reasoning, particularly as they relate to the just war tradition (Pierce 2004). Mary Kaldor (2006) famously argued that von Clausewitz's ideas are only relevant to 'old wars'; 'new wars' are conflicts that do not take place between states on a battlefield for clear political purposes, but are found in terrorism, intervention and civil wars for profit purposes.

Rather than make an empirical judgement about whether or not war is old or new, let me step back and consider the political nature of violence. One political theorization of violence comes from Frantz Fanon (2001 [1961]), whose *The Wretched of the Earth* served as a clarion call to many revolutionary movements on its publication in 1961. Fanon's analysis of violence in the context of colonialism explored how violence can be an enabling act, something that not only frees the individual from domination by more powerful agents, but also gives political agency to individuals who, under a colonial regime, had been completely deprived of a voice. To some extent, his ideas draw on the Hegelian notion of recognition; that is, one can only be truly human if one is recognized by the other, an idea discussed in more detail in Chapter 7. For Fanon, if one is so deprived of any respect and recognition by the other, there needs to be a violent act that will bring about that recognition, a process that will provide agency for the one who has undertaken the violence. Violence becomes a means by which individuals, acting with and through the emerging national community, can assert their presence on a political stage.

There is, however, a danger in this approach. While political action is a value, which rules and structures of dominance restrict, a world of violent political action is not one in which most of us wish to live. Rules do provide a good, the ability to retreat after political action to peace of a sort, to a home in which we can be assured that our door will not be knocked down in pursuit of the next threat. They structure the world in which political action can even be possible; they constitute our world. How do we balance the need for political action – a need that Fanon correctly identifies as absent from the colonial context – without creating a world in which we have no space to recoup for the next political engagement?

Fanon's analysis of violence as a means by which the individual might engage in the public sphere, a public sphere constituted by the native's attempts to dismantle the colonial structure, was criticized by political theorist Hannah Arendt in her book *On Violence* (1972). Fanon was not her only, or even main, target in this essay; she was responding to the student movements of the late 1960s in the US and Germany in particular, and the general student unrest that seemed to be shaping the political world at that time. *On Violence* provides an alternative conception of the relationship of violence and politics, one that, while resisting violence, echoes Fanon in some ways.

Arendt's overriding concern in the essay was to decouple the concepts of violence and power that had become linked in various Third World and Marxist discourses (Owens 2008). She begins the text not with the student justifications of violence, but by noting that while war has long been part of the human condition, the advent of nuclear weapons has created a world in which any link between power and violence has been severed: 'The technical development of the implements of violence has now reached the point where no political goal could conceivably correspond to their destructive potential or justify their actual use in armed conflict' (Arendt 1972: 105). She compares this technological power of the state with the student movements that had taken up violence in their revolutionary efforts. She suggests that to better understand violence, we need a better understanding of power, which she supplies:

> Power corresponds to the human ability not just to act but to act in concert. Power is never the property of an individual; it belongs to a group and remains in existence only so long as the group keeps together. (Arendt 1972: 143)

Violence, on the other hand, is the utilization of implements to coerce others. Violence can be undertaken in the name of a group, but it is not what power is, namely, the coming together to act in the political realm. Violence is a tool, one that cannot have any meaning in and of itself, whereas power is a truly political action.

This distinction leads to an even more important point. For Arendt, power is the foundation of government, but it does not give legitimacy. On the other hand, violence can never be legitimate, it can only be justified:

> Power needs no justification, being inherent in the very existence of political communities; what it does need is legitimacy. The common treatment of these two words as synonyms is no less misleading and confusing than the current equation of obedience and support. Power springs up whenever people get together and act in concert, but it derives its legitimacy from the initial getting together rather than from any action that then may follow. Legitimacy, when challenged, bases itself

on an appeal to the past, while justification relates to an end that lies in the future. Violence can be justifiable, but it never will be legitimate. Its justification loses its plausibility the farther its intended end recedes into the future. No one questions the use of violence in self-defence, because the danger is not only clear but also present, and the end justifying the means is immediate. Arendt (1972: 151)

Arendt argues that to engage in violence is not irrational or even inhuman; she points out that at times violence is the only way to set things right, to achieve justice. But violence is always just a means, and a short-term means for Arendt. It is the most dangerous of means, for political action is about the action itself, not about its consequences, according to Arendt's conception of political action.

Some theories of nonviolence also explore the nature of power and politics. Ian Atack has examined how political theories relate to violence and, more importantly, nonviolence. Atack (2012: 75–7) points to the ways in which pacifist writers from Leo Tolstoy to Mohandas Ghandi were keenly aware of the relationship between politics and violence. For instance, Tolstoy, arguing from an anarchist Christian perspective, claimed that the state could never be nonviolent, and so nonviolence means removing oneself from the rules and laws of the traditional political community. Gandhi, on the other hand, believed that the use of nonviolence can be part of an effort to re-create the state and move it towards new forms of justice (ibid.: 77–9). Atack, after reviewing these and other positions on nonviolence, points towards the values of Arendt's understanding of power and violence. He argues that a political theory of nonviolence needs to take seriously issues of the state and power, which his use of Arendt and other thinkers allows us to do.

Arendt's definition of power and its relation to the idea of violence is a useful one. Naturally, it is linked to a set of wider concerns, ones that rely on her ideas about what it means to act politically. Rather than wholeheartedly accepting her definitions, they at least suggest for us a slightly different understanding of violence and power than is often found in international affairs. It is important, however, to understand that any evaluation of violence, war and conflict in international affairs needs to be undertaken in relation to an idea of what does and does not count as political; that is, is violence part of political life or separate from it? The political context is important in two ways when it comes to war and violence. The first is that specific contexts, with cultural and political codes and processes, generate the kinds of rules and codes that govern the use of violence. One cannot understand a specific ethical injunction without understanding its origins in a particular place. This point is difficult to square with international norms, rules and laws, for it is assumed that such ethical injunctions are not grounded in any particular place but reflect a kind of commonly shared humanity. The international system may well be moving in this direction (Sullivan and Kymlicka 2007), but those movements generally start from some particular place with a particular tradition.

A second dimension of the political context that is important to emphasize is the role of authority, which was addressed in Chapter 1. If it is the case that the cultural and broader national context determines normative codes, the role of an authority structure to interpret those codes in specific situations is also central. This is not a Hobbesian point that the sovereign determines what is right and wrong; rather, it is that decisions to use force generally come from some authority structure. Indeed, to convince people to sacrifice their lives or kill others requires more than a simple wish on the part of an individual. Instead, it requires the acceptance by individuals that the use of force not only corresponds to a set of norms but is authorized by a legitimate structure. As a result, in all the traditions explored below, authority is a central consideration. The just war tradition has formalized the centrality of authority for decisions to use force, although research on what constitutes just authority has waned in recent years (Lang et al. 2013). As competing authority structures, for example states, the UN, NATO and the EU, compete and play more important roles in the governance of international security, questions on authority will become more and more central to scholarship in this field.

Keeping in mind the relationship of violence to power, authority and the political is central if we want to do more than simply make judgements about the rightness or wrongness of using force. In the following overview of different traditions of thought about violence and war, I highlight how these approaches treat these more fundamental questions. That is, rather than a review of the ethics of war and peace, this chapter provides a review of political theories in which questions of war and peace play a central role.

Classical approaches

Keeping in mind the importance of the political as described above, this section provides an overview of some important efforts to evaluate war and violence that have arisen from the religious and classical traditions of thought. The Judeo-Christian Bible includes as one of the Ten Commandments: You shall not murder (Exodus 20: 13). There is some disagreement among biblical scholars on this translation, for the Hebrew root word does not convey exactly the distinction between murder and killing. Moreover, in other contexts in the Bible, the same root word is used to refer to unintentional killing (Deuteronomy 4: 41ff; Joshua 20: 3). Whatever the translation, though, this rule was not absolute, as is reflected in the record of war and violence found throughout the historical books of the Bible.

Rather than appeal to a simple rule, to capture the complexity of the biblical tradition, one needs to consider some of the norms that can be found within it. One is the idea of *herem*, sometimes translated as the 'ban'. This concept refers to those things that are to be sacrificed to God after a war – including the enemy population (Numbers 31: 1–54). Such norms may have made sense in a particular type of community, but as the ancient Israelite community evolved and its authority structures changed, the ethics governing war also evolved. For instance, during a period when the Israelites were trying to establish their dominance in the region of Canaan, killing through deception and trickery became more common. Stories from the Book of Judges demonstrate these new norms, especially those concerning Ehud (Judges 3: 15–25) and Jael (Judges 4: 17–22). The context in which such actions took place, however, was one in which there were competing authority structures; the book famously ends with the lamentation: 'In those days, there was no king; all the people did what was right in their own eyes' (Judges 21: 25). In comparison to the next stage in Israelite history, when the kingdoms of Saul, David and their successors created a more formalized set of norms governing warfare, the time of the Judges created more space for uses of violence that were less rule governed. In some ways, we might argue that these moments of violence were outside the 'political', for they took place in a context of shifting authority structures and without any clear guidance from larger normative frameworks. At the same time, one might argue that they were necessary acts of violence designed to create the conditions for the creation of a political community. In other words, violence might sit outside the political but perhaps it is necessary to create those structures.

The arrival of Jesus of Nazareth produced a new tradition, that of Christianity. The stories of Jesus, found in the Gospels, describe an individual who refused the normal modes of political authority, including the use of violence. The Gospel of Luke includes some of the clearest expressions of this resistance to using force, captured in passages such as calling his followers to love their enemies (Luke 6: 27–36) and his refusal to allow his disciples to protect him with violence as he is arrested (Luke 23: 50–3). Yet, other biblical passages suggest Jesus did not renounce violence completely, as when he deals with Roman soldiers without chastising them for their profession (Luke 7: 1–10). These conflicting accounts within the Christian Bible have generated a great deal of debate about Jesus' views on war and peace (Hauerwas 1985; Koontz 1996; Yoder 1994).

The biblical sources are not the end point of debate about the use of military force in the Jewish and Christian traditions. The rich writings of the Jewish legal tradition and rabbinical commentary demonstrate how Jewish views on violence and war evolved through the centuries. As a community largely without a territorial identity (after being expelled from Palestine in the early 1st century), the rabbis took the texts of the Bible and developed a complex set of justifications for war and violence. Because of this lack of a territorially defined identity, Michael Walzer (1996: 96) points out: 'Jews are the victims, not the agents, of war.' The development of Jewish thought in the medieval period has been the subject of recent reformulations, some of it focusing on philosophers such as Maimonides (Feldman 2005; Ravitzky 1996).

With the creation of an authoritative structure within which Jewish thought and practice about war could develop, that is, the state of Israel, ethical reflection on security developed further. The state of Israel is not formally Jewish, but norms, rules and laws concerning warfare draw on a mixture of Zionist political thought and Jewish reflections on war. As a result of the regional political context in which Israelis have found themselves, their reflections on war and peace have addressed some of the issues of importance to the larger international community today, such as pre-emptive versus preventive war and counterterrorism policies. Other theorists have sought to contribute more broadly to international ethics on questions of war and peace from a Jewish perspective (Gopin 2002). As a living religious tradition that is responding to the political situation of a particular state, these reflections will most certainly continue (see Walzer 2000).

The Christian tradition also evolved from its biblical roots. The early Christian Church largely adopted a pacifist approach, a position that was linked to the refusal to serve in the Roman Empire but also to Jesus' statements on peace (Bainton 1961). When Constantine made Christianity the official religion of the Roman Empire in the mid-4th century, Christianity moved away from these pacifist origins. The most important figure here was Augustine of Hippo (354–430 AD), who served as a bishop in North Africa (Brown 1969). In Augustine's corpus, there is not a single text on war and peace; rather, his ideas are spread throughout his writings, sermons and letters. His attitude towards war is that it is necessary for the creation of an acceptable order on earth, but this earthly order can never match the heavenly order, which is where the only true justice is to be found. Even more importantly, he sees war as an evil that must never be embraced but should be undertaken reluctantly, so that mercy and justice discipline war.

Unlike modern approaches to security and war, Augustine does not emphasize self-defence as the primary justification for war. Because he sees war as something that an authority should use to create a particular kind of order, he argues that punishment is the one of the most just reasons for waging war: 'Just wars are defined as those which avenge injuries, if some nation or state against whom one is waging war has neglected to punish a wrong committed by its citizens' (Augustine, cited in Reichberg et al. 2006: 82). Connected to the importance of punishment, in Book 19 of the *City of God*, he argues that peace should be the ultimate goal of war. The human person naturally wishes for peace; even those who wage war seek to create peace in the end (Augustine 1967 [418–427 AD]: 866–70). And peace within the Roman Empire required the use of force at times, just as political order within a society requires punishment. In a letter to one commander in the field, Augustine reminds him that while the goods of this world are ephemeral, they do at least create a state of peace that is necessary for human existence (Letter 189, to Boniface, reprinted in Augustine 2001 [410–427 AD]: 214–18). Both punishment and war are understood to be tools for keeping order but tools that should be used with great discretion and even sorrow.

Augustine's views on war need to be understood in his particular political context. As a bishop of a new faith that was being blamed for the collapse of the Roman Empire, Augustine felt the need to demonstrate that Christians could engage in combat as much as the Romans could. In light of his physical location on the outskirts of the empire, where various groups were engaged in attempts to topple the authority of Rome, Augustine saw the need for the judicious use of force.

After Augustine, reflection on war and peace in the Christian tradition evolved in different ways. One, the just war tradition, will be explored in more depth below. Another, the holy war or crusading tradition, flourished as the Christian community undertook large-scale military actions to recapture the Holy Land, primarily Jerusalem, for Christianity (Reichberg et al. 2006: 98–103; Riley-Smith 1987). This tradition of thought was promulgated by popes who gave sanction to the use of military force against Muslims, Jews and even Eastern Orthodox Christians. Outside the just war and crusader traditions, pacifism was another route the Christian tradition took concerning matters of war and peace. As noted above, the early Christian Church was largely pacifist, although there continues to be debate about this. Erasmus (1466–1536), a key figure in the Renaissance tradition, argued against the just war tradition and sought to emphasize the classical and Christian sources of pacifism (Dallmayr 2004; Reichberg et al. 2006: 233–9). The 'peace churches', such as the Quakers and Mennonites, have continued this tradition.

Alongside the Judeo-Christian tradition, the other influential tradition in Western political thought can broadly be defined as the 'classical' approach, one which draws on Ancient Greece and Rome for its inspiration. Perhaps the most important text within this tradition is Homer's *Iliad*. The *Iliad*, the story of the war between the Greek city-states and the Asian power Troy, became the touchstone for understanding war and peace throughout the Greek and Roman eras. Drawing norms from this largely oral epic are difficult, not least because translations of the Ancient Greek text do not always capture the complexity of the normative assumptions that structure military life at the time (Adkins 1972). Moreover, most scholars assume the war described took place around 1200 BCE, while the final written form of the *Iliad* probably appeared around 800 BCE. As a result, there is a mix of normative assumptions throughout the text, ones combining different social and political structures over a 400-year period.

Despite these difficulties in history and translation, one can identify key norms within the *Iliad*. The first and most important is honour. This is best seen in the fact that rather than large unnamed enemies fighting each other, the *Iliad* names each and every warrior as he engages in battle. Nor is the naming limited to one side; Greeks and Trojans are remembered through their unique histories as they fight and die. Another key norm is the importance of respecting the bodies of the dead. Ironically, this norm is emphasized in its breach, most famously in the scene where Achilles desecrates the body of Hector after their hand-to-hand combat.

But the *Iliad* does not simply celebrate war, as some modern commentators believe (Kaplan 2002). The opening lines of the text emphasize that war emerges from rage, an uncontrolled emotion that does not deserve to be celebrated; indeed, Ares, the god of war, is often characterized as being unable to control his emotions. At the end of Book 5, Zeus, the king of gods, describes how much he hates Ares because he cannot be controlled and wrecks so much havoc on humanity. One author even points to the fact that Ares is really the god of violence, while Athena, goddess of wisdom (traditionally pictured in a war helmet), is actually the goddess of 'organised, disciplined, rationally conducted collective activity', that is, war by a city-state (Neff 2005: 16).

The Greek tradition evolved, and new norms emerged in what is sometimes called the 'Classical period'. Captured in the historian Thucydides' account of the Peloponnesian War, these norms continue to emphasize the Homeric norms of honour, but the individual becomes less important as the city-state emerges as the central agent war (Crane 1998; Garst 1989; Johnson 1993). For Thucydides, three norms motivate the warrior: honour, fear and profit (Lebow 2003). One of the most interesting shifts is the importance of *ad bellum* justifications for war. The *Iliad* famously starts in the middle of the war; we know the reasons for the war only because we know the myths of Greece and Troy. The *Iliad* was not concerned with justifying why war broke out because war had been something that had long been in existence. In Thucydides' account, on the other hand, there is an extended discussion of what justifies the Athenians waging war against the Spartans. These justifications are not the same as those we might invoke today, but included debates over colonies. Thucydides (1972 [411–404 BC]: Book 1) claimed these justifications could be boiled down to the fear that the Spartans felt of growing Athenian power. While these are not moral justifications, the point is that they are justifications for the war.

The Greek tradition informs the Roman tradition. Rome rose to power in the 2nd century BC, dominating the Mediterranean region and large parts of Europe and North Africa for the next 600 years. Its dominance was embodied in warfare, particularly its ability to extend its empire through military means. Unlike the Greek tradition, where norms and rules can be found in a few specific texts, the norms and rules – and eventually laws – that governed the Roman approach to war are not so easily located. This may be because Rome, as an ever-expanding empire, slowly constructed a set of rules that evolved into an international legal structure concerning the use of force.

Roman international law as it relates to warfare begins with a largely religious process, the *ius fetiale*. This originated in the role of the College of Fetials, essentially a body of priests who were also important in diplomacy. As described by the Roman historian Livy (1960: 69–70), the rules included a formal demand for redress by the Romans against their enemies, who were allowed 33 days to respond. If they did not offer anything for their affront to the Roman state, one of the priests would throw a spear across the border, an act that had to be undertaken in the presence of at least three enemy soldiers. These procedures evolved as Rome began to wage war outside its immediate borders, including consecrating a part of the Roman Forum as 'enemy territory' into which the spear was thrown (Neff 2005: 28).

This largely symbolic procedure seems more about actually declaring war than imposing any norms, rules or laws on it, about which there is some debate among classicists (Harris 1979: 166–74). Some argue that the procedure moderated aggressive war by forcing the Romans to demand redress for some affront; while it could certainly be a false justification, the need to justify the war to the Roman community and the enemy at least disciplined the urge to war and expansion (Weidemann 1986). Cicero (1991: 15–16), the Roman philosopher who some see as central to the early just war tradition (Bellamy 2006: 19–20), saw the *ius fetiale* as important for disciplining warfare, which he believed provided a set of clear rules that should guide war.

Yet another tradition of thought is important to consider, as it has come to shape debates and conflicts in the current international order in recent years. Islamic conceptions of war and peace have appeared in the public eye recently as a result of various political and military interactions between the US, Europe and parts of the Islamic world. From the Iranian revolution of 1979 to the current 'war on terror', debates about what role Islam does and should play in the international normative order have created a cottage industry of books and articles. Surprisingly, not much of this literature has directly addressed the issues of this chapter, namely, the ethical and political dimensions of war and peace; instead, much of it tends to be alarmist and often uninformed.

To understand the Islamic approach to war and peace, certain features of the tradition are important to keep in mind. First, unlike Christianity, the founder of Islam was the leader of a political community. When Muhammad immigrated to Medina at the invitation of the elites of that city in 622 AD, the beginnings of a formal political community were inaugurated (Watt 1961: 82–101). This community soon engaged in a systematic expansion, pushing forward the new religion of Islam into communities that were most often receptive to it. As a result, while fighting did take place, a number of communities embraced the new faith, giving Muhammad and those who followed him experience in war and diplomacy.

The second important feature of Islam is the centrality of law. Islam, like Judaism but perhaps less so Christianity, is a highly law-governed tradition. Most debates about specific norms, rules and laws in Islam are based on the interpretation of legal texts (see al-Azami 1996; Schacht 1979). While the Quran is the primary text, it does not yield so easily to interpretation. Unlike the Judeo-Christian scriptures, the Quran does not follow a chronology nor does it have a specific set of norms spelled out concerning war and violence. The second important text, and sometimes more important, is the Sunna (also called the Hadith), a body of writings on the activities of the Prophet Muhammad as they relate to his activities surrounding the daily life of the individual Muslim and the political structures and policies of the rapidly growing community. These texts have led to the creation of sharia, the body of Islamic law that governs the life of the individual Muslim and the Islamic ummah, or community, as a whole. The interpretation of these texts as they relate to the dilemmas of daily life is the central issue for understanding the rule-governed and political contexts relating to war and peace in an Islamic perspective.

For obvious reasons, much of this debate about how to interpret these texts takes place in Arabic. At the same time, Muslims are not solely in the Arab-speaking world; the largest number of Muslims in any one state is in Indonesia, and a growing population exists in Europe. Even more relevant for the purposes of this chapter, when individuals such as Osama bin Laden produce interpretations of these texts, sometimes referred to as 'fatwas', which justify violent actions in relation to North American and European populations, these interpretations become part of a larger discursive community. The debate over who should be allowed to interpret these texts has been subject to a great deal of controversy in the Islamic world. Traditionally, only the ulema, or scholars of the law, could undertake such authoritative interpretations, ones that took place within the confines of the four traditional schools of Islamic law. While interpretations by individuals such as bin Laden have received the most interest, the power to interpret these sacred texts has been altered in recent years by the emergence of new communities of young Muslims (Mandaville 2007).

As a result of this wide range of interpretations and texts, it is difficult to identify a single Islamic view on the ethics of international security. A few scholars in the field of international law and ethics have sought to make sense of this wide range of texts. One of the most important works in English is Majid Khadduri's translation of Muhammad Shaybani's *Sharia Kitab Al-Siyar*, one of the first texts on international law in the Islamic tradition (Khadduri 2001 [1961]; also see Khadduri 1955). Shaybani was an 8th-century Islamic philosopher, a leading figure in one of the Islamic schools of law. The text explores not only questions of war and peace but also how the Islamic empire should relate to other communities through diplomacy. For Shaybani, the use of military force was allowed but it was to be moderated by concerns about innocents and injunctions not to force conversions of individuals to Islam. At the same time, within the realm of the Islamic empire, Shaybani emphasized the authority of the caliph in establishing order, through force if necessary.

A concept developed at the time of Shaybani's text was the distinction between the *dar al-Islam* and the *dar al-harb*, or the abode of Islam and the abode of war. This geographical distinction was intended to differentiate the ethics of war allowed within the Islamic community and those outside it, as described in Shaybani's work. Today, this distinction is evoked in some interpretations of Islamic ethics, although others have questioned its applicability in a world in which Islamic governments are rare and Muslims live throughout the world (Ramadan 2004: 62–101).

Some have argued that there is a strong parallel between Islamic teachings on war and peace and the just war tradition. John Kelsay (2007) has made this case most clearly, arguing that there are *jus ad bellum* and *jus in bello* norms that map quite closely on to the Christian-inspired tradition. Sohail Hashmi (1996, 2002) has connected Islamic political ethics directly to issues of war and peace.

The just war tradition

The previous historical overview left out one of the most important traditions of thought about war and violence, the just war. The core of the just war tradition rests on the idea that not all ends justify the use of force and that even when ends are accepted as just, not all means are justified to achieve these ends; at the same time, it privileges the pursuit of justice over the benefits of peace (see Box 5.1). The just war tradition, therefore, proposes certain legitimate reasons to go to war (*jus ad bellum*) and criteria of acceptable behaviour during war (*jus in bello*). In recent years, a third category of ethical reflection has been added, *jus post bellum*, or the norms, rules and laws that should guide the way a post-conflict situation is handled. It is important to keep in mind that the just war tradition is a framework for evaluating the use of force and 'not a weapon to be used to justify a political conclusion or a set of mechanical criteria that automatically yields a simple answer, but a way of moral reasoning to, discern the ethical limits of action' (USCCB 1983: 6).

The just war tradition is the Christian tradition. This is not to say that other traditions do not have theorizations of war and violence. But, it is important to note that the just war tradition we have today largely originated as a response to the pacifism of Jesus and the early church. The

---

BOX 5.1   The just war: tradition or theory?

The just war is understood by some as a tradition and by others as a theory. One might say this is not an important distinction and is only an example of academic debate with no real purpose. In fact, there is an important, but subtle difference. If one thinks of the just war as a tradition, then it should be read as an ongoing dialogue between theorists of the past and those of the present. This means that reading Augustine or Aquinas should be about understanding their ideas in a context and responding to them in their terms. Historians of political thought have just as much a role here as moral philosophers. Those who view it as a theory often see it as an analytic construct by which to evaluate wars in the current order. If a historical figure provides some insight, fine; otherwise, their contexts (often religious in this case) may remove them from the debate. When seen as a theory, the history of just war becomes a museum piece by which we can demonstrate how thought has evolved. This chapter presents the just war as more of a tradition of thought than a theory, although those who take the latter view have provided some of the most insightful and innovative ideas about just war over the years.

For just war as a tradition, see: Johnson 1975, 1981; Rengger 2013. *For those who view it more as a theory, see:* Fabre 2012; McMahan 2009; Rodin 2002.

thought of Augustine was also described above; he is sometimes seen as one of the originators of the just war tradition, for it is Augustine who turned Christian thought away from its largely pacifist orientation. After Augustine, Christian reflections on war and peace moved to the cannon lawyers, who helped turn its theology into practical rules of statecraft. Much of this work focused on commentaries on respected authorities, such as Gratian's *Decretum*. Gratian, a 12th-century medieval monk, sought to harmonize a large body of legal rules, papal decrees and real-life political and religious dilemmas. The text is organized in terms of answers to hypothetical cases covering a wide range of issues (Reichberg et al. 2006: 104–24). Case number 23 deals with questions of war and violence. Interestingly, the text focuses on a hypothetical case in which a group of bishops have committed heresy and the justification for using force to discipline them. As a result, a large part of the text deals with the use of force to punish rather than to act in self-defence. But in clarifying when violence can be used by a public authority, Gratian plays a key role in the development of the just war tradition (Johnson 1981: 122–71).

As with almost every element of Christian thought, Thomas Aquinas, the 13th-century Dominican theologian/philosopher, played a key role in pushing the tradition forward. His important work on natural law was described more extensively in Chapter 2. Aquinas is crucial for the development of the just war tradition, but his works on war and violence are not located in one place nor are they easily accessible to a modern-day reader. The *Summa Theologica*, his famous work, is structured as a dialogue between him and different authorities, primarily the Bible but also theologians and philosophers. He begins by asking a question, provides responses from those authorities, and then his replies to those authorities. He does not disagree with them, for to do so would undermine their authority. Rather, he reinterprets their works to develop a new synthesis.

The question of war and violence is dealt with in a number places in the *Summa*. He firsts asks questions about peace in Question 29, concluding that while peace is a virtue, it must be in relation to the wider good of humanity: 'Hence, true peace is only in good men and about good things. The peace of the wicked is not a true peace, but a semblance thereof' (Aquinas, quoted in Reichberg et al. 2006: 173). In Question 40, he turns directly to the question of war, listing the three conditions that make war licit, or allowable: right authority, just cause and right intention. As noted below, these become a central part of the just war tradition. He writes more extensively on a range of topics related to war and violence, including the question of civil war, or what he calls 'sedition'. In his discussion of these matters, Aquinas is less willing to allow for civil war, and he even suggests that it may be necessary to live under tyranny in order to protect the civil peace. He also argued that while force cannot be used to propagate the Christian religion, it might be justified against heretics (Reichberg et al. 2006: 192–3).

These elements of Aquinas' work stand outside modern ideas of just war, for the punishment of heresy is no longer considered acceptable. Yet, at the same time, the idea of punishment as a justification for force – found in Augustine, Gratian and Aquinas – may be said to have reappeared in some types of intervention or even collective security. For instance, if an intervention is undertaken to force a regime or leader to conform to human rights norms, it might include hurting that regime in pursuit of that end. This punitive war or intervention has echoes in the medieval tradition, although the norms being protected are no longer the same (Lang 2008).

In Chapter 2, I described the work of Christian theologians who drew on Aquinas and developed the ideas of natural law. It is in these works, including Vitoria, Grotius and Vattel, that the just war tradition flourished. In the next section, I explore Grotius's work in more depth, but let me here jump forward to the 19th century. During the 19th century, the emergence of positivism as a foundation for international law meant that the just war tradition, with its explicit combination of law and ethics, faded into some irrelevance (other than in Catholic social and political thinking, where it continued to play a prominent role). In the mid-20th century, however, just war returned to some prominence. The failure of international law to regulate the outbreak and conduct of both world wars led some to recognize the need for a return to alternative sources for the norms and rules that could moderate war. Two further developments generated renewed interest in the just war tradition. First, the rise of nuclear war as a potential and the creation of a Cold War climate led a number of thinkers to return to the tradition (Ramsey 1961, 1968; Tucker 1978). When the US Conference of Catholic Bishops addressed this issue with a pastoral letter in 1983, it raised the prominence of the tradition in public discourse (USCCB 1983).

One of the most important works on just war appeared at this time. Walzer (1977), a political theorist, argued in *Just and Unjust Wars* that the tradition is actually the language through which we talk about war. In his original introduction (the book has been through four editions), Walzer stated that he wrote the book in part because of his frustration with how discourse about war was being framed in the US in the aftermath of the Vietnam War. Finding that particular war unjust did not mean that all wars were unjust. Drawing on an array of historical 'examples', as he called them, Walzer constructs an argument based on the 'legalist paradigm', or the idea that states are members of an international society that is governed by the broadly conceived rules found in the just war tradition. This argument relies, to some extent, on his communitarian philosophical leanings

(Erskine 2008). His argument reveals a tension between the *ad bellum* and *in bello* elements of the tradition, when he points out that if a war is truly just, then all means would be allowable. This complicates his own analysis at points, such as when he justifies the 'supreme emergency' defence, the idea that if the existence of a community is in jeopardy, then anything is allowed to save it. Walzer's effort to deal with situations like this is to emphasize the idea of responsibility, the responsibility of leaders to reason through the categories of the just war and the more limited responsibility of the soldier, who cannot be held liable for the war itself but is liable for their conduct on the field of battle.

Nicholas Rengger (2013) argues in response to Walzer that the idea of the supreme emergency, along with others, creates more exceptions to rules because of its move away from the problem-based tradition in which it originated. That is, rather than a tradition that seeks to find answers to particular problems in the context of a wider ethical framework, it has moved towards a tradition of rules and rule following that does not conform well to political life. Rengger's larger critique of the just war as it exists today suggests that the move towards making just war a rule-based tradition has undermined its utility to bring about peace.

This idea of the individual soldier's responsibility has been a focus of attention among a more recent body of work addressing the just war tradition, or, more accurately, just war theory, as they would call it. These works have critically engaged notions of responsibility and liability. David Rodin's book, *War and Self-Defense* (2002), provides a good example of this approach. In it, Rodin (2002) argues that the most well-founded justification for war, self-defence, collapses once it is set within the context of global rights. This results from the structure of rights discourse (where he explicitly draws on Hohfeld's theory of rights, explained in Chapter 3) and the fact that the nation-state cannot be a 'self' in the way that persons can. Jeff McMahan (2009) has contributed in important ways to this approach to just war. In his most recent work, he has argued that the distinction between the *in bello* and *ad bellum* elements of the tradition assumes that individual soldiers should not be held responsible for unjust wars and that civilians should not necessarily be considered innocent. Fabre (2012) has also recently contributed to this approach in her attempt to develop a 'cosmopolitan just war'. Fabre argues that the primary principle of cosmopolitan theory is that individual persons are the focal point of ethical analysis, no matter where they are located. She goes on to defend an individual's right to go to war in defence of their rights. This account results in arguments about private military companies and humanitarian interventions that rely less on nation-state boundaries or authority structures and more on the rights of individual persons.

The just war theory propounded by thinkers such as Rodin, McMahan and Fabre has been growing in influence in recent years, in some ways eclipsing the natural law tradition within which it originally rested. This shift has positive and negative implications. It is positive in that the cosmopolitan universalism of the theory makes it less liable to abuse by Western leaders as justifications for their own wars. At the same time, by pulling the tradition from its foundations in the European Christian tradition, certain key principles such as that of mercy and compassion may be lost (May 2007).

As is evident from this overview, the just war tradition is understood in a variety of ways by those who engage with it. But most every account draws on the categories or principles that frame it. These categories allow us to raise some further important points about the tradition and its relevance for modern warfare.

Making judgements about war

The just war tradition has traditionally been framed in terms of two sets of standards, or questions to be asked about any use of force, which are usually categorized as follows.

Jus ad bellum questions:

- Is the cause of going to war just?
- Is there a right authority waging the war?
- Is the agent conducting the war acting from a right intention?
- Is the war a proportional response to the situation?
- Is the war the last resort, or have all other options been considered?
- Is there a probable chance of success?

Jus in bello questions:

- Is the war being conducted in a proportional way, that is, are the tactical and strategic decisions being made in proper response to the attacks being undertaken?
- Is the war discriminating between soldiers and civilians or legitimate and illegitimate targets?

In this section, I use these categories to provide an overview of some issues that arise when considering war and peace. These draw on some elements of the just war tradition, but, in the spirit of the tradition not being a set of rules but a set of categories by which we can ask important questions, I also point to how other approaches, ethical and legal, might provide answers to these questions.

Just cause

The first question to ask is if the war is just, or is force being used for a justifiable reason? Traditionally, there were three just causes: self-defence, punishment and retaking what had been taken. As international legal norms and rules came to dominate the international order, the primary just cause came to be self-defence against aggression. Some have explored the return of other just causes, such as punishment (Lang 2008; O'Driscoll 2008).

Another development in the just cause category, one related to the question of self-defence, concerns pre-emptive and preventive military actions. Prompted by the attacks of 9/11 and the Bush administration's decision to attack Iraq on the basis of a possible future threat, a debate arose about the justification for preventive war (Lang et al. 2003). The US administration developed its argument for this new approach to self-defence in its 2002 National Security Strategy document, one that fundamentally redefined the notion of pre-emption (Bush 2002). Some traditionally liberal IR theorists have proposed normative reasons for creating an institutional structure for waging preventive war (Buchanan and Keohane 2004; Doyle 2008). Legal theorists have struggled with appropriate rule-governed responses to preventive military action (Dershowitz 2006). A number of philosophers have also addressed this issue at some length (Shue and Rodin 2007). A few ethical arguments have been made to support preventive war (Kaufman 2005). Richard Miller (2008) has used the concept of just cause to critically assess the 2003 war against Iraq, determining that a rigorous use of the category undermines the justice of the war. Jeff McMahan (2005) has generated debate about the principle of just cause by linking it to the issue of individual liability in warfare (see also Hurka 2007).

Right authority

Right authority is the second criteria of *jus ad bellum*. It suggests that war must be declared by those who are responsible for public order not private groups or individuals. The intent of this condition is to narrow the spectrum of entities able to wage war, and to ensure that the decision to wage war is made by a legitimate authority. Who is considered the legitimate authority, however, is an issue of contention (Lang et al. 2013). Over the course of history, shifts in just authority have occurred, the largest one marked by the creation of the Westphalian system (named after the Treaty of Westphalia in 1648). Considered a pivotal stage of power transition, the Westphalian system was the first step in the shift of legitimate authority from religious institutions to sovereign states. With the advent of democracy in the 19th and 20th centuries, state leaders became accountable to their citizens, who demanded to know why they were being forced to take up arms for the national interest.

The central dilemma of authority is what role should be played by the UN and other international structures in authorizing the use of force. As the concept of peacekeeping has developed in recent years, the authority of the UN has become more of a contentious issue. When the UN Security Council was avoided by the great powers in the Kosovo (1999) and Iraq conflicts (2003), important questions were raised about its legitimacy when it comes to the use of military force (Cronin and Hurd 2008). Others have suggested normative justifications for how international organizations can be more formally structured to respond to a broad range of threats (Keohane et al. 2006).

Right intentions

The third question to ask concerns intentions. Like other moral theories, the just war tradition suggests that the intentions of the agents are important to consider in evaluating actions. This is related to the just cause criteria, but different in an important way. For example, one might argue that, objectively, a war can be labelled just because it leads to the destruction of an evil regime. But, if those undertaking the war intend to simply increase their nation's power, advance their personal financial or political interests, or achieve fame and fortune, then the validity of the war may be called into question. In fact, it is more accurate to call this category 'right motive', as Terry Nardin (2006: 10) has suggested. In philosophy, an intention is the declared reason for action, while a motive is the issue or concern that motivates an individual to undertake an action. In other words, the category of right intention should probably be known as right motive.

Walzer (1977: 26) has pointed out that no individual or government really ever has truly pure motives. But, at the same time, the question of hypocrisy is one that bedevils anyone interested in ethics and international affairs. That is, if individuals profess to be acting for morally good reasons but are discovered to be acting for morally suspect ones, then their future actions will constantly be called into account. Those who have criticized the recent surge in moralism in humanitarian intervention and other uses of military force rely heavily on this kind of critique (Chandler 2002; Chomsky 1999). Chris Brown (2003) has critically assessed this concern with motives, particularly in terms of humanitarian intervention, arguing that an excessive focus on intentions may well lead to a failure to act in crucial moments. As a result, the tradition's emphasis on the centrality of right motives is an important discipline on excessive moralism.

Last resort

The last resort question is a difficult one to answer. Walzer (2004) has pointed out that there is never a last resort, because something could always be tried before launching a war. This criterion reveals why the just war tradition is not really best understood as set of criteria to be met before launching a war, but a set of issues to be considered. This criterion is perhaps better understood as a prudential rather than a moral one. This means that there is a need for judgement when it comes to war, judgement that we often leave to political leaders. One could not logically put this criterion into legal or moral terms, but one could make sure any leader considering war should carefully think through whether or not a war makes sense or if diplomatic or other means are better used.

Importantly, though, the last resort should not be seen as a means to stop war from ever happening. Consider one case in which force was not used but perhaps should have been. In January 1994, a UN official sent a cable to the UN headquarters saying that it would appear groups in Rwanda were stockpiling small arms and other weapons and were using the radio to incite hatred. This warning was not taken up by the UN office for peace-keeping, which instead turned to other methods to try to resolve the situation (Barnett 2002). Only a few months later, a genocide broke out which left almost one million people dead. UN officials, schooled in the importance of diplomacy and wary of too many African conflicts in which various sides fought over a variety of issues, did not advise the great powers to undertake any military action. The US, scarred by its failure in Somalia, also sought to use other methods (or none at all, in fact). As a result of these failures, which might be seen as operating under the idea that force should only be the last result, there was a horrible outcome that might have been prevented had military force been used.

Probable chance of success

Probable chance of success is also a prudential category, for there can be no rule that states force should only be used if we are sure of success. It is important, however, that leaders considering the use of force do not abandon their responsibilities to the welfare of their people by throwing them into conflict for purposes that may not result in a positive outcome.

This is also a problematic criterion, though, for it means that individuals or political communities may be counselled to abandon resistance because there is no hope they will succeed. In fact, in some situations, it may simply be right to use force even if there is little chance of success. So, for instance, one would not fault the Polish military standing up to the invasion of Nazi Germany in 1939, even though they were fighting with cavalry in response to German blitzkrieg attacks. Again, though, this is where thinking of these as questions from a political perspective rather than a singular moral standard is helpful. We would agree that the Polish people were morally right to stand up to the Nazis with force, for what choice did they have? One can then ask whether or not a political judgement, one fully informed of the situation and with some knowledge of the wider European and global context, would have counselled the same choice. It might have, but this is open to judgement rather than a strict application of a rule.

Proportionality

Proportionality is a criterion of *jus ad bellum* and *jus in bello*. In terms of *jus ad bellum*, it attempts to ensure that the damage and costs of war, in human and physical terms, is proportionate to the benefits expected as an outcome of war; that is, it seeks to take into account the grand strategy of pursuing a war rather than specific strategies and tactics of war. In light of the overwhelming military superiority of the US military, some believe that any use of force by the US will violate the proportionality criterion. Neta Crawford (2003) has argued that the US response to 9/11 raises precisely this issue. The growth of US power in the international system has created what many argue is a situation of asymmetry, which may increase the chances that opposing states and non-state actors will utilize terrorist and irregular warfare, further complicating the ability of the US to respond proportionately to attacks.

In *jus in bello*, the proportionality criterion reflects the commonsense assumption that warring communities should not reply in excess to attacks on them. There is no mathematical formula to determine what is proportional, however, so evaluating proportionality remains a matter of prudential judgement (Franck 2008). One could argue that attempts to place limits on the collateral damage that noncombatant entities may sustain during a war, in the hopes that the good outweigh the costs of a war, represent a form of proportionality. While it is acceptable to have a certain ratio of noncombatant/combatant casualties, it is imperative that the intent of the attacks is to produce more good than bad. In other words, means must justify the ends and those means utilized to pursue just ends must be set in a morally restrictive framework.

One version of the proportionality criterion is the idea of double effect. This concept, articulated by Aquinas among others, stipulates that if a military action is not intended to kill civilians but does so in the course of accomplishing a military objective, then it can be considered morally licit.

This is a contested concept, however, for it allows individuals to explain away violations of the proportionality criteria without having to consider the seriousness of their violation.

One area where the question of proportionality has become prominent is in aerial warfare. The Hague Conventions of 1899 and 1907 do not include any laws concerning aerial warfare, although there is an important 1923 document called *The Hague Rules of Air Warfare* (Roberts and Guelff 2003: 139–53). Ward Thomas (2001: 87–180) has explored how a set of norms evolved concerning aerial warfare. On the one hand, a set of norms drawing on the protection of innocents meant that aerial warfare failed to live up to the norms and rules governing this new technology. At the same time, those developing this new technology would argue that actually targeting civilians might lead to a quicker end to war, for it would make it too unbearable for civilian populations. The tension between these different norms resulted in an evolving and sometimes confusing set of ideas surrounding the justification for aerial warfare.

Discrimination

The last principle is discrimination. It states that just authorities engaged in combat must only fight persons also engaged in combat. Bystanders must not be targeted, and cannot play a role in combat unless either participating in a formal military service or uniformed militia. Furthermore, prisoners of war are entitled to specific rights and treatment. These elements of the tradition have been most clearly translated into laws rather than simply rules or norms. These laws have been codified in the Geneva Conventions of 1949 and the Additional Protocols of 1977.

The Conventions and Protocols are often presented in the popular press outside their political contexts. That is, they appear as international laws that military officers are expected to uphold. Yet, there are tensions built into these documents that render them problematic. The four Geneva Conventions were passed in the wake of the Second World War, designed primarily to give greater protection to civilians in the context of warfare. Yet they were also constructed in response to political dynamics in which understandings of rights and authority were shifting. For instance, one of the crucial elements of the Geneva Conventions concerned the definition of a prisoner of war, which was ultimately about defining who is a legitimate soldier and who is a civilian. The definition, found in Convention III, Article 4, includes four criteria:

- must serve under a unified command structure
- must wear a distinctive emblem

- must openly carry arms
- must act in conformity with the laws of war.

These four criteria helped to discriminate between soldiers and civilians.

With the rise of the decolonization movement in the 1960s, some of which arose from revolutionary military movements, those who succeeded in creating new states wanted to redefine this distinction. There were many who believed that the colonial powers had used the Geneva Conventions to criminalize efforts to remove colonial regimes in places as diverse as Vietnam, Malaysia and Algeria, by claiming that revolutionary fighters were hiding behind civilians rather than openly fighting. As a result, in 1977, the Protocols to the Geneva Convention were passed. These Protocols included the following section from Protocol I, Article 44:

> 3. In order to promote the protection of the civilian population from the effects of hostilities, combatants are obliged to distinguish themselves from the civilian population while they are engaged in an attack or in a military operation preparatory to an attack. Recognizing, however, that there are situations in armed conflicts where, owing to the nature of the hostilities an armed combatant cannot so distinguish himself, he shall retain his status as a combatant, provided that, in such situations, he carries his arms openly.

This language somewhat loosened the criteria by focusing only on the nature of openly carrying arms rather than the unified command or the emblem issue. These changes are perhaps important for military necessity, but they resulted from a particular political moment in time. It is important to note, as well, that the US has never signed on to the Protocols, in large part because it objects to language such as this.

Distinguishing soldiers and civilians may seem to be an easy task, but modern warfare has made this much more complicated. As some theorists have noted, new forms of 'humane warfare' have challenged our understanding of what constitutes a soldier (Coker 2001; Ignatieff 2000). The increased role of civilians in the technology of warfare has also raised important questions about how they should be considered; for instance, what is an individual sitting at a computer terminal who does not necessarily wear a uniform but may control battlefield operations (Dunlap 2004)?

Jus post bellum

This leads to the last set of questions, which is, as noted above, a new one for the tradition. One of the results of the focus on discrimination is the creation of different kinds of judicial structures to deal with the aftermath of war. War crimes tribunals and international criminal courts have flourished since the end of the Cold War. Some theorists have linked the courts back to the just war tradition (Johnson 2004; May 2007), although others have raised important normative questions about what these courts can and cannot do (Branch 2007; Simpson 2007).

As the international community has progressively become engaged in the reconstruction of post-conflict societies, analysts of international affairs have focused their attention on these dynamics. In point of fact, 'reconstruction' is not a new endeavour for the international community (Williams 2006). Much of the literature on post-conflict reconstruction, however, has focused primarily on the more recent past. Some writers have focused on creating a peaceful order, while others have addressed the difficulties of creating a just political order (Kerr and Mobekk 2007; Mani 2002; Richmond 2002; Teitel 2000; Zaum 2007).

Whether to focus on peace or justice is an ethical dilemma. The distinction between the two is not that clear, but attempts to create peace sometimes focus on the short-term imposition of policies rather than long-term attempts to reconstruct political institutions. At the same time, in situations where violence is just below the surface, the need to impose a peaceful order may take precedence. In light of the importance of authority this book has highlighted, efforts to construct political institutions, particularly those labelled as 'rule of law' initiatives, are becoming more important. This rule of law approach has become a central part of many UN-led post-conflict interventions. For instance, in East Timor and Kosovo, the UN had full judicial authority for short periods, a much more extensive form of control than in other post-conflict situations, where the role of the UN was mainly to facilitate the creation of new judicial institutions (Chesterman 2004: 154–82).

To understand the issue, consider humanitarian intervention. When international forces undertake a humanitarian intervention, usually involving a strong military presence at first that only eventually transitions into more civil society programmes, attention is paid to the creation of a secure environment through force of arms. When it comes to ensuring public order and obedience to the law, too often military/police forces, which are not backed up by a functioning prosecutorial, judicial and penal structure, will end up detaining and even informally punishing those who serve as 'spoilers' or even common criminals. These punitive measures undertaken by those whose primary goal should be the investigation of crimes and arrest of suspected criminals distort the just application of sentencing procedures. Rather than engage in just punishment, these military/police forces, often internationally trained and even including international police forces, distort the rule of law and justice. Such issues raise ethical and political complexities that are being addressed through legal and ethical literature (May 2012; Orend 2002).

This overview has presented some different perspectives on the problems of war and peace, using the categories of the just war tradition to frame those issues. There are many other issue that could be considered, and one might also use different starting points to make these judgements, such as the growing volume of work on international humanitarian law. But, as highlighted throughout, the crucial issue to keep in mind is that using violence in any capacity raises issues of authority, rights and rules.

Hugo Grotius

This final section focuses on one significant figure in the history of the just war and international legal traditions. Hugo Grotius was a Dutch Renaissance thinker whose work spanned law, theology, politics and statecraft. He stands at the point where moral and religious thought about war and peace was evolving into something more like international law. He also wrote in the midst of the Thirty Years War, which concluded with the famous Treaty of Westphalia, sometimes read as a marker for when the European political order shifted to something like the modern state system. Finally, Grotius helped to redefine the idea of natural law as something that could not just be derived from biblical or even natural sources but also comes from the actions of historical and contemporary contexts. For all these reasons, Grotius gives us a fascinating insight into the international political theory of war and peace.

Grotius was trained in the tradition of Renaissance humanism, in which he excelled (Edwards 1981). He wrote from a very early age, including a range of works on theology, philosophy, law and even literature. But he was not simply a scholar; he was involved directly in the complicated politics of his homeland, a political context that is helpful in understanding some of Grotius's ideas. For the purposes of this chapter, two contexts matter: the political relationship of the United Provinces to each other and to the Spanish Empire; and the economic context of the Dutch East India Company as a quasi-political entity engaged in the use of military force against the Portuguese in the East Indies region. These two contexts shaped the background structure against which Grotius developed his ideas; indeed, he was not removed from politics but rather served as an official state representative during a period of conflict among the United Provinces and later as an ambassador of Sweden to France. Instead, especially in understanding his conceptions of political authority, appreciating the conflicts over political authority that defined the Dutch Republic and the questions about the authority of mercantile companies like the Dutch East India Company must be taken into account.

Theorists of the international society approach to IR sometimes locate Grotius in terms of the Thirty Years War (1618–48) (Bull et al. 1990). But, I would argue that the more relevant context for understanding Grotius is the Dutch Revolt against Spain that began in 1566. In 1551, Philip II of Spain inherited the 17 provinces of the Netherlands, which roughly correspond to the Netherlands and Benelux countries of today. The social and political conditions of the northern provinces were based on a series of overlapping political structures, with a great deal of power remaining in the cities and villages of the different provinces. As statehood became more centralized in places like Spain, England and France, the provinces retained political structures that were 'medieval, political and administratively atomised' (Wilson 1961: 8). The Union of Utrecht in 1579 brought together the seven northern provinces, led by Holland, the wealthiest, into a defensive alliance against the power of Spain (Tracy 2008).

As a number of historians have emphasized, this union was not one that led to a single unified state. While there existed the office of Stadholder, originally the lieutenant of the Hapsburgs in the region who became the military leader of the republic after the revolt led by William of Orange in 1566, true power rested in the States General, or meeting of the delegates of the seven provinces that took place in the Hague. One historian notes that rather than a parliament, this institution was more like a meeting of allies, with the requirement that any decision be unanimous rather than the result of the majority. This structure was even more surprising in light of the vast diversity of economic power between the leading provinces such as Holland and the smaller ones. This constitutional structure gave more power to 'local liberties at the expense of central direction' (Haley 1972: 74).

While the Dutch Republic was born as a loose federation in response to a need to defend the provinces against the Spanish Empire, it soon saw political and military struggles of its own, conflicts in which Grotius was enmeshed. Johann Oldenbarnevelt, the delegate from the city of Rotterdam, one of the leading cities of Holland, had taken on Grotius as one of his protégées in 1601. Oldenbarnevelt became involved in the religious controversy surging through the region when he argued that the strict Calvinism of the Dutch should be modified to allow for less emphasis on predestination. This conflict resulted in the Synod of Dordt in 1618–19, at which Oldenbarnevelt and the moderates were defeated, leading to his execution by the Stadholder, Prince Maurice of Orange. Grotius ended up being imprisoned as a result of his association with Oldenbarnevelt, escaping in 1621.

Hence, Grotius lived through a political experience in which his life was jeopardized by a religious-political conflict. He had other interesting roles as well. In 1601, Oldenbarnevelt asked him to be the official historian of Holland, a task that led him to write some unpublished and eventually published accounts of the constitutional structure of Holland and the Dutch Republic as a whole. This historical work makes its way at various points into *De Jure Belli ad Pacis*, and appears in other published works by Grotius. The point to emphasize here is not that Grotius's experience of living through and writing about the history of his political community determined his theoretical output, but rather that his narrative of the Dutch Republic was essentially about competing authority structures in a contested political space.

The second political context is Grotius's relationship to the mercantile company that dominated the expansion of Dutch trade throughout the world in the 17th century, one that connects to some of the discussion about wealth in Chapter 4. Dutch economic power emerged in the late 16th century as a result of its location in a key trading route between the northern and southern regions of Europe. The Dutch became a pivot in the trade system of Europe, buying goods from the Baltic regions and selling them to Spain, France and England. Not only did they trade in the north, however; the various Dutch republics soon expanded into the Mediterranean as well, again serving as middlemen in the trade system of Europe (Israel 1989). Eventually, they expanded to Africa, the Caribbean and the East Indies.

It is their expansion into the East Indies that is most relevant for Grotius. In the 1590s, Dutch merchants realized the potential profits to be found in the spice trade from the region. The primary competitor was the Portuguese crown, which controlled most of the economic activity within the region. In contrast, Dutch merchants acted on their own, pursuing profits through investment companies that combined the interests of merchants, investors and the political leadership. After competition among the Dutch merchants, for the trade increased in the last years of the 16th century, they turned to the leaders of Holland for help. This resulted in the creation of the United Dutch East India Company in 1602. The company was unlike previous economic organizations, however:

> Never before had a joint-stock company been created which organized investment, and balanced the interests of different towns and regions, on the basis of a federal concept of management. Nor, clearly, could this have been attempted had the United Provinces not been a federal republic, organized to prevent the concentration of power at any one centre. (Israel 1989: 69)

As with the Dutch political structure, this mercantile company, which became the engine for Dutch economic expansion in the East Indies, was decentralized. Importantly, it was also a quasi-governmental structure. While not controlled by the Dutch republics, it was incorporated by the state of Holland that also invested in it.

The Dutch East India Company used military force in pursuit of its interests in the region. Oldenbarnevelt encouraged the company to establish military bases to counter the power of the Portuguese. As one historian puts it:

> As far as the States of Holland and Zeeland were concerned, the VOC [the Dutch acronym for the company] was an arm of the state empowered to deploy armies and navies in Asia in the name of the States General and to conduct diplomacy under the States General's flag and seal. (Israel 1989: 70)

Grotius's relationship to the company came in two phases. In 1602, he wrote a legal defence of a Dutch merchant who had captured a Portuguese ship carrying a significant amount of goods from the East Indies. The capture may have been a spur to the creation of the Dutch East India Company, which was created only months later. Grotius's defence of this individual became the core of *De Jure Pradea* (Law of the Prize), written in 1604. In 1605, the Dutch took over a Portuguese fort in the region, further stoking the conflict between the company, the Dutch Republic and the Portuguese crown.

In 1608, the company requested that Grotius take this longer text and turn it into a shorter pamphlet in the context of the ongoing dispute between Portugal and the company. This request produced *Mare Liberum*, for which Grotius became quite famous in his day and which many believe influenced the ideas behind his *De Jure Belli ac Pacis*. This text formed the basis of Grotius's ideas about the freedom of the seas, arguing that no state could control them as the Portuguese claimed. As Richard Tuck (1999) notes, *Mare Liberum* also included a discussion of *ius gladii*, or the right to punish, a right based not on sovereign authority but on the just cause for which an actor is fighting.

The central point of this episode is that Grotius's conception of what justified the use of force arose in the context of a largely economic actor using military force (van Ittersum 2006). While the Dutch East India Company was one of the first such mercantile companies, it was not the only one to emerge in Europe. As Janice Thomson describes it, these mercantile companies, although first created by states, soon needed to be controlled by the state in order that they base their sovereignty on the control of violence. Comparing mercantile companies to mercenaries and pirates, Thomson

(1994) examines how the state system in Europe was only able to create truly sovereign states by limiting the capabilities of these quasi-public institutions to use military force. In other words, controlling these non-state agents became a central part of the creation of a sovereign state system.

Grotius's ideas about force can be understood as arising from a political context in which authority and rules were much more complex than we might assume. The political authority of the emerging Dutch Republic was not a traditional 'sovereign state' that could be seen as a clearly defined 'just authority' in either the international legal or even modern just war theory sense. Rather, it was a complex political structure that included disagreement over not only who was in charge, but also how the power of governance related to things like religious belief. And, if we consider the economic and political links between the Dutch East Indies Company and the Dutch political leadership, the fact that the 'rules' governing force were designed to promote the economic interests of these actors makes the situation even more complex and interesting.

Let me briefly explain, then, what Grotius wrote about the use of force, although it is important to keep in mind the above historical context. Grotius is most well known for his *De Jure Belli ac Pacis*. It is translated in two different ways because he wrote in Latin and the word *jure* lends itself to different translations: some call it *The Rights of War and Peace*, while others call it *The Laws of War and Peace*. In the following, I will keep to the Latin title, although the complicated relationship between natural law and natural right theory, discussed in Chapter 2, can be seen as a result of this transitional issue (Finnis 1980).

De Jure Belli ac Pacis (Grotius 2005 [1625]) is divided into three books. The Prolegomena provides the basis for the text as a whole, building on the natural law arguments of *Mare Liberum*. Book I defines war, justice and right, drawing on a wide range of Christian and classical authors. Book II begins by extending the just causes of war introduced in Book I, but then explores the foundations of right, property and punishment. These foundations result from the fact that Grotius, like the just war tradition within which he was writing, assumed that there were three just causes for war: self-defence, retaking of property unlawfully taken, and punishment of wrongdoing. Book III then examines what may be justly undertaken in war, or what is today called *jus in bello*.

Grotius's intellectual and political contexts resulted in a nuanced understanding of the relationship between political authority and war. That understanding can first be found in his natural law reflections on what constitutes just authority and the reasons for which a just authority can use force. It can also be found in the political context in which he wrote, one in which different kinds of agents fought to establish their rights to defend life and property. The combination of a natural law framework that privileged the reasons for using force with a political context in which authority was in a state of flux resulted in an understanding of just war that stands in stark opposition to the modern focus on the state that characterizes just war theory and international law.

Grotius is known as a theorist of natural law, in his day a relatively new approach to morality and politics and one which was explored in Chapter 2. Grotius's contribution to the natural law tradition was to explore morality in the context of one of the least law-bound human practices, war. Grotius's contribution to natural law was controversial in his day because of one sentence, which later became known as the 'impious hypothesis'. In establishing the reality of natural law in his Prolegomena, he argued: 'And, indeed, all we have now said would take place, though we should even grant, what without the greatest Wickedness cannot be granted that there is no God, or that he takes no care in human affairs' (Grotius 2005 [1625]: 89). The challenge Grotius presented to the solely Christian conception of natural law did not rely only this sentence, but the fact that Grotius drew on classical Greek and Roman writers and, most controversially, the practices of states, both ancient and contemporary, as evidence for the reality of natural law.

His definition of natural law seeks to elide the conflict with divine law:

> Natural right is the Rule and Dictate of Right Reason, shewing the Moral Deformity or Moral Necessity there is in any Act, according to its Suitableness or Unsuitableness to a reasonable nature, and consequently that such an Act is either forbid or commanded by GOD, the Author of Nature. (Grotius 2005 [1625]: 150–1)

Rather than rely purely on God's commands, however, Grotius also notes that, as Cicero argued: 'The Consent of all Nations is to be reputed the Law of Nature' (ibid.: 161).

After establishing what constitutes natural law, Grotius argues that this law does allow for the use of force. Beginning with every animal's instinctual desire to defend itself, but then extending into reason, sacred history and secular history, Grotius establishes the principle that defence of oneself is the primary reason for using force. This reason, however, is extended to the concept of a natural right to punish in Book II, a concept that raises important challenges to authority. For Grotius, punishment is a justified reason for using military force. But, unlike most conceptions of punishment, his does not rely on a clearly defined sovereign undertaking that punishment. Rather, his justification relies on the nature of the wrong committed.

Grotius does not simply list punishment as a potential cause for war. Rather, he develops a much larger and extensive analysis of the philosophical purpose behind punishment. It is in Book II, Chapters 20 and 21, 'On Punishment' and 'On the Sharing of Punishments', that Grotius extends the argument that war can be waged for the purposes of punishment. Grotius does not assume the necessity of a single community headed by a sovereign who has the responsibility to punish. Rather than argue that the right to punish derives from the inherent dignity or authority of the sovereign, he posits that punishment derives from the character of the violation:

> But the Subject of this Right, that is, the Person to whom the Right of Punishing belongs, is not determined by the Law of Nature. For natural reason informs us, that a Malefactor may be punished, but not who ought to punish him. It suggests indeed so much, that it is the fittest to be done by a Superior, but yet does not shew that to be absolutely necessary, unless by Superior we mean him who is innocent and detrude the Guilty below the Rank of Men, which is the Doctrine of some Divines. (Grotius 2005 [1625]: 955)

Rather than punishment being defined by the existence of a sovereign, it is defined by the objective fact of a criminal violation.

In Section 37 of Chapter 20, Grotius turns to the question of war being waged to inflict punishment. He notes: 'the Desire for inflicting Punishment is often the Occasion of War' (ibid.: 1018). He then turns to the question of whether a king whose subjects have not been harmed may launch a war to punish one who has harmed another community. He argues yes, those who commit crimes 'against nature' may be punished by any sovereign state through war. Grotius's argument that punishment is a just cause for waging war arises from his natural law framework. But, as the above section noted, his understanding of political authority resulted from a different political context than we live in today. We could simply state that punishment is no longer a legitimate cause for war (Lang 2008). But Grotius is not simply adding punishment as one possible reason for war; rather, this is at the core of his understanding of war and peace, an understanding that still impacts us today. That is, underlying Grotius's ideas about war are complicated political, moral and economic contexts that resulted in a much stranger story than we are used to in the modern world.

Conclusion

This chapter has moved through a wide range of ideas, from many different traditions. Throughout, however, I have tried to emphasize the importance of the political nature of the rules that have arisen to govern violence in the current international order. The last discussion of Grotius points to how his political context shaped some of his ideas, and also suggested why some of his less well-known ideas, such as his support of punishment as a reason for military action, might still be relevant.

In conclusion, let me return to the issue raised at the outset of this chapter, the use of drones. Political leaders argue that they use force only in self-defence. But, especially if we consider the use of drone strikes, do these not have a punitive dimension to them? While they may take out high value targets that might in the future use force against us, they also target those who have used force against great powers in previous episodes. One of the earliest uses of drone strikes came against a carload of 'terrorists' who were travelling in Yemen. On 4 November 2002, a US Predator unmanned aircraft launched a Hellfire air-to-ground missile at a car travelling through a remote region of Yemen. This strike killed six people, including Ali Qaed Senyan al-Harthi, who was a suspect in the attack on the USS *Cole* in 2000 and had been a close associate of Osama bin Laden. As the debate over drones suggests, this was only the first moment in a longer term campaign against terrorist suspects. The descriptions of the attack focused particularly on the role of al-Harthi's role in the attack on the USS *Cole*, which suggests a punitive logic was at work along with a self-defence one. This suggests that perhaps underlying the use of force, there is still a punitive dimension. Can we rely on Grotius's defence of punishment as a legitimate means of using force? One might further consider how Grotius's justification was linked to his economic purpose, or the economic purpose of the Dutch East Indies Company. It is difficult to make the exact link here, but one might think about how uses of force are often tied to economic actors, who wish to promote their agendas and use political and even military means to do so.

This discussion of Grotius, his context and its relevance for today raises more questions than answers. But, that is the point of political theory. It is not designed to give you answers to complex questions of the global realm. It is, however, through an engagement with the past that we can come to a more productive means to think critically about what may seem like obvious reasons for using force and how those reasons relate to much more complicated questions about authority, rights and rules in the global system.

Further reading

Iain Atack. 2012. *Non-violence in Political Theory*. Edinburgh: Edinburgh University Press.
   Explores the nature of nonviolence in political theory. Using a critical lens, explores why nonviolence is often left unexamined in the tradition of political theory and how it is linked to ideas that have arisen from practices of nonviolence.

Alex Bellamy. 2006. *Just Wars: From Cicero to Iraq*. Cambridge: Polity Press.
   Overview of just war theory that combines a historical discussion with efforts to explore its contemporary relevance. Clearly written and well developed. The author has written extensively on the use of force from a broad range of perspectives that he brings to bear in this text.

Stephen C. Neff. 2005. *War and the Law of Nations: A General History*. Cambridge: Cambridge University Press.
   Excellent historical treatment of how the laws of war developed, stretching back to the ancient world. Written by an international lawyer who has written extensively on this historical dimension.

Steven Pinker. 2011. *The Better Angels of Our Nature: A History of Violence and Humanity*. New York: Penguin.
   Far-reaching analysis of the human use of violence, arguing that over time violence has decreased in frequency. Pinker draws on evidence from his own field of cognitive science along with material from medicine, social science and neurobiology to explain this decline. He argues that various civilizing processes have led to the decline in violence, looking to diverse causes, including the moderating role of the novel in the 18th and 19th centuries.

Ruti Teitel. 2011. *Humanity's Law*. Oxford: Oxford University Press.
   A leading international legal theorist argues that there has been a shift from traditional international laws concerning force to an international humanitarian law, which focuses on human rights and the protection of civilians. Excellent historical and theoretical treatment of the shift in international laws concerning the use of force.

Richard Tuck. 1999. *The Rights of War and Peace: Political Thought and International Order from Grotius to Kant*. Oxford: Oxford University Press.
   Written by a historian of political ideas, one of the best efforts to trace the structure of political theories concerning war and peace. Starting with Grotius, goes through the crucial early modern and Enlightenment period, with important insights on all the theorists addressed.

Michael Walzer. 1977. *Just and Unjust Wars*. New York: Basic Books.
   Standard text on just war theory, clearly organized and presented. Uses the idea of responsibility, the responsibility of soldiers to act in accordance with the *in bello* criteria and commanders to act in accordance with the *ad bellum* criteria. Draws heavily on examples, and written in an accessible, interesting style.

Chapter 6

Nature

In 2007, the Intergovernmental Panel on Climate Change (IPCC) issued its Fourth Assessment Report on the state of the world's climate, which warned: 'Warming of the climate system is unequivocal, as is now evident from observations of increases in global average air and ocean temperatures, widespread melting of snow and ice and rising global average sea levels' (IPCC 2007). The report presents further evidence to establish what it calls the 'anthropogenic drivers' of climate change, that is, the actions brought about by human beings as opposed to those resulting from atmospheric changes. The report is clear that the causes attributable to human action, particularly fossil fuel use, have greatly increased climate change over the past 200 years. The consequences of climate change are dire, as the report warns, including potential harm to vast numbers of inhabitants of the planet. The next IPCC report is due out in 2014, and its conclusions seem destined to reinforce those already established by the previous report.

While some have questioned the conclusions of the IPCC reports over the years, there seems to be a global scientific consensus concerning the fact of climate change. What is missing is a global consensus about who or what is responsible for this change. One can argue that human beings are central to this change, but when it comes to determining responsibility more precisely, this point is not helpful. It is unhelpful because the scope of climate change is global and, in some way, all humans seem responsible for it. But the idea of responsibility is problematic here. Not every person consumes the same amount of fossil fuels or food. Moreover, individual persons are located in political communities that organize their political and economic activities in ways those individuals may or may not be able to control. The policies of these communities, particularly powerful states, concerning economic development have been the most important influence on climate change. This would suggest that rather than persons, states should be held responsible for global climate change. Within IR theory, various theorists have tried to clarify the idea that states are responsible agents (Erskine 2003; Isaacs and Vernon 2011).

One effort to make states more responsible for climate change has been through the international legal process of a creating a multilateral treaty, one that proposed a slightly revised conception of responsibility. In 1992, at the Earth Summit in Rio de Janeiro, the United Nations Framework

Convention on Climate Change (UNFCCC) was drafted and entered into force in 1994. This treaty was originally more aspirational than action-able; that is, it had little in the way of obligations and commitments that bound states to act. This changed in 1997 with the passage of the Kyoto Protocol to the treaty. The Kyoto Protocol demanded that states begin a progressive reduction in carbon emissions through a series of mechanisms such as carbon trading, or the ability to 'buy and sell' credits for carbon emissions. Controversially, the Kyoto Protocol also introduced the idea of 'common but differentiated responsibilities', which placed a heavier burden on developed states to lower their carbon emissions more quickly than the developing countries. The treaty was signed by almost all coun-tries and came into effect in 2005.

The proposal for common but differentiated responsibilities has not gone down well with powerful states whose responsibilities under the terms of the treaty are much greater than other states. The US, which has not ratified the Kyoto Protocol because of its objections to the idea of common but differentiated responsibilities, has argued, in the words of Secretary of State John Kerry (2013): 'Plain and simple, all nations have a responsibility to make near-term emissions reductions.' Admittedly, the US under the administration of President Barack Obama has sought to respond to climate change in more active ways than the previous US administration. Yet, it is undoubtedly true that the US does not see its responsibility to respond to climate change through the lens of a differ-entiated one, but through a simple one of all states making roughly equivalent contributions. American leaders argued that the Kyoto Protocol serves more as a means for debate about climate change and a forum for developing countries to criticize Europe and North America than a means to move forward with real solutions (Helm 2012). In 2012, Canada withdrew from the Kyoto Protocol, arguing that it cost too much to its economy and also that it was failing to change the world's environ-mental problems, although its interests in exploiting fossil fuels in the Arctic region, coupled with a conservative government, undoubtedly played a role in its decision.

Climate change raises not just the issue of responsibility but all the conceptual issues that have been the focus of this textbook: rights, rules, responsibilities and authority. The debate has been about which countries are responsible for the emissions that are generating climate change, with most concluding that the advanced, industrial states are most responsible. At the same time, large developing states – China, India and Brazil, for instance – are now also generating levels of emissions that are causing the same, if not more, of the problems being faced by the international community. This means that these states are increasingly responsible for the problems facing the international community. But these and other developing countries are responding that they have just as much of a 'right' to development as the advanced countries. They argue that to force them to limit their emissions undermines their rights to a fully developed economic order.

Powerful states like the US have tried to respond to climate change while eliding the international legal structure created by the Kyoto Protocol, developing a series of initiatives to limit its own climate emissions. More importantly, at the level of US states and even cities, there are a number of efforts seeking to move forward on reducing emissions (Hoffman 2011). The contrast between the US position on the UNFCCC and its own internal efforts raises the problems of rules and authority. The US government does not see the authority of rule making from the UN system as useful for addressing this issue. As is evident from the US attitude to a number of other global issues, it is unlikely that the US political elite or even many of its citizens see the international legal system or the UN as a source of legitimate authority that can generate binding rules on its behaviour. This is a big question, one that can be seen in the background to many of the issues that have been raised in this book.

This chapter begins with this issue because it raises some of the most important questions of authority, rules, rights and responsibilities at the global level. But, the chapter will step back from these issues at first to think more critically about how humans relate to nature, particularly in their political activities. One could argue that the problems concerning climate change have more to do with flaws in the UN or the state system, both of which are true to some extent. But, even if these problems of authority were somehow resolved, it is unclear if changes in rules that govern the behaviour of individuals would address the core of climate change. For what climate change and a range of other environmental issues suggest is that some of our standard frameworks for addressing these issues may be inadequate; as some environmentalists have pointed out, our patterns of consumption, social and economic structures, and political organs are nested within a particular understanding of the human relationship to the natural world. It might be more useful to ask deeper questions, questions about how we understand the concept of 'nature' and how it relates to our assumptions about our place in this world.

Unlike other issues addressed thus far in this book, some argue that there is not a single classical or early modern theorist to whom we can point for answers to global environmental problems, as the environment has only come to be a focus of attention for the world in the past 100 years. While there is some truth in this idea, this chapter will use the idea of nature rather than the environment as a starting point. In so doing, it allows us to see how various traditions of political thought have addressed the relationship of the human person to the natural world. One theorist who helps us think about this relationship is Aristotle, whose naturalist approach to the world launched so much of political theory, including the rich tradition of natural law discussed in Chapter 2. The point of exploring the work of Aristotle is not that he provides us with an answer to climate change; rather, Aristotle helps us to locate our understanding of humans as beings in nature, a location that can force us to think more critically about how to tackle some of the problems raised in the climate change debate and a number of other environmental issues. Moreover, he also constructed a moral and political theory that draws on the idea of virtues, which might be one way to reframe the idea of rights and responsibilities concerning the environment. Indeed, the virtue ethics tradition provides a means to transcend the discourse of rights and responsibilities, as these concepts may not be the most helpful in dealing with problems such as climate change.

The chapter first explores the idea of nature, and suggests some ways to think critically about this core concept in relation to politics and the study of politics. It then turns to a discussion of Aristotle's political theories and locates those in relation to some of the themes addressed thus far in this book. The chapter then moves on to discuss various climate change issues and responses, some drawing on ideas of rights and responsibilities, but some providing alternative formulations of our relationship to the environment. It concludes that rather than assumptions about rights and responsibilities, perhaps the only way to address problems like climate change is to reorient our lives to a completely different relationship to nature and the place of humanity in that world.

Nature and politics

Our relationship to the natural world has long been a concern for humankind. Only recently, however, has that concern manifested itself in terms of efforts to 'protect the environment', for the environment has not been something humans have understood as a separate realm from themselves until recently. Yet, one could argue that, in many ways, humans have understood themselves through the natural world for much of their history.

One effort to link humans with nature is the natural law tradition discussed in Chapter 2, but this is not the only way in which nature is deployed in political argument and analysis. Indeed, it is now much less common than a range of other meanings for 'nature'. The following are some possible underlying meanings for 'nature' or 'natural':

- Nature is the physical reality of the entire universe, a kind of ontological reality. That is, nature is everything that exists. This would mean that nature is not simply planet earth, but all planets, the solar system, the Milky Way galaxy, and the entire universe as we understand it. This is not a common meaning for the term, but it might be one that some use at times.
- Nature is the physical reality of the earth, which includes all living and non-living elements. One version of this meaning is the 'Gaia hypothesis', a term proposed by James Lovelock in the 1970s. It assumes that the planet earth is 'alive' in some broad sense of that term and that the interaction of organic and inorganic entities creates a kind of living organism that can evolve.
- Nature is the organic and inorganic matter on earth that has *not* been impacted by humans. This is the meaning that comes from Romantic views of nature, as beautiful and unspoiled, often contrasted with city life or machinery. It relies on an aesthetic understanding of nature, one that seeks to appreciate its beauty rather than view it in scientific terms.
- Nature, or more accurately natural, is an adjective to describe human behaviours that are not the result of rational deliberation but are instinctual. This is also a Romantic idea of 'letting go' or 'acting naturally' rather than being bound by social rules or conventions.
- Nature is a set of rules or laws that constitute the world around us, particularly as these relate to human behaviour. One version of this is the idea of natural law, which has already been discussed. Another could be the modern scientific notion of finding the causal laws in the natural world that incorporate findings from physics, chemistry and biology, or what has been called 'naturalism' by some philosophers (Rosenberg 2000).

The last point about naturalism has been a focus of attention not just in scholarly works about international affairs but in the wider debates in the world of ideas. For instance, Steven Pinker, a psychologist, argues that the social sciences and humanities have failed to integrate science into their scholarship. Pinker claims that more attention to scientific discoveries would radically change the way we understand ethical and political issues:

> The worldview that guides the moral and spiritual values of an educated person today is the worldview given to us by science. Though the scientific facts do not by themselves dictate values, they certainly hem in the possibilities ... And in combination with a few unexceptional convictions – that all of us value our own welfare and that we are social beings who impinge on each other and can negotiate codes of conduct – the scientific

facts militate toward a defensible morality, namely adhering to principles that maximize the flourishing of humans and other sentient beings. This humanism, which is inextricable from a scientific understanding of the world, is becoming the de facto morality of modern democracies, international organizations, and liberalizing religions, and its unfulfilled promises define the moral imperatives we face today. (Pinker 2013)

A version of this point appears in Pinker's (2011) book, where he argues that violence has declined in recent years, much more extensively than many believe. Not only does he provide historical evidence to back up this claim, he also provides recent psychological and neurobiological research, which reinforces his arguments that the human person has become less violent over time as a result of wider social and psychological evolutionary mechanisms.

Underlying Pinker's claims is a philosophical position known as 'naturalism'. Naturalism is the idea that all reality results from mechanisms or processes that can be found in the world around us. This is a stronger claim than defences of the scientific method made by social scientists; instead, it is the argument that all explanations of human action and behaviour can be found in causes that exist within the natural, physical world. That is, ideational claims, such as those based on ethical, political or cultural norms, should not be made in explanations of human behaviour. Another position against which naturalists sometimes argue is that there is a divine presence, that is, God, directing the mechanisms of nature. In opposition to these views, naturalists argue that evidence should be drawn from the physical realities discoverable through physics, chemistry and biology. Defenders of naturalist positions range from the popular science writer Richard Dawkins (1991) to philosophers such as Alexander Rosenberg (2000).

The point at which naturalists and their opponents sometimes come into conflict is the idea of evolution. In 1859, Charles Darwin published *On The Origin of Species* (1958 [1859]), a book that revolutionized not only the science of biology but politics, ethics and religious belief. Darwin's ideas, based largely on his and others observations of plant and animal life and the inability to account for the divergence of different species, led him to conclude that all life evolved through the mechanism of natural selection. This selection takes place in different ways, such as a competitive struggle for existence in certain environments or sexual selection among species. What Darwin called a 'struggle for existence' in the first edition of the book became 'survival of the fittest' in later editions, a term introduced by Herbert Spencer (Darwin 1958 [1859]: 74). Darwin's ideas have been developed and refined for the past 150 years, resulting in a strong scientific consensus about the truths of their claims.

The political consequences of Darwin's ideas have been mixed. One of the most problematic is social Darwinism, introduced by Herbert Spencer. Spencer and others drew on the idea of evolution, which included not only the works of Darwin but figures such as Jean-Baptiste Lamark, to create an ideological framework that supported two key principles: a laissez-faire approach to social life that militated against efforts at social reform, and support for competitive economic and political doctrines that reinforced capitalism and colonialism in the 19th century (Hofstadter 1954). There is some question as to whether or not Darwin himself supported what came to be called social Darwinism. As one commentator argues, Darwin may have held views about colonialism that stood counter to these ideas, but his ideas helped to constitute a worldview within which the ideology of social Darwinism made sense; that is, his ideas created the justifications for various policies and ideas that he himself may not have supported (Hawkins 1997: 35–8).

Social Darwinism gave ideological support not only to colonialism but to the racial justifications for colonialism that came to dominate thinking in Europe and North America. Already in early 19th-century America, ideas such as 'manifest destiny' were providing justifications for policies of aggressive expansion across the American continent. The idea that the fittest survive reinforced attitudes towards Native Americans and blacks in the US and American and European dominance over Africa and Asia. Social Darwinism gave a scientific and natural basis to the imperialist polices of many countries, and even provided a normative justification:

> To be sure, power politics and the pursuit of American interests in international affairs did not require social Darwinism. But Darwinian ideas proved particularly well suited to represent and justify them; it was nature's way that inferior races yield to superior races. This was not merely a question of power, but of right; for inferior races were inherently incapable of establishing institutions of liberty. This had to be done for them by superior races, even if that sometimes required force and imposition. (McCarthy 2010: 80)

These theories retained their popularity until the Holocaust, when they were linked to theories of eugenics and especially theories employed by the Nazis to justify the Holocaust.

The abuse of Darwin's arguments to support colonialism or racism should not be used to discredit his overall claims. Ultimately, Darwin presented a scientific explanation for the diversity of species in the world, not a theory of society or political life. But the fact that Darwin may not have intended his arguments to be used in this way does not mean that others could not do so. Further, the idea that arguments derived from 'nature' can be employed to draw conclusions about social and political life is widespread and can result in opposing positions on contentious political topics. Consider, for instance, homosexuality. Arguments made against LGBT rights sometimes take a naturalist form – because homosexuality is not 'natural' but somehow a deviation from the norm, it should not be protected by rights. The Catechism of the Catholic Church states that homosexuality violates the natural law, for it goes against the idea, traced back to Aquinas, that sexual actions must be open to procreation, which is one of its 'natural' elements (although in the same document, the Catholic Church argues against discrimination on the basis of sexual orientation). Psychologists classified homosexuality as a form of deviance largely on the basis that it was not natural, a classification that was not changed until the 1970s.

At the same time, a naturalist argument could be made to justify acceptance of homosexuality. One might highlight the fact that the animal kingdom demonstrates a range of homosexual behaviours. Moreover, as one author notes, while there is less evidence of homosexual orientation as opposed to homosexual behaviour among non-human animals, there also is no evidence of homophobia of any sort among species where homosexuality takes place (LeVay 1996: 193–4). So, one could argue that on the basis of observations of the non-human animal world, homosexual activity is just as natural as heterosexual activity. What this debate suggests is that appeals to 'nature' can result in very different outcomes.

As a result, some seek to move away from naturalist accounts, because they do not suggest clarity about what counts as evidence; in the case of homosexuality, how does the fact that animals do or do not engage in homosexual behaviour indicate anything about its moral status? In the same vein, why is it that the Catholic Church's claim that sexual acts are naturally oriented towards procreation mean that homosexuality is not natural and, hence, not morally supported? Partly as a response to these kinds of problems, the social critic and philosopher Michel Foucault (1990 [1977]) argued against the idea that there is anything 'natural' about sexual orientation, pointing out that, in Ancient Greece, it was normal for a man to have boys as lovers when younger and then turn to a heterosexual relationship when older. This does not mean that homosexuality is not an orientation, but it does open up the possibility that appealing to nature may not necessarily resolve the issue. In effect, it suggests that much of what we see as 'natural' is constructed through social and political practices and norms.

Naturalism has made advances in the study of politics, or its methodology. Scholars seeking to explain human behaviour have been turning to neurobiology, or the study of the brain, to understand political behaviours. John Hibbing (2013) has defended this approach, arguing that the study of a correlation between certain biological factors and social behaviours is not necessarily deterministic or reductionist. In response to Hibbing, one commentator pointed out that a resistance to the use of biological arguments in understanding politics comes from the liberal assumption of freedom; that is, we want to believe that we are free to act as we wish, a narrative that is ingrained into the human person, which might reinforce the idea that certain behaviours or assumptions are 'natural' (Marcus 2013). While Hibbing's approach to neurobiology reflects a largely positivist method, political theorists who find their inspiration outside positivism have also looked to the natural world for insights into human behaviour; William Connolly (2002, 2011), for instance, has drawn on research in neurobiology to explore elements of political life such as speed, creativity and the self-organization of collectives in political life.

The concept of 'human nature' is also a place where divergent ideas of nature play themselves out. One use of the idea of human nature in IR theory can be found in certain forms of classical realism, such as that of Morgenthau. Morgenthau argued that the pursuit of power is intrinsic to the human condition. His theory relied on the idea that humans are 'naturally' disposed to competitive pursuits of power, as he famously noted in *Politics Among Nations*:

> The situation is, however, different when we deal not with social arrangements and institutions created by man, but with those elemental biopsychological drives by which society is created. The drives to live, to propagate and to dominate are common to all men. (Morgenthau 1948: 17)

This 'first image' assumption about politics informs not only Morgenthau's but a number of other thinkers' views on international affairs (Waltz 1959). It assumes that politics can be explained on the basis of traits inherent to the human person or, in other words, traits that are somehow 'natural'.

Recent political theory has begun to more critically engage the idea of nature. One recent edited volume introduces the idea of 'second nature', or the claim that both nature and the political are imbricated with each other. They argue, for instance, that:

> Where an ideal of nature *sans* humanity portrays proper politics as distinct from, rather than enabled by, the human relationship with nature, an ideal of humanly controlled nature fails to acknowledge sufficiently how human relationships with nature often exceed, challenge, and transform human agency. (Archer et al. 2013: 15)

Nature here is understood as more than simply an inert thing, but something that is inherently part of the political process and shapes that process in important ways. I will return to one version of this in the final section of this chapter, but it is important to note that there are alternatives emerging not simply in terms of rules and rights about nature, but in the very idea itself as it relates to political life.

As such, we can see that appeals to the natural or nature in political life can be used in a variety of ways. The one I wish to explore in the remainder of this chapter concerns the environment, but underlying environmental arguments are often unarticulated ideas about nature. The point of this section has been to highlight the fact that appealing to nature does not necessarily solve a political problem, either domestically or internationally. Rather, it often opens up questions about the very meaning of nature, questions that should not be closed off by appeals to the authority of science alone.

The environment and politics

Of course, the most common use of nature in political life concerns environmental issues. As noted above, seeing the environment as a subject of political attention is relatively recent. Ancient peoples lived in the same material world that we do, but they were unable to influence or impact the environment in the same way that we can today. In the 19th century, though, as industrialization surged, it became clear that human activity can change not only the aesthetics of the world around us, but the actual reality of it. Smog-filled cities and despoliation of landscapes from factory production and new modes of transport revealed how radically humans could change their world. As a result, those engaged in political life became more aware of how their activities were changing the world around them.

We saw one response to these changing economic and social dynamics in Chapter 4; Karl Marx's communism. A different response came from Romanticism, a broader cultural and literary project that focused on the individual, especially the individual's emotional response to the world around them. It was helped by the emergence of a wider reading public and the availability of novels as a means to see the perspective of others. For some Romantics, a turn to nature provided a kind of respite from the ugliness of the modern, mechanistic world, and 19th-century America saw one of the first efforts to combine this Romantic inclination with an appreciation of nature. In 1836, Ralph Waldo Emerson published an essay entitled *Nature* (1990 [1836]), in which he argued that humans needed to change their relationship with the physical world. The essay, which launched the idea of transcendentalism, was his reaction against the rationalist religious traditions dominant in the early American Protestant tradition, but it had important political implications as well. For one, it encouraged greater respect for the natural world and a more 'holistic' appreciation of the world. Rather than something to dominate or conquer, nature was seen to be infused with the spirit of the divine and should be valued on its own terms rather than as something useful to humans. Perhaps because his essay is more about spirituality than about politics or ethics directly, Emerson's *Nature* is not usually seen as an instance of environmentalism; at the same time, it was part of a reconsideration of the natural world, one that linked the human person to their surroundings in a different way.

Emerson's essay was read by a young student at Harvard University who also sought to rethink the relationship of humans to the natural world. Henry David Thoreau, a native of Massachusetts, worked as a journalist and surveyor before deciding to retreat from a society he found to be unjust as a result of its dependence on slavery. His friendship with Emerson enabled him to explore these philosophical beliefs in more depth. In 1845, Thoreau moved into a cabin he had built on land owned by Emerson, where he lived for two years. During that period, he refused to pay his taxes because of his objection to slavery and the Mexican–American War and, as a result, spent one night in jail. He wrote an essay in which he justified this action, which was published under the title *Resistance to Civil Government* but became better known as *Civil Disobedience*. The essay developed an argument for peaceful resistance to unjust government, something that influenced figures such as Martin Luther King, Jr (2000 [1962]: 433).

This essay does not explore nature directly, but another work of his further develops the ideas that Emerson presented in his essay on nature. After leaving his cabin, Thoreau spent the next few years writing a book on this experience, one that connected some of his political views with his philosophical ideas about the self and nature. This work, entitled *Walden*, was published in 1854 and has become a central text in the history of American political and social thought. On the one hand, the book is the philosophical and spiritual journey of a single man. On the other, it has clear political implications, ones that direct the reader to a greater awareness of how their actions impinge on the natural world. In one chapter, entitled Higher Laws, Thoreau seems close to the natural law arguments described in Chapter 2. Yet it is not the natural law tradition that celebrates reason alone, but rather one that has spiritual and emotional resonances. Moreover, it is one that celebrates that more animalistic element of the human person:

> The wildest scenes had become unaccountably familiar. I found in myself, and I still find, an instinct toward a higher or, as it is named, spiritual life, as do most men, and another toward a primitive rank and savage one, and I reverence them both. I love the wild no less than the good. (Thoreau 2000 [1854]: 181–2)

His relationship with nature, then, is not about learning from it as the natural law theorists did, for example, drawing rational lessons concerning self-defence. Rather, it is embracing all nature, including the savage and wild in him, an embrace that reflects his conception of the higher law.

Thoreau is also surprisingly global in his thinking, with an almost environmental cosmopolitanism. Throughout the text, he refers to Indian and Chinese traditions of thought. Even more importantly, the concluding chapter challenges national boundaries through a deeper understanding of the environment and its relation to nation-state politics: 'The wild goose is more of a cosmopolite than we; he breaks his fast in Canada, takes a luncheon in the Ohio, and plumes himself for the night in a southern bayou ... The universe is wider than our views of it' (Thoreau 2000 [1854]: 254). Clearly, for Thoreau, the environment transcends national boundaries, a lesson that he sees not just for the goose but for our own philosophical and political understandings.

Appreciation of the natural world, especially in its aesthetic sense, continued throughout the 19th century, leading to the creation of national parks in the US and elsewhere. But an aesthetic appreciation was not the only approach to nature and the environment. Scientists and other practitioners began having an impact in the later 19th and early 20th century. One of the most influential examples of this is Aldo Leopold, who is often seen as a crucial figure in the development of modern environmental thinking. An American scientist and forestry manager, Leopold published *A Sand County Almanac* in 1949. The book proposed what Leopold (2003 [1949]: 39) called the 'land ethic': 'The land ethic simply enlarges the boundaries of the community to include soils, waters, plants, and animals, or collectively: the land.' His argument, often posed in terms of ethics rather than politics, is most certainly a political theory as the reference to an enlarged community in the quote above suggests. Another scientist in the US, Rachel Carson, published an influential book in 1962 entitled *Silent Spring*. Carson (1962) revealed the impact of pesticides on the wider environment, highlighting the ways in which efforts to improve agricultural yields were having long-term serious impacts on the wider environment. Her book became a surprising bestseller, one that generated a greater awareness about the problems of traditional methods of agriculture.

The 1970s saw the publication of some important works on the philosophical issues arising from the environment. In 1972, Arne Naess, a Norwegian philosopher, first proposed the idea of 'deep ecology' in opposition to environmentalism, as an alternative understanding of the ethical and political issues arising from the environment. Naess argued that environmentalism as a political movement and philosophical idea failed to address the conceptual and practical needs of the global environmental crisis. Instead of continuing to understand the problems of the environment in terms of how they relate to humanity, he argued that all life needed to be the starting point for ethical reflection and practical political movements. In a later publication, he argued that deep ecology assumes that 'the well-being and flourishing of human and non-human life on Earth have value in themselves. These values are independent of the usefulness of the non-human world for human purposes' (Naess 2003 [1986]: 264). Interestingly, for such a radical statement, Naess argued that it makes no sense to keep this idea for a select few philosophers and activists, but that advocates of deep ecology need to employ rhetorical strategies that will reach beyond the few and build on wider social and political norms in order for it to succeed. For instance, he suggested reaching out to religious traditions and movements in order to find resources within them for greater environmental awareness. The fact that conservative and fundamentalist Christians in the US have recently been supporters of environmental causes suggests that Naess may have been more prescient in his views than others might have assumed.

Another important work that appeared at roughly the same time was Peter Singer's book, *Animal Liberation* (1975). Singer, whose work on global poverty has been discussed in Chapter 4, made a strong case for the rights of animals. Rather than simply an embrace of all life, however, Singer argued that ethical and political concern should be directed at beings that have 'interests'. He posed his argument against environmentalists and animal welfare campaigners who put their arguments in terms of species rather than individual animals. Those animals that can feel pain (vertebrate animals) are ones that have interests in not being harmed. Building on his consequentialist philosophical position, Singer argued that political actions designed to harm individual animals who can feel pain cannot be morally defended. This means that modern environmental movements need to go beyond just saving species and orient themselves towards the protection of individual animals, a much harder task.

These two thinkers prompted a diverse array of arguments ranging from the nature of 'value' to greater awareness of plurality and conceptual diversity in understanding the environment and the political strategies being employed to protect it (Light and Rolston 2003). Their arguments, in a sense, are inherently international, as the environment is an issue that obviously crosses border; so, unlike other contexts, the task of reading 'international' issues into these ideas is less difficult here. What is perhaps worth mentioning though is that, at first glance, the environment tends to be more 'global' than it does 'international'. Because, as Thoreau notes, the goose does not take into account nation-state boundaries, the issues and concerns of the wider environment are not bound by our sovereign state system. At the same time, policies and options designed to address environmental issues must still progress through the sovereign state structure. Even if initiated by an international organization like the UN, these practices are bound by the structures of the existing international order, which means an order defined by the sovereign state system. A body of literature has emerged, for instance, that addresses environmental issues in the context of security. Sometimes called 'human security', these approaches argue that rather than the traditional sovereign state's security, human security concerns – the environment, poverty and a range of other issues – endanger individuals. Policies must be designed to respond to these threats. Put differently, these analysts suggest that the environment needs to be 'securititzed' (Dalby 2002). While this literature ostensibly goes beyond the state in the traditional sense, by employing the idea of security, it fits political responses to environmental issues back into an international context.

While understanding the importance of the state and seeing the environment in terms of security is one way to address these issues, I want to suggest some alternatives, particularly alternatives that seek to address the normative nature of these issues. I will use climate change as a way to think more practically about some of these themes, but before doing that, I want to step back and use a thinker who relied heavily on the idea of nature.

Aristotle, nature and virtue

While determining his exact dates is somewhat difficult, Aristotle is traditionally believed to have lived from 384–322 BC. He was born in modern-day northern Greece, in what is today the region of Macedonia. He was educated, however, in Athens, taught by Plato, whose work was discussed briefly in Chapter 4. After his education in Athens, Aristotle returned to Macedon, where he served as the tutor to Alexander the Great, the Macedonian prince who went on to create one of the largest empires in the ancient world. Once Alexander became king, Aristotle moved back to Athens where he created his own school. It is during this period that he lectured widely on a range of topics, the results of which are the texts we have today.

Aristotle is best understood as a systematic thinker. His writings cover numerous topics, including logic, physics, biology, zoology, ethics, politics and literary theory to name just a few. The core of his thought relates to the idea of nature, which in Ancient Greek is *phusis*. The word does not correspond precisely to our understanding of nature but is closer to the idea of 'reality' or 'essence', although there are other translations of these words in Ancient Greek. In *Physics*, Aristotle (1949: 237) explains nature as a combination of the material essence of a thing, its form, its principle of change or motion and the ends towards which it progresses.

Aristotle also calls these four elements the causes of a thing. A cause for Aristotle is more complex than our understanding of this word (see Box 6.1). There are four causes for everything: the material, the formal, the efficient, and the teleological (1949: 240–1):

1. The *material* is the material stuff from which something is made, that is, wood of a table.
2. The *formal* cause is that class in which a thing belongs, a table is that which has four legs and a flat top.
3. The *efficient* cause is closest to what we would understand by cause, that is, that which brings something into existence. In the case of the table, the efficient cause would be the carpenter who built it.
4. The final cause is the *teleological*, from the Greek word *telos*, which means goal or fulfilment. This is one of the more difficult ideas to capture, but is crucial for understanding Aristotle's wider philosophy. The end or purpose of the table could be multiple: a place to write, a place to eat, or a place to hold artefacts. There are, of course, some things we know a table is not designed for, such as locomotion or weaponry. We might use a table for such things, but these do not reflect its true purpose, as it is not designed for such things; for instance, a better designed weapon would not be so large and unwieldy and a vehicle would have wheels or sleds on which to move forward. The table's three causes feed into its purpose, its *telos*, by making it fit for purpose.

Aristotle uses these four causes not just in understanding natural phenomena, but the human condition as well, which he does in *Nicomachean Ethics* and *Politics*. In particular, what structures his ethical and political thought is an understanding of the *telos* of the human person or that which defines the person in opposition to the rest of reality. In *Nicomachean Ethics* (2000), Aristotle begins by noting that the ideal to be pursued is happiness. Happiness is not only about pleasure, but a life lived in accordance with the particular human characteristics that differentiate us from animals or plants or the rest of reality. These characteristics provide the basis for what Aristotle calls 'virtue', in Ancient Greek *arête*. In fact, the Greek word *arête* means excellence, for virtue is the practice of an activity in the best possible way. So, the virtue of a carpenter is to create the best kinds of wood crafts (or most efficiently fix things in a household and so on).

BOX 6.1 Causation

Social and political science assumes that most questions can be answered using the scientific method. As discussed briefly in the Introduction, this results from the dominance of positivism in the social sciences. An important part of the modern positivist tradition is a particular understanding of causation, one that is sometimes called 'Humean causation', named after the Scottish Enlightenment thinker, David Hume. Hume argued that we cannot truly find causes in the world, but what we can find are correlations among events in the world. We can discover these correlations best through statistical analyses, or the discovery of repeated conjunctions of events. If event A follows event B often enough, we begin to assume that A has caused B. Modern statistics have become a central part of the way political and social scientists establish claims for causation. But, as some scholars have been arguing recently, this approach to the study of the social and political world does not get at the true nature of reality because it does not capture what is really causing events. Instead, they have argued, following the natural sciences, that there are events and patterns that cannot be observed but are nonetheless very real. This 'scientific realism' has made important inroads into IR theory, led by individuals such as Colin Wight (2006). Milja Kurki (2008) has focused in particular on the idea of causation and has suggested that the study of IR needs to reintroduce Aristotle's fourfold notion of causation to capture this deeper reality. The work of these scientific realists has raised important questions about how to study the political and social world and demonstrated a new relevance for the approach that Aristotle introduced.

While it is a somewhat easy matter to define what constitutes the best possible carpenter or teacher or student, it is more complicated to define what is the best possible person. In modern liberal theory, defining what constitutes a good person is left to individuals to determine. We may believe that certain characteristics are good or bad for persons, but generally today we do not seek to define the best person. Aristotle differs from our approach in this fundamental way. Using a quasi-scientific method, Aristotle proposes two characteristics that differentiate us from the rest of reality, particularly the animal world: we live in organized political communities and we use our reason. As a result, those virtues that are most important, and which Aristotle details in the text, are the moral and the intellectual. The former are those virtues focused on the practice of daily life, particularly those that result from living in a community with others in which we cannot simply pursue our own desires and appetites; living politically requires that we moderate our behaviour in ways that allow others to live with us. The latter are those dedicated to the life of contemplation, the task of philosophers. Unlike his teacher Plato, however, Aristotle does not privilege thinking above action; rather, as one commentator notes, philosophy is not complete unless it is political philosophy (Nichols 1992: 7).

One of the virtues that combine the political and the intellectual is that of 'prudence', or *phronesis* in Greek. This virtue is intimately connected to very nature of virtue and Aristotle's teleological project, for it is the ability to reason about how to obtain the good. It is the ability to know what is good and to act on it, thus combining the intellectual with the moral realms. *Phronesis* does not arise from the mere accumulation of factual knowledge, but comes from a life lived in a community in which individuals must negotiate their differences and come to some common standards of behaviour (Box 6.2).

Nicomachean Ethics concludes with a discussion of how to create a community within which individuals will be able to live virtuous lives. Aristotle uses this conclusion to transition to *Politics*, where he proposes a similar model by using the idea of the purpose of a state to construct an argument for what is the best state. The state is understood as a 'natural' thing, something which evolves from the particular needs of humans; he calls man a 'political animal' on the very first page of *Politics*. While human perfection comes through reason, reason expresses itself through speech – the Ancient Greek word *logos* means both reason and speech.

BOX 6.2 *Phronesis* in IR theory

Phronesis as a concept has appeared in IR theories, particularly among classical realists. It has often been used to understand the nature of diplomacy, as it is diplomats who must combine intellectual and practical knowledge. In fact, the practice of diplomacy, which is sometimes seen as amoral or even immoral – reflected in the famous adage that a diplomat is an honest man sent to lie abroad for his country – has an important normative element to it. Morgenthau (1948), the famous classical realist, argued at the end of his book, *Politics Among Nations*, that diplomacy is the only real way to achieve the goal of peace in the modern world. More relevant for this chapter, Morgenthau also lectured on Aristotle's *Politics* each year of his life, lectures that have recently been published (Morgenthau 2004; see also Lang 2007). In those lectures, Morgenthau directly linked the idea of Aristotle's prudence, the word that some use to translate the word *phronesis*, to what it means to be a wise leader and diplomat. More recently, critical theorists such as Richard Shapcott (2004) have found a place for *phronesis*, arguing it can be used by global citizens to think critically about the world through a cosmopolitan lens.

And speech only exists in community with others. As Mary Nichols (1992: 15) explains:

> Politics is therefore natural – a way in which we fulfil our natural capacity for reason and speech. Politics involves argument about advantage and justice, deliberation concerning alternatives, choices among them, and action to attain them. Implicit in Aristotle's presentation of the human good is our need for others, with whom we share our deliberations, choices, and actions. When Aristotle speaks of the human good as the end of our most authoritative association [the state], he indicates that this good comes to us through association – not in isolation from others (1252a1–7).

The text of *Politics* explores the nature of the state, or what is better translated as the 'city-state', the *polis*. Keeping in mind that the *polis* is the entity that will provide the framework within which human perfection can come about, Aristotle not only explains political life, he also evaluates it in terms of which kind of state is best for the human person. Again, unlike his teacher Plato who created a hierarchical state in which classes are fixed in place to serve particular ends, Aristotle argues that the best state is one in which there is a strong middle class and individuals can serve as both citizens and statesmen. The idea here is that to truly appreciate and embrace the excellence of moral and political virtue, individuals must be able to rule and be ruled. The state can be subject to disruption, and one reading of *Politics*, especially its emphasis on the importance of the middle classes, can be read as a way to prevent revolution, which is discussed in Book VII of the text. The text also concludes with an extensive discussion of education, where the state will cultivate in its citizens the kinds of virtues necessary not only for the state to be the best possible state but for them to be the best possible human beings.

As with his approach to the study of the human person, Aristotle's study of the state is also driven by a scientific method. *Politics* is the result of a comparative study of the constitutions of over 100 Greek city-states of his day (Aristotle 1996). We only have his description of the Athenian political system, although there are references to other state structures throughout the text of *Politics*. This comparative approach reflects modern-day social science, which often draws on a range of cases to develop generalizations. Unlike much of modern social science, however, Aristotle's conclusions are both empirical and normative; that is, his conclusions not only explain things such as how leaders can prevent their states from falling into a revolution, they also describe the best kind of state through a focus on the idea of virtues.

We have strayed, it seems, away from the focus on the environment, although as I have tried to emphasize here, the focus remains on the idea of nature. Aristotle's approach is naturalistic, at least as this was understood in his day. In addition, his approach to the political world differs in important ways from the more 'mechanistic' approaches of figures such as Hobbes (Meyer 2001). In fact, the naturalism of Aristotle's theories persisted throughout the medieval and early modern period; Aristotle was seen as the source of most scientific knowledge, and during the medieval period he was known simply as 'The Philosopher'. Yet, after a time, this dominance came to stultify efforts to understand the world, and many early modern and modern philosophers and scientists argued against Aristotle in an effort to move towards a more experimental approach to knowledge.

But Aristotle provides us with one way to see the ethical and political dilemmas of global environmental issues through a lens that has lapsed in recent years. This is the tradition of virtue ethics. Virtue ethicists position their arguments in opposition to utilitarian or deontological theories. A utilitarian moral theory presumes that actions ought to be oriented towards maximizing the amount of good for the greatest number of people. A deontological theory presumes that actions ought to conform to rules derived from logical deductions of what is right. A virtue ethics theory seeks to cultivate particular kinds of characteristics in people, ones that will allow them to make judgements about the right and good in moments of choice. It seeks to cultivate the virtue of *phronesis*, or the ability to make choices that reflect an understanding of the context and that seek to reconstruct contexts to improve the lives of themselves and all others into the future. Virtue ethics can be described as partly self-interested, in that it assumes that individual moral action need not be a sacrifice to standards that are difficult to achieve but should be about creating people who will want to act in good ways because it benefits them and their wider communities (Statman 1997).

The challenge is to uncover what types of characteristics should be cultivated in persons, particularly in relation to concerns about the environment. As noted above, Aristotle argued that the best possible person is one who employs rationality and political acumen (understood in terms of leadership and citizenship) to the best possible means. Aristotle's conclusions as to what type of person is best drew on his 'scientific' study, that is, what characteristics differentiate us from the rest of the world. Can we use the same method today to determine what kinds of virtues should guide our actions? Modern-day science has established that we are closer to the animal world than we thought, and also provides more information about what characterizes the human condition; for instance, perhaps it is not just our reasoning abilities that make us different. An alternative scientific approach locates us much more clearly within a wider ambit of the natural world. Fritjof Capra (2003) has recently argued that there are a wealth of ways in which human life is linked to the natural world. This takes place not simply on a conscious level, but in mirrored processes of cellular biology and human social interaction. That is, there is a wider systemic structure in place in the world within which we fit as humans and which does not give us the kind of differentiated position described by Aristotle.

Neither Aristotle's nor Capra's accounts provide pragmatic responses to environmental issues, although they might help orient us to different ways of seeing our relationship with nature. Aristotle's characteristics remain helpful, however, although they need not be justified in terms of how they demonstrate our differences from the rest of the animal world. It might well be that a focus on cultivating the intellect and political acumen can help us deal with issues such as the environment. In a recent book that draws on Plato rather than Aristotle, Melissa Lane (2011) suggests that a focus on the virtues can be crucial in helping us to deal with the environment. In the area of climate change, for instance, Lane suggests that we have a responsibility to be able to comprehend and address the science behind climate change. For Lane, this corresponds to Plato's idea of the best human person being one who is able to use reason to the best of their ability. But, is knowledge alone the way to deal with global environmental problems? Clearly, the issues facing the world today are not just about science, they are about political leadership at the global level.

As noted above, Aristotle adds to Plato's focus on the intellectual virtues the importance of the practical or political virtues. This suggests that we might supplement Lane's account with a focus on Aristotle, who combines the intellectual and practical virtues. So, we might add to Lane's account of the importance of knowledge the ability to engage in political life, as citizens and leaders, in order to advance solutions to climate change. That is, rather than stand outside the fray and complain or abandon the hope of making any changes in the climate change realm because of an inability to make any real practical change, we need to garner support and advance political solutions that can move the planet towards alternatives. An Aristotelian sensibility about the virtues might be a way forward in dealing with global environmental problems. In the final section, I turn towards some accounts of the ethics and politics of climate change to suggest how the political and intellectual virtues might help us move forward.

Some international political theories of climate change

In this section, I survey some proposals for dealing with the environment and its challenges. In so doing, I use the Aristotelian idea of the virtues, in particular the virtue of *phronesis*, or judgement, as a position against which to evaluate some of this literature. This particular virtue points to the ways in which individuals need to make judgements about their position in the world, judgements that build on intellect and practical experience. This virtue-based approach points towards the idea of responsibility rather than rights as a framing device, which moves us in a different direction from some of the previous theorists we have explored. Moreover, it highlights that responses to climate change must include scientific knowledge and diverse political practices, including the ability to advance new ideas (leading) and follow shared rules (following).

There are some works that begin with a notion of rights as a means to address the environment. One such argument explores the need to make concrete the right to a clean environment perhaps through a state's constitution. Tim Hayward (2004), for instance, argues that there is a universal right to a clean environment, which ought to be made part of each state's constitution. Hayward adopts a Hohfeldian set of assumptions about rights and obligations, which means that any right generates a set of corresponding duties or obligations (a framework discussed in Chapter 3). So, while his account leads to a conception of responsibilities, it arises from a particular understanding of how rights relate to responsibilities. This account, located in the liberal tradition of rights, is important, but is perhaps limited. By keeping environmental issues in the framework of rights alone, it does not leave space or create ways of seeing how political action might lead to new possibilities.

A second variation on this rights-based account comes from Andrew Dobson (2003), who proposes a form of 'environmental citizenship'. Dobson's account of citizenship moves beyond the state, however, and even beyond the liberal focus on rights. Instead, he argues for a more republican-inspired notion of citizenship, one that prompts new forms of political action that transcend obligations to a single community and instead seek to formulate responses to the global problems of the environment. He argues for a form of 'ecological' citizenship rather than merely environmental, the distinction being one that draws on an understanding of the human relationship to the environment, which goes beyond merely protecting the human race and moves towards a deeper appreciation of the natural world. Dobson focuses his practical responses on education, arguing that even in traditional liberal societies, there is a responsibility to teach future generations about the environment in ways that go beyond their own communities. This account is perhaps closer to Aristotle, for it highlights the idea that citizenship is not just about holding rights but also having responsibilities for acting differently.

Elizabeth Cripps (2013) examines the nature of our responsibilities towards the environment and each other in her recent book on climate change. She proposes what she calls a 'weakly collective moral duty' to alleviate climate change. It is collective rather than individualized because she recognizes that individuals alone cannot make any serious changes to climate change. Yet, she also confronts the question explored briefly in Chapter 3 concerning the nature of collective responsibility; that is, can groups be held responsible and also have duties to act? Her argument is that they do, but that these are 'weaker' perhaps than individualized responsibilities. She explores the nature of choice that individuals must face when considering the problems of the environment, choices that will often lead to tragic outcomes, especially when one is seeking to balance commitments to individuals with whom one has a close relationship and the wider community of fellow humans. Balancing these competing claims is precisely the kind of judgement that Aristotle proposes we must engage with in the use of *phronesis*. Cripps (2013: 191) interestingly explores Aristotle and the virtue tradition, but wishes to keep her account distinct from this approach, because she does not see it as taking seriously the 'impersonal moral point of view'. While Cripps's conclusions are powerful and convincing, I would suggest that her account might be improved by exploring not simply the nature of virtue, but also Aristotle's account of *phronesis* and the cultivation of the intellect and political virtues that follow from this.

Hayward, Dobson and Cripps focus on themes arising from the state, rights and citizenship, although they seek to transcend them. Other efforts to deal with climate change and environmental issues begin with international elements but turn those into local action. The first comes from an innovative book by Walter Baber and Robert Bartlett, *Global Democracy and Sustainable Jurisprudence*. Baber and Bartlett (2009) address head-on one of the problems of environmental politics – the debate surrounding the scientific evidence about various issues, which leaves many individuals around the world unwilling or unable to act politically to change it. They argue that there is a responsibility not only to act but also to understand more clearly what is happening in the environment, something they do not believe can be left to the scientific community alone. As such, they propose the use of deliberative democracy as a means to generate political change. Importantly, writing from the perspective of international law, they suggest that communities need to be created around the world that can play a role in translating environmental science and political action into various forms of legislation. These communities of deliberation can be structured around specific problems in communities but then translate these problems into a global scope and begin linking them together. Such groups would include scientists, political activists and lawyers in an effort to create materials that could be turned into national, regional or even international law. This approach maps well with the Aristotelian account of the virtues, because it calls for the ability to understand the scientific knowledge claims being made about the environment while encouraging direct political engagement by a wider community.

Matthew Hoffman (2011) provides evidence for how activism around climate change has emerged at a range of levels, often in response to the failure of international legal efforts to create multilateral treaties. His argument is less a normative one and more of a descriptive and explanatory one, in which he explores various 'experiments' for dealing with climate change that have arisen since the Kyoto Protocol. Hoffman's account points to the ways in which schemes such as regional cap and trade agreements in North America, ones which cross the US–Canadian border, or municipal efforts to limit carbon emissions have emerged in the face of national failures to act. The US Congress, for instance, has failed to act on its commitments to the Kyoto Protocol, which has resulted in US governors and mayors acting in their place. Additionally, Hoffman points to how multinational companies like Cisco Corporation have worked with NGOs such as the Clinton Foundation to encourage greater internet connectivity in cities to lessen the carbon impact of commuting. These efforts are prompted by the idea of responsibility, and an acknowledgement that the international legal responsibility of states has not been translated into action. As such, actors at a number of different levels have moved responsibility from the state to state treaty-making process to forms of political action. Again, we see echoes of the Aristotelian idea of the virtues, although not directly. Rather than propose a virtue-based account of politics, Hoffman's work demonstrates how individuals prompted by their knowledge of climate change are choosing to act through different political communities in order to achieve their objectives.

The previous examples point to ways in which political action can arise from discourses of responsibility. The last example I wish to highlight is a more radical one, drawing on a deeper ecological sentiment than the previous analyses, which, as a result, challenges our accepted meanings of agency and responsibility (one that mirrors the idea of second nature, discussed above). Moreover, this last suggestion highlights how dealing with environmental problems might benefit from a deeper engagement with the very idea of nature and its relation to the human person.

Jane Bennett (2010) argues in *Vibrant Matter* that an anthropocentric approach to political life fails to appreciate the complexities of agency. She suggests that distinguishing between matter and life, as much philosophical and political discourse does without thinking, ignores various ways in which political life is shaped by non-human materiality. For instance, she looks to an essay by Charles Darwin whose study of worms ended with the pithy observation that they 'make history'. She acknowledges that this is a form of anthropomorphism but embraces this accusation rather than defend against it. Using Rancière's notion of democracy as a form of irruption, she argues that such irruptions in political life need not come from intentional human persons but can come from various forces in the wider world. Darwin's point was that worms keep in place certain artefacts and destroy others, making them authors of a kind of history. This agency is vital to how history evolves and how humans understand themselves.

Bennett only briefly refers to climate change. Early in her text, she highlights how responsibility assumes an intentional agent who we can identify and reward or punish if necessary. Drawing here on Connolly's (1991) critique of the politics of responsibility, Bennett suggests that if we relax our assumptions about human agency and allow other forms of agency to develop, our ideas about responsibility will also evolve. Using the idea of an assemblage, Bennett (2010: 36) argues that responsibility is better located in 'human-nonhuman assemblages'. Rather than the assumption that no one is to blame, however, Bennett encourages us to consider how to respond as persons to this situation of political responsibility. She argues that we must resist a politics of blame and instead consider how we should relate to the human–non-human assemblages in which we are enmeshed.

Bennett's account moves us away from the standard accounts of rights and responsibilities. It also moves away from the Aristotelian account of virtue that I have proposed as one way to think about climate change and environmental problems. At the same time, Bennett's account does suggest one way that a 'naturalist' account might be developed. This is, however, a much more radical naturalist account than others, because it is asking us to rethink our relationship to nature, including locating ourselves in relation to 'non-living' things. This expands our understanding of nature to the idea that nature is somehow everything, which, interestingly, locates us back in terms of Aristotle's idea of *phusis*. In other words, Bennett highlights that if we wish to take seriously our relationship to reality, we might need to expand our understandings of what is alive and what is not in such a way that our political actions might be radically altered. Indeed, this is precisely what political theory ought to do – point us to the unexplored elements of our social and political lives in ways that might lead to alternative possibilities for our ability to interact with each other and the world.

Conclusion

This chapter explored the idea of nature, and used that idea to address some fundamental issues at the global level. The chapter has not provided an answer to the problems of climate change but it has pointed to some ideas and tools that might lead to new ways of 'being' in the world. From the naturalism of Thoreau to the naturalist philosophy of Aristotle, there is a wealth of resources outside the traditional liberal accounts that have been explored in other chapters. While I have also pointed to some of those liberal resources in the works on climate change, I think they may need to be supplemented by some alternative accounts in order to speak to the core problems of our relationship to the natural world.

Further reading

Crina Archer, Laura Ephraim and Lida Maxwell, eds. 2013. *Second Nature: Rethinking the Natural through Politics*. New York: Fordham University Press.
Edited collection that arose from a conference of political theorists interested in environmental issues. Like this chapter, they focused more on the question of nature than the environment. Chapters include studies of cremation and what it tells us about the human relationship to bodies and nature, along with more standard environmental issues.

Fritjof Capra. 2003. *The Hidden Connections: A Science for Sustainable Living*. London: Flamingo.
Creative work by a scientist, who links current research on genetics, biology, astronomy and social science to make connections across various ranges of reality, arguing that there are many parallels and connections from the natural to the human.

Andrew Dobson. 2006. *Green Political Thought*, 4th edn. London: Routledge.
Excellent introduction to debates within green political theory, using environmentalism and ecologism as framing devices. Points to key historical texts and arguments and presents the most important debates concerning environmental issues.

John M. Meyer. 2001. *Political Nature: Environmentalism and the Interpretation of Western Thought*. Cambridge, MA: MIT Press.
Interpretive study of how environmentalism has been shaped by two strands in Western political thought, the naturalist and the mechanist. Traces the former to Aristotle and the latter to Hobbes. Poses the tensions that exist in both, and how they may or may not speak to current environmental issues.

Mary Nichols. 1992. *Citizens and Statesman: A Study of Aristotle's Politics*. Lanham, MD: Rowman & Littlefield.
Clear, accessible overview of the main themes from Aristotle's *Politics*. While it does not necessarily speak to the issues raised in this chapter, it gives the background to Aristotle's arguments and locates them in various strands in IPT.

Chapter 7

Belief

In June 2013, the Russian Duma passed a law making 'homosexual propaganda directed toward children' illegal. Some days later, it passed another law making it illegal for same-sex couples to adopt children. In response to criticism of these laws, President Vladimir Putin claimed: 'We don't have a ban on non-traditional sexual relations. We have a ban on promoting homosexuality and paedophilia among minors' (BBC Online 2014). Some have argued that attitudes in Russia towards gay and lesbian rights have been partly shaped by the Russian Orthodox Church. In 2007, in an address to the Council of Europe, Patriarch Aleksii, the then leader of the Russian Orthodox Church, argued that homosexuality was a sickness and a sin (Anderson 2012). Patriarch Kirill, his successor, has made similar statements. He has criticized the efforts of the European Court of Human Rights, an organ of the Council of Europe of which Russia is a member, to protect the rights of gays and lesbians. He has gone even further than this, stating:

> This [homosexuality] is a very dangerous apocalyptic symptom, and we must do everything in our powers to ensure that sin is never sanctioned in Russia by state law, because that would mean that the nation has embarked on a path of self-destruction. (Manson 2013)

The position of the Russian Orthodox Church does not, however, shape the policies of the Russian government, but the presidency of President Putin has seen efforts to reinforce Church principles in social life. This is not to claim that Putin is a strongly religious person; indeed, he comes across as more pragmatic in his approach to the Church, using it to reinforce his policies about social unity rather than being directly inspired by a religious agenda (Anderson 2007). What is more interesting, however, is how the Church sees its role as protecting Russia against the dangers of liberalism, particularly the liberalism of Europe, which it interprets as advancing positions such as gay and lesbian rights. Church representatives have warned against democracy as something that creates divisions in society; Patriarch Kirill positioned his understanding of Russian democracy against other models in the following way: 'Russian democracy is not a model of division, competition and clash of opinions. The model is one of unity and agreement, even whilst taking into account different opinions and interests' (quoted in Anderson 2007: 191). More relevant for this book, Kirill and others in the Russian Orthodox Church see divisions as being foisted on Russia from Europe, where what they believe to be the excesses of liberalism and democracy have undermined any moral truths and paved the way for radical pluralist ideas. The Church and the government of Putin have proposed something they call 'managed pluralism', or a pluralism that allows for very little divergence from shared norms in order to keep social unity (and support for the government) strong.

The Russian Orthodox Church is not the only Christian or religious institution to take this position on gay and lesbian rights. As a result of its historical development, however, it gives us an example of a church that is more closely tied to a state and a nation. Religious institutions play a crucial role in the political life of many nation-states, and in an age of globalization, these institutions, many of them already globalized, play a prominent role in international affairs. Religious traditions, as embodiments of truth claims about the world, force us to consider the ideas of relativism and pluralism. That is, how can truth claims that cross boundaries and seek to impose a universal position be reconciled with the diversity of those very truth claims as they are manifest in religious traditions and other worldviews? One possible answer was reviewed in Chapter 6, the scientific one: that is, answers to normative questions can be reduced to either evolution or biology or some other scientifically observable process (Pinker 2011). Chapter 6 raised some questions about our assumptions about science and nature, which I will not focus on as specifically in this chapter.

A second answer, and the one that will be more the focus in this chapter, is that answers to normative dilemmas can be found in some reality outside our own, whether that be a divine being who makes the rules or some sort of idealized spirit in which humans participate. This answer relies on some notion of belief, belief in a reality that we cannot observe and that structures our ways of seeing the world, particularly the political world. There has been a resurgence of interest in the intersection of international politics and religious beliefs, prompted by efforts to engage with Islamic thought in relation to events in the Middle East and genealogical analyses of strands in IR theory that find in the origins of IR a focus on Christianity. There are other efforts to understand the importance of religious beliefs for the lived realities of many worldwide, particularly when it comes to how ordinary people address ethical dilemmas or problems; these approaches tend, more than IPT theorists perhaps, to turn to religious traditions and ideas as ways to navigate the complexities of modern life.

While this turn to religion and belief has generated many new insights for IPT, it is also perhaps problematic. By locating answers to normative questions outside the sphere of politics, global religions (and the world of science) may limit our ability to recognize and acknowledge each other in the spaces in which we practise politics. Scientists and religious believers are, of course, focused on human beings. But the way in which they provide that focus tends to be through the creation of singularities, or clear authoritative answers to questions that are perhaps better understood as the product of diversity and pluralism. This is not to say that science and religion are the same, however, for they arise from different processes and ways of seeing the world. Moreover, there are a number of ways in which religion and science can be understood less as means of finding certainty and more as efforts to understand one's location in the world. So, for instance, the scientific method is designed not to rest on certainty but to continue to use various means to challenge existing knowledge claims in the hopes of better understanding. In addition, religious belief can be seen as something like a wager, a best guess as to what is the true nature of reality. In other words, through religious practice, individuals may be searching for answers rather than resting in truth.

But, too often, when religious belief is yoked to political practice, it becomes a means to assert certainty rather than a method for resolving conflict or understanding differences. While Chapter 6 highlighted some of the problems of scientific certainty, this chapter will focus more on religion. The overall point being made here is that when the certainty of religious belief is seen to be the source for all our answers, we no longer need to respect different positions and standpoints and can easily rest in the certainty of our individual answers.

Instead of science or religion as a way to answer the problem of diversity and relativism, then, I suggest two interrelated responses to the problem of relativism: a right to recognition and a politics of pluralism. To explain the first idea, I turn to the idealist philosophy of Hegel, the early 19th-century German political thinker. Building on his work, there has emerged a body of literature that explores rights through a theory of constitutive recognition, which I explain briefly. The latter idea is developed through an engagement with the ideas of Connolly and Flathman, two theorists whose ideas about pluralism go deeper than many other accounts. Connolly and Flathman find inspiration for their pluralism in the work of William James, the early 20th-century psychologist, who connected the idea of pluralism with different ways of experiencing religion. These ideas about pluralism connect to theories of recognition, in that they allow us to see the importance of political life as a shared experience in which we respect and embrace others, all the while in search of some means by which we can find answers to core global political problems. In making this argument, I also suggest that by doing political theory, that is, engaging in the practice of thinking about and responding to political problems at the global level, we embody a pluralist ethos.

The chapter proceeds as follows. The next section briefly introduces the 'rise of religion' in IR theory and practice. The following section looks at the darker side of this revival of religion, which crystalizes in Samuel Huntington's idea of a 'clash of civilizations'. This concept is critically assessed from the perspective of postcolonial theory, which demonstrates that the idea of a unified 'civilization' and perhaps even a religious tradition is problematic because of its failure to confront the diversity of voices existing within and across cultures, civilizations and religions. The chapter then explains the ideas of recognition and pluralism as counters to these presentations of certainty in religious belief, suggesting how they might give us ways to see international affairs in a new way. I conclude this chapter by returning to the issues raised by the Russian treatment of its gay and lesbian citizens. I suggest that by deploying the ideas of recognition and deep pluralism, we can construct spaces in which religious believers and defenders of various forms of rights can coexist. Importantly, this coexistence is partly enabled by locating dilemmas such as these not just in particular national contexts, but also in a wider global context where numerous viewpoints can be deployed in defence of different positions. The response I suggest is not that the Russian Orthodox Church must abandon its belief structure concerning sexuality, but rather that if it sees itself in a wider global context, perhaps one of divergent Christianity rather than a singular denominational/national context, we can perhaps find space for alternative identities and belief systems.

Belief, religion and relativism

The word 'belief' has multiple meanings, but it generally means an acceptance that something exists or is true without an appeal to evidence. Belief can be contrasted with knowledge, in which there is a certainty about truth claims because of some procedure by which evidence is deployed to support the claim being made. As described in Chapter 6, science provides one form of evidence, or at least a procedure by which evidence can be used to test truth claims. Beliefs do not require such standards or procedures.

This is not to say, however, that there are no grounds for believing something. Belief can rely on a range of foundations, from intuitions to emotional states to logical arguments. But these foundations do not have the same wide acceptance as the scientific method. As such, they are sometimes seen to be relativistic, since there is no shared means by which they can be grounded but only assertions that they are true. This point simplifies both the nature of belief and the nature of knowledge, including scientific knowledge. One might argue that the scientific method requires a kind of belief, the belief that this particular mode of generating and testing evidence will bring about knowledge. Or one might claim that beliefs about the nature of the world or a divine being can be provided by means of rigorous logical argument. Or, one might argue that personal experiences can provide evidence of a spiritual reality that cannot be ascertained by other modes of knowledge generation.

This book is concerned with politics, particularly international or global politics, so the nature of belief versus knowledge is not its central concern. But, the consequences of contrasting and conflicting belief claims are important when it comes to IR. Often times, these conflicts are interpreted in terms of moral relativism. Moral relativism is the idea that there is no single truth claim when it comes to ethical codes and/or specific moral injunctions. One can simply describe differences among the different cultures or peoples of the world, although when people use the term 'moral relativism', they tend to mean it in the deeper sense that there is no one true moral position.

There are many responses to moral relativism, but perhaps the first is to highlight its underlying moral position and be clear that there exists a universal moral claim within it. That is, the idea that there is no universal truth is itself a universal truth claim. A different response is to argue that while there might seemingly be different moral codes, they all eventually result in the same overarching idea of morality. C.S. Lewis (1943) famously argued that we can find the same basic moral values across all religious traditions, although for Lewis this conclusion was used to make a different claim, that is, that these moral codes are proof of God's existence. This relates in some ways to the natural law tradition, especially its Christian heritage, particularly as the tradition has extended into secular arguments, as noted in Chapter 2.

The diversity of religious traditions is often cited as the best evidence of moral relativism. This is perhaps better understood as a deeper form of what one might call 'metaphysical relativism'; that is, there are not simply differing moral codes, there are contrasting moral universes in which the standards and foundations of morality differ in very important ways. To see how this relativism operates, let me briefly review some ideas about religion and politics.

One body of ideas derives from events since the Iranian revolution in 1979, which many saw as the first step in the rise of political Islam. When the Ayatollah Khomeini arrived in Tehran in February 1979 proclaiming an Islamic revolution, he confounded many who had come to accept the secularization thesis that political scientists had been arguing for since the 1950s. This was the argument that religion would become less significant over time as a way for individuals to understand their place in the world, and as part of the 'development' of Third World countries, religion would recede into the background or at least into private life. Political Islam as a way of integrating faith and political life undermined this thesis. The rise of political movements that embraced Islam in the Middle East, Southwest and Southeast Asia revealed a wide range of approaches as to how this faith tradition could speak to political life in new ways (Mandaville 2007). One scholar of political Islam claimed that along with resurgence of interest in Christianity and Judaism, this represented the 'revenge of God' (Kepel 1994).

There is a large body of literature on political Islam, more than can be addressed here. What is important to emphasize is that this resurgence of interest is seen by some as a way in which individuals in various parts of the world have sought to negotiate the tensions of modernity by turning to their religious heritage. In other words, political Islam today is not the recovery of an ancient belief system but a reimagining of Islam in light of challenges from the modern world. This leads to peaceful and progressive forms of Islamic thinking along with hostile and violent forms; that is, the strands in political Islam parallel the diversity of moral and political positions in the modern world.

It is not only Islam that has become more prominent in political life. For instance, Philip Jenkins (2002) has argued that Christianity in Africa has become an active (and conservative) tradition, partly in response to the rise of political Islam but also in an effort to find meaning in a modern world that so often seems resistant to such meaning making. IR scholars have tried to explore this growth in religious belief around the world and how it may be shaping international affairs (Haynes 2013; Snyder 2011). Some work has explored the nature of secularism in the international political order; rather than assuming its truth as modern scholarly practice often does, these works inquire into its political origins and current status (Shakman Hurd 2008).

In many ways, these religious revivals are responses to modernity. But to reduce them to this would be to ignore their truth claims; that is, adherents to these traditions do not see themselves as simply responding to modern dilemmas. Rather, they believe that their traditions provide them with truths that come from a divine source, which can guide their lives. If they believe these truths to be universal, which almost by definition they must, then they may well seek to promote their belief systems through proselytization or even violent acts such as terrorism. This is not to claim, of course, that all or even most religious believers will adopt these tactics, nor is it to say that proselytizing and violent actions are the same. Rather, the point is that the truth claims in religion can lead to assertions of certainty that do not necessarily lend themselves to an acceptance of plural ethical and political positions.

Religions, then, can generate moral and cultural values that divide individuals and political communities, even to the extent of causing military conflict. The most famous argument along these lines came from Samuel Huntington. In 1993, Huntington (1993) wrote a short article in the prestigious journal, *Foreign Affairs*, in which he argued that future conflicts would be between 'civilizations' rather than states. Huntington compartmentalized the world into eight civilizations, which he argued were defined by identity politics and cultural values. This argument generated a wide range of responses, from empirical critiques of the existence of civilizations to normative ones that highlighted how Huntington's views would produce more conflict rather than simply describe a new phenomenon. Huntington's argument was not only about religion, as he argued that civilizations are more than their religious belief systems. Nevertheless, religion plays a central role in his argument, as it constructs many of the civilizations he describes. Interestingly, Huntington fails to acknowledge other writers who have made similar arguments. For instance, Arnold Toynbee (1972), an English historian and philosopher of history, developed an account of history that argued that civilizations grow and decline on the basis of their religious beliefs. Eric Voegelin (1987), a German political theorist, proposed a 'new science of politics', in which he argued that there is a motivating spirit underlying political structures.

Huntington's failure to cite these previous instances suggests that he may not recognize the heritage of historical and philosophical studies he is part of, a heritage that is problematic for the way its taxonomic structure leaves out crucial experiences, places and belief systems. More importantly, perhaps, the critique one might make of these efforts is that their attempt to combine politics, religion and historical experience under labels of order or civilization imposes a rigid framework onto highly diverse political and religious systems of thought and practice. In relation to Islam, Peter Mandaville (2007) has argued that the diversity of voices engaged in interpreting Islam through spaces on the internet and global television has made it difficult to see this as one tradition. And Christians are well aware of the diversity of traditions found within their shared tradition, from Evangelical traditions to Catholicism to Orthodoxy. Indeed, in every one of these Christian traditions, there exists a multiplicity of voices and experiences that make it difficult to generalize across them all.

Outside the diversity of these traditions there is another problem. Approaches such as Huntington's replicate a colonial structure that reinforces essential distinctions as if they are somehow 'real' but which are the result of historical developments such as colonialism. In one effort to critically assess Huntington, Mark Salter (2002) points to the ways in which the idea of a civilization, and particularly Huntington's formulation of how those competing civilizations come into conflict, reveals how certain groups become 'barbarians' while others remain 'civilized'. Salter's argument provides a corrective to simplistic accounts of the current international order, revealing, for instance, the barbarian nature of the American war on terror, especially in its use of torture, reversing the dichotomy so often found in media accounts where the Middle East is filled with barbarians who need to be civilized. Salter is drawing on wider discourses in what is sometimes called 'postcolonial theory', some of which is prompted by the theories of Edward Said (1978) and others which confront IR theory or world history more directly (Seth 2013).

But religions can also be sources for engagement with others and diverse ways of confronting some of the dilemmas that appear in this book. For instance, R. Scott Appleby (2000) has found the resources for peace making in religious traditions; his argument is that religions do not just cause conflict, but their institutions and belief systems can lead to peace. Others have argued that there are resources in religious traditions that might help in creating new relationships with the natural world. For instance, Oliver Smith turns to the Russian intellectual and Orthodox religious tradition to find a different way of dealing with nature and the material world, one that combines an attentiveness to the spiritual dimensions of life with an appreciation of science and technology. Drawing on theological resources, Smith (2011) demonstrates that science and technology need not stand counter to a deep spiritual awareness and can, in fact, enable a more spiritual or belief-based relationship with the natural world. Many other examples could be found; the point is that religious belief need not lead to the clash of civilizations that Huntington promotes but could be a prompt for new ways to think about international political life.

A different kind of role for religious belief can be found in efforts to find in political and IR theory a heritage of religious belief, particularly its Christian heritage. Carl Schmitt (2005), the German legal and political theorist, argued that all political concepts in use today are really religious ones. Schmitt's heritage in political theory is somewhat compromised by his association with the Nazis, but his insights are powerful, in that they provide a critical distance from the liberal tradition that is so dominant in much legal and political theory. From a different starting point, Jean Bethke Elshtain (2012) argued in a series of lectures that the central idea of IR, sovereignty, can be best understood through a genealogical reading of Christian theological and philosophical debates about the human person and political life. This radical reading of sovereignty argues that we cannot put aside religious categories in interpreting political life today. Another, albeit related effort has been undertaken in IR theory, where scholars have identified the influential role of Christian theology in realist theory, especially in the link between the theologian Niebuhr and the classical realism of figures such as Morgenthau (Guilhot 2010). This work is less about a particular event in world history that demonstrates the centrality of religion but more about how our received, supposedly secular categories of politics are really a species of religious thought. This can lead to the important insight that despite the tensions that might emerge from religious belief among divergent peoples, we cannot escape its hold on our collective human experience.

So what do these writings have to do with relativism? For one, they demonstrate that there is no one answer in religious belief systems about the true nature of the world. As the diversity within religion suggests, there are just as many answers to political and ethical dilemmas within religious systems as there are in the non-religious world. So, just as turning to science cannot answer our relativist's dilemmas, a point made in Chapter 6, neither can turning to religion. In the next two sections, I suggest some alternatives, which seek to mediate among the confusing and contested order(s) in the current international system and propose an understanding of pluralism that might be a way forward.

The right to recognition

As noted in the Introduction, one of the most contentious issues in the current international order concerns the rights of LGBT peoples. When the UN Human Rights Council and the High Commissioner for Human Rights advanced a campaign to raise awareness of violations of the rights of LGBT peoples around the world, religious and cultural critiques were raised by many in diverse contexts. These responses focused on the fact that while there might exist human rights, they do not give a right to engage in forms of sexual activity that are outside traditional heterosexual marriage norms. The response of the Russian Orthodox Church described at the outset of this chapter captures these sentiments and adds an additional dimension to them. Not only does the Church object to recognizing gay and lesbian identity as a reality, it also sees the promotion of this identity as the result of efforts by liberals in Europe to promote a particular idea of the human person. The Church's objection to the idea of gay and lesbian rights is a moral and a political one.

A simple appeal to 'human rights' might be one way to address this dilemma, which is exactly how the UN system has responded. Yet, as the Russian Orthodox Church's position makes clear, this particular understanding of rights is limited in important ways. Is there any other way to respond to deep disagreements about rights and sexuality, especially in ways that protect individuals from harm and discrimination but also respect belief systems in which understandings of sexuality might be grounded in sacred or naturalist claims about the world?

Briefly, recognition theory argues that individuals reach their fullest potential through a discursive and agonistic engagement with each other. As Costas Douzinas (2000: 287–8) describes the idea:

> Human rights do not just confirm or enforce therefore certain universal personality traits. The fact that rights are always extended to new groups and expanded to novel areas of activity, indicates their deeply agonistic character. The recognition bestowed by human rights does not extend just to external objects, such as property or contractual entitlements. It goes to the heart of existence, addresses the fundamental other-appreciation and self-esteem of the individual beyond respect, and touches the foundations of her identity. This concrete recognition cannot be based on the universal characteristics of law, but on a continuous struggle for the other's unique desire and concrete recognition.

Douzinas's emphasis on the social and the agonistic, or conflictual, nature of recognition theory is important to keep in mind. Additionally, the theory is one that assumes a certain ontological status for the human person; that is, it is through recognition of others that we ourselves become fully human.

This idea is sometimes traced back to the philosophy of Hegel. Hegel (1770–1831) was born in southern Germany and lived through the tumultuous era of change, during which the Enlightenment shifted to the Romantic era in European thought. One of his most important works is *The Phenomenology of Spirit* (1977 [1807]), which lays out a metaphysical framework in which the dualism of the human condition can be overcome through the evolution of the 'spirit' in time and space. The text moves through the ways in which 'reason' and 'spirit' interact in the individual person, then within society and the state, and finally into religion. These steps provide a framework for understanding how persons can come to fulfilment not just in the perfection of their own inner selves but also in a life lived in community with others in such a way that those others participate in the 'ethical life' of the state.

The state in Hegel's thought is not what we would think of as the nation-state today. In *Elements of the Philosophy of Right* (Hegel 1991

[1821]), Hegel argues that the political structure of the state can embody the 'spirit' and hence provide the fullness of the human person if it is structured in such a way that it enables a particular type of freedom. In this way, like Kant, Locke and Mill, Hegel is privileging freedom, but unlike them, his freedom is more 'restricted' in some ways. It is restricted in the sense that he understands true freedom to exist only if there is the possibility for individuals to achieve their fullest selves in their interactions with each other under the structure of a constitutional state. Part of this fulfilment is the recognition of others as persons, which can lead to the further development of the self (Hegel 1991 [1821]: 69). The state provides the space in which this fulfilment can come about, but it is a particular type of state, one that embodies the spirit and reason: 'The State is the actuality of the ethical idea – the ethical spirit as substantial will, manifest and clear to itself, which thinks and knows itself and implements what it knows in so far as it knows it' (Hegel 1991 [1821]: 275). For Hegel, the state becomes a kind of 'earthly divinity', a position that has led some to argue that Hegel is a theorist of the kind of state worship found in fascism. But Hegel means only that the state, when it is properly actualized, provides the space in which human persons can come to their fruition. This happens not only through a conscious effort to come together as a community; it also comes about through the emergence of the spirit in the legal and constitutional structures of the state, a process that comes through the movement of ideas in human life.

Hegel is complicated, to say the least, and the few points here do not capture the fullness of his thought. His thought is also tainted by how some of his ideas result from his historical context; for instance, he did not believe that certain civilizations could develop or be able to provide the kind of space in which a truly human person might emerge (Grovogui 2013). He also argued that states, in order to be fully actualized, must engage with other states in practices such as war, although this is also heavily contextualized by Hegel himself (Hegel 1991 [1821]: 370). The most important point for this chapter, however, is his contribution to the theory of recognition. Hegel was not exploring human rights or even rights directly, but his ideas give us a way to see how rights are essentially about recognizing the humanity, or personality, of others. This does not necessarily happen in an easy way, but sometimes through the agonistic dialogue described by Douzinas above. That is, it is through confronting each other, in a respectful way, that we come to recognize the humanity of others. So, we may disagree strongly with each other, but only if we recognize others as legitimate persons who are part of a dialogue with us can we achieve our full personality. One crucial point to keep in mind about recognition theory is that it means there is not one final answer to why we have rights or should respect the rights of others; only through continued political engagement, engagement that can be conflictual or cooperative, can we achieve some form of rights. We must continually recognize persons as they emerge and especially as they display a diversity of differences in how they live in and engage with the world around them.

Hegel's ideas have influenced the idea of recognition, which can be found in a number of places. In the Introduction, I noted IPT scholars such as Frost (1996), whose constitutive theory draws on Hegel's ideas, although Frost explores the nature of the state as an agent that comes into its fullest existence through the recognition and respect for other states. This international society version of Hegel's ideas can map onto certain modes of international political theory, for it locates the diversity of the human condition in an IR framework. Hutchings (1999) has also drawn on Hegel and uses his ideas to find a way to negotiate the particularity of specific persons and cultures with the cosmopolitanism that defines so much of IPT. Patrick Hayden (2012) has also suggested that the 'right to healthcare' might be better understood and evaluated through a theory of recognition, one that does not simply use scientific data or natural rights claims to assert the right to health, but situates that right within a societal context in which persons engage with each other in a political realm defined by contestation.

How does this theory of recognition speak to the problem of relativism? As noted above, relativism can lead to conflicts when different individuals or groups assert the truth claims of their own tradition. Recognition theory allows for individuals to seek the truth and believe they may have access to it, but requires that they respect the truth claims of others. It demands a political practice of engagement, which will, hopefully, lead to the fulfilment of persons. Alone we cannot find that truth, but only through the recognition of others and a fully fledged respect for them can we find our true humanity. In the conclusion of this chapter, I will use this idea to suggest that the fullest recognition of ourselves should not just come through participation in the state, as Hegel suggests; instead, an even fuller recognition of ourselves can come about through an engagement with the world, the community of humanity. This is not necessarily a cosmopolitan argument, although it may be the basis for one. Rather, the point I am making here is that if the recognition of the other provides a means by which we can more fully realize who we are, our humanity will be enriched even more if we locate ourselves in relation to the vast diversity of the globe rather than the more limited diversity of our nation-state.

The politics of pluralism

Before continuing on to this point, it is perhaps worth considering an alternative to the theory of recognition. Within the liberal tradition, one response to differences, locally and globally, is the idea of pluralism. To understand pluralism, we might contrast it with toleration. To tolerate someone or something is to accept it, but to accept it grudgingly and perhaps even with some distaste. We often do not value that which we tolerate, as it is something with which we are forced to live. Pluralism, on the other hand, implies an understanding and acceptance of different views in a way that incorporates them into one's own context. A pluralist will see differences as the source for greater understanding of the world, perhaps, or a celebration of the diversity of the human condition. That is, rather than 'tolerate' others, a pluralist will embrace the benefits of differences.

This is a moral position, one that is sometimes more carefully described as 'ethical pluralism'. Pluralism also has a meaning in political theory, one that derives from mid-20th century debates in political science about how to understand the role of groups in a democracy. Robert Dahl (1961) argued that American political life was best understood through the behaviour of various interest groups. Underlying this largely positivist and behaviourist account of political life was a commitment to ethical pluralism (Blokland 2011). This pluralism drew upon older conceptual traditions in American political thought, including the philosophy of James Madison, as expressed in *The Federalist Papers* (Rossiter 1961) and the pragmatism of John Dewey (1927).

This political idea of pluralism has been extended by others, although it has been subject to criticism in American political science. The more interesting and relevant extension of the theme of pluralism for the purposes of this book comes from political theorists who find in the idea a resource for understanding the deeper dimensions of political life. One such theorist is William E. Connolly, who has engaged with the idea of pluralism throughout his career (along with numerous other ideas). Soon after the concept appeared in the work of Dahl and others, Connolly (1969) explored its intellectual heritage among a range of theorists and provided some critical perspective on the way in which positivist theorists were deploying it. After his work took a more genealogical and international turn, Connolly continued to explore pluralism (Connolly 1995). In one book, provocatively entitled *Why I am Not a Secularist*, Connolly (1999) argued that secular politics and philosophy failed due to the same certainties and exclusions that religious traditions had traditionally assumed. This book demonstrated what it means to be pluralist in a way that much work on pluralism failed to do. In response to the 9/11 attacks, for instance,

Connolly sought to further his explorations of pluralist political life at the global level, turning to Islamic political theory in an effort to critically engage a form of religious political thought that many saw as the cause of the attacks. Connolly's critical analysis of the work of Sayyid Qutb presents a model of how to conduct pluralist political theory; he does not uncritically embrace it, but explores its origins and seeks to connect it with strands in American political thought and practice that might make sense of it in a more nuanced way. The chapter in which Connolly (2005: 11–37) engages with the thought of Qutb explores the discourse of 'evil' that dominated public debate in the wake of the 9/11 attacks, but which Connolly turns into a deeper discussion of how evil functions in political life. Drawing on the idea of recognition, one might say that Connolly 'recognizes' Qutb's ideas and appeal by locating them in relation to his own political and national context.

Connolly's genealogical and critical investigations point to one approach to the question of pluralism. Another comes from Flathman, whose work on authority appeared in Chapter 1. Flathman's account of pluralism turns in a different direction than Connolly's and others; rather than begin with the politics of pluralism, Flathman (2005: 1) starts his account by pointing out that we are all pluralists, in that we experience a plurality of things in the world. This might seem a simplistic point, but Flathman develops his account in dialogue with the philosophy of William James. James, a late 19th and early 20th-century American thinker whose insights into psychology, pragmatist philosophy and religious thought were widely read during his day, argued that rather than a universe, we should see ourselves as living in a multiverse. This multiverse resulted not only from the reality of different things but also from an internal pluralism, a recognition that we have numerous 'selves' inside us that reconfirm our diverse outer experience. One might let this lead to a kind of simplistic relativism, or even a schizophrenia, resulting in a failure to act or seek to change the world around us. Instead, James also argued that we have a duty to meliorate this multiverse, to act in ways that are within our power to help improve the world. This melioration is, partly, a result of our ability to recognize the diversity in the world, to embrace this multiverse (Flathman 2005: 43).

James's work speaks directly to the themes of this chapter, especially in the lectures he gave that were eventually published as *The Varieties of Religious Experience* (1987 [1902]). The lectures present his research on the great variety of religious experiences that shape the modern world. In describing these experiences, he notes that they arise from a grounding that is neither rational nor subject to proof in the scientific sense. Yet, they are profoundly real and intense experiences, ones that shape the reality of people around the world (James 1987 [1902]: 73). He valorizes what he sees as the 'empirical' evidence of these experiences, taking them seriously in a way that many in his profession of psychology refused to do. That is, he argued that with this great variety of religious experience, experiences that we could explain away but which seem to come back in so many different forms, we are left with a body of evidence about belief that is perhaps overwhelming in its truth claims.

In a later set of lectures, James takes some of this evidence of the diversity of religious experience, along with his reading of a range of philosophers, and develops a critique of what he calls 'monism', or the idealist philosophical position that emerged in the late 19th and early 20th century, which built on Hegel's philosophy. Oxford University was a home to many leading thinkers of this approach, leading to a school of thought known as 'British idealism' (Boucher 1997). These approaches argued for a kind of unity of spirit, an overarching reality that structured the entire universe. In response to this idea, James argued that the diversity of human experience simply did not allow for such a unified reality. Instead, there must be a kind of multiverse, a diversity of experience that cannot be subsumed under the unity of rationalism or monism. This is not a disjointed or meaningless multiverse, though, for these diverse experiences and realities are connected to each other in their external expression, a point that has political implications for James (1987 [1909]: 776):

> Everything you can think of, however vast or inclusive, has on the pluralistic view a genuinely 'external' environment of one sort or another. Things are 'with' one another in many ways, but nothing includes everything, or dominates over everything. The word 'and' trails along after every sentence. Something always escapes. ... The pluralistic world is thus more like a federal republic than like an empire or a kingdom. However much may be collected, however much may report itself as present at any effective centre of consciousness or action, something else is self-governed and absent and unreduced to unity.

James was not a political theorist in the formal sense of the word, although as the above quote suggests, and as demonstrated by the way in which he inspired Connolly and Flathman's ideas of pluralism, his conception of the multiverse has some important political implications.

James delivered these lectures on pluralism at Oxford of all places, the heart of Hegelian idealism; in so doing, he seems to embody the theory of recognition described above. That is, rather than critique the Oxford idealists from a distance, James chose to speak directly to them and with them. The lectures also reflect his reading of these thinkers, which he does not dismiss but treats in a respectful way. He does not agree with them in any sense, but his disagreement is not hidden. Through dialogue, actual dialogue that undoubtedly took place following the lectures, James embodied the Hegelian ideal of a dialectic process through which truth might emerge.

Hegel and James had different things to say about the nature of the universe and our place in it. Yet, together, their works can provide some inspiration to us about how to understand the nature of belief in the current world order. They do not give us answers, but provide positions against which we can evaluate our own responses to the complexity of belief and its role in political life. These thinkers leave us with a pluralism that recognizes the bewildering diversity in the world, embracing it and using that diversity as a way to construct new political spaces and move towards new political horizons. Coupled with the theory of recognition, a deep pluralism of the sort described here might be a way forward for theorists of international political theory in understanding current world political conditions.

Conclusion

This chapter began with a conflict involving contrasting beliefs which, when yoked to a political system, resulted in the deprivation of the rights of a group of people. The Russian Orthodox Church has carved out its position concerning gay and lesbian rights as one of conflicting values. Their claim is that the belief system of the Church does not allow space for homosexuality and, as a result, must support the legislation passed by the Russian Duma that prevents gay and lesbian citizens from adopting children or 'propagating' their lifestyle, although it is unclear what this means. In addition, the leaders of the Church have argued that their beliefs on this issue are threatened by the moral relativism of Europe as found in the rulings of the European Court of Human Rights and the wider Council of Europe. In opposition to this position, liberals in Europe and elsewhere have argued that the Church is failing to respect the liberal rights of gay and lesbian citizens and should, as a result, be condemned along with the Russian government that is allowing such polices to proliferate. The Russian Orthodox Church wants a unified Russia, one with a shared set of cultural values that does not leave space for too much religious or political diversity.

Can the ideas raised in this chapter provide any insights into how such a conflict might be rethought? It is unlikely that any Russian Orthodox Church officials will read this text and, even if they did, will change their views. Rather, what we might do is use this episode as a way to think critically about how to engage each other in a deeply diverse religious and political world.

First, if we adopt the idea of recognition, especially a theory of recognition that is located in the global rather than the national, we can see how locating ourselves in the context of the entire human community might reshape this dynamic. For instance, if we see the world of humanity composed of a deep radical diversity of persons, attitudes and behaviours, we can see that to recognize this diversity does not mean that we simply accept all persons and behaviours. Rather, our first task is to simply delight in the diversity of the human condition and to see that human condition as mirrored in our selves. Rather than base our identity claims on appeals to single human nature, we can, like James, recognize that there is diversity within ourselves. This might include the recognition of various sexual orientations in all of us, rather than a singular set of identities that are fixed through time and space. To make such a claim might be uncomfortable for some; indeed, sexual identity claims are some of the most personal we might hold. But, acknowledging the complexity of human sexuality might be a first step in recognizing the deep plurality of the world.

A second form of recognition might come from the other direction. That is, those who object to the moral teachings of the Russian Orthodox Church on this matter should realize that there is great diversity in religious belief. Even within a single denomination, such as the Russian Orthodox Church, there will be believers with a wide range of beliefs. Of course, at a certain point, there must be some sort of core of shared beliefs for all Christians. Despite the way such matters are often relayed in the press, however, those core beliefs tend not to be focused on matters of human sexuality. Instead, they tend to focus on the divinity of the person of Jesus of Nazareth, whose life and actions embody an ethos of joy in the diversity of life, whose life and teachings structure the belief systems of all Christians, including those in the Russian Orthodox Church. From the accounts we have of him in the Christian Gospels, Jesus does not appear to be someone overly concerned with sexual morality; indeed, it rarely figures in his teachings. He seems more concerned with matters of poverty, religious intolerance, forgiveness and healing. This is not a book of Christian theology, however, so it is not the place to argue for the merits of this particular belief system. The point I wish to make here is that Christianity cannot be reduced to a single unified belief system; instead, it is a diverse and dizzying array of beliefs and ideas about the human condition that cannot be reduced to any singular truth claim.

The danger of the Russian Orthodox Church's position on this issue is that when religious belief is linked to a state, it serves to reinforce a particular identity as the way to truth. One reading of Hegel, as noted above, hints at this view; that the state provides the ultimate location for belief systems and can give the space in which the human condition is perfected. But, as I have suggested above, a different reading of Hegel allows us to move out of the state into the global political community as the place where conflicting belief claims can be located and addressed. Coupled with James's ideas about the multiverse, we can find in that diversity great wonder and joy. If we see ourselves as part of a global community, we might better discover and celebrate the diversity and plurality of the world, a diversity and plurality that is found both within and outside us. And, through recognizing that diversity, we can change ourselves.

Further reading

William Connolly. 2005. *Pluralism*. Durham, NC: Duke University Press.
Written by a leading American political theorist, one of the best books on the nature of pluralism. As described above, Connolly interrogates liberal assumptions about pluralism, forcing us to go deeper in our engagement with alternative political ideas, such as those of Islamic fundamentalists. Also includes Connolly's reflections on his own ideas about faith and belief, making it more personal and accessible.

Richard Flathman. 2005. *Pluralism and Liberal Democracy*. Baltimore: Johns Hopkins University Press.
Another leading American political theorist (and colleague of Connolly's) grapples with the nature of pluralism. Flathman turns inward, though, to emphasize how our ideas of pluralism need to be enriched by an appreciation of the distinctions among us that we may not be able to articulate. He draws more directly on William James, supplementing the approach in this chapter.

Conclusion

This book has explored the nature of international political life by engaging with the theories and ideas of a range of individuals. Each chapter has focused on a few central theorists, although always in relation to a wider body of literature, drawn from IR theory, international law and ethics. The insights from these thinkers arise from a number of different historical, regional and cultural contexts. As such, they provide their insights into contemporary political life in ways that are not always obvious and do not necessarily lead to straightforward conclusions.

This book is the result of a series of conversations I have had over the years. Some of these conversations have been with my students, undergraduate and postgraduate, who have been in my lectures, seminars and tutorials on international political theory. While I have shaped the reading lists they engaged with, I have followed their ideas and insights in writing this book. The chapters in this book have been read by them in draft at a number of different stages, and this conversation has largely shaped my idea of what international political theory can be. The second set of conversations have been with professional colleagues and friends who have read the same material or pointed me to new bodies of literature that I did not myself think to consult. Their suggestions have surprised me at times, challenged me at others, and enriched me and this book. The third set of conversations are with the thinkers described herein, constructed conversations, of course, but ones that have allowed me to grapple with difficult concepts.

In my view, this is how international political theory ought to be done, as a series of conversations. Michael Oakeshott (1991 [1961]: 489–91), the British political theorist, described the nature of conversation in the following, which warrants quoting at length:

> In a conversation the participants are not engaged in an inquiry or a debate; there is no 'truth' to be discovered, no proposition to be proved, no conclusion sought. They are not concerned to inform, to persuade, or to refute one another, and therefore the cogency of their utterances does not depend upon their all speaking in the same idiom; they may differ without disagreeing. Of course, a conversation may have passages of argument and a speaker is not forbidden to be demonstrative; but reasoning is neither sovereign nor alone, and the conversation itself does not compose an argument. ... In conversation, 'facts' appear only to be resolved once more into the possibilities from which they were

made; 'certainties' are shown to be combustible, not by being brought in contact with other 'certainties' or with doubts, but by being kindled by the presence of ideas of another order; approximations are revealed between notions normally remote from one another ... Properly speaking, it is impossible in the absence of a diversity of voices: in it different universes of discourse meet, acknowledge each other and enjoy an oblique relationship which neither requires nor forecasts their being assimilated to one another. This, I believe, is the appropriate image of human intercourse, appropriate because it recognizes the qualities, the diversities, and the proper relationships of human utterances. As civilized human beings, we are the inheritors, neither of an inquiry about ourselves and the world, nor of an accumulating body of information, but of a conversation, begun in the primeval forests and extended and made more articulate in the course of centuries. It is a conversation which goes on both in public and within each of ourselves.

As Oakeshott so aptly describes, a conversation is not designed to prove a point or solve a problem. Its task is to orient us, to enrich us, to allow us to see the world through a new and different light. I have not invited enough individuals into this conversation; I am conscious of how little is included from non-Western contexts or traditions such as feminism. The book, like a conversation, is derivative of those who are involved, in that it proceeds through an engagement with others. In this way, it embodies the Hegelian idea of recognition, for it respects the thought of a diversity of people and uses that diversity to enrich our understanding of political life. It is also pluralist, in that it seeks to advance competing metaphysics in order to find some deeper truth. It is not fully pluralist, though, in that there is perhaps not enough attention paid to gender, sexuality, race and ethnicity as frames through which to understand international affairs. Yet I would hope that the book is written in such a way that it invites such voices into the conversation, oriented around the themes raised here, but open to challenges to those themes and the assumptions they bring with them.

I might, however, diverge slightly from Oakeshott, because I do believe that there are possible outcomes of having the conversation about IPT that might speak to the world's problems, that is, might lead to ideas about how to change the world for the better. Unlike policy proposals, these possibilities can be found in the very nature of thinking. If we take seriously the challenge of thinking, we can see that this entails a kind of work that has direct relevance for political practice. This does not mean advising world leaders on what they should do next but rather cultivating particular sensibilities in ourselves and others that can lead to new ways of seeing global political life. The framing conditions of the modern political world –

authority, rules and rights – lead us to see the dilemmas surrounding wealth, violence, nature and belief with new eyes. There will continue to be problems in the international political order that do not bend to our normative efforts to resolve them. This does not mean we give up thinking about such matters, nor do we give up reading theorists, both past and present. It means that we should continue to engage in the difficult task of thinking, which can be enhanced by the more enjoyable task of conversing with figures past and present.

Political theory, including IPT, is sometimes dismissed by political scientists or others as 'just theory'. Activists or those in the policy world may also critique it on the grounds that reading Locke, for instance, cannot inform our efforts to respond to the suppression of LGBT rights in Russia or the failures of the international community to come to an agreement on climate change. To both these criticisms, I would respond that political theory is a kind of action. To think hard about a particular normative dilemma, to critically investigate your own assumptions in your responses to those dilemmas and to frame your answers through various theoretical traditions that require you to cultivate a certain respect for their positions is what political theory demands. So, I do not believe that IPT is about theory rather than practice. IPT is a kind of practice, a very difficult one indeed. I hope this book provides you with some guidelines on how to do political theory. Only in so doing can we develop new and innovative responses to the world. If we agree to do that thinking out loud and in conversation with others, we may well be able to change the world.

Bibliography

Adkins, A.W.H. 1972. *Moral Values and Political Behavior in Ancient Greece: From Homer to the End of the Fifth Century*. London: Chatto & Windus.

Adler, Immanuel and Michael Barnett, eds. 1998. *Security Communities*. Cambridge: Cambridge University Press.

Agamben, Giorgio. 2005. *State of Exception*, trans. Kevin Attell. Chicago: University of Chicago Press.

Al-Azami, M. Mustapha. 1996. *On Schacht's Origins of Muhammadan Jurisprudence*. Cambridge: Islamic Texts Society.

Alford, C. Fred. 2010. *Narrative, Nature and the Natural Law: From Aquinas to International Human Rights*. Basingstoke: Palgrave Macmillan.

Anderson, John. 2007. 'Putin and the Russian Orthodox Church: Asymmetric Symphonia?' *Columbia Journal of International Affairs* 61(1): 185–204.

Anderson, John. 2011. 'Conservative Christianity, the Global South, and the Battle over Sexual Orientation'. *Third World Quarterly* 32(9): 1589–605.

Anderson, John. 2012. 'Rocks, Art and Sex: The 'Culture Wars" Come to Russia?' *Journal of Church and State* 55(2): 307–34.

Anghie, Antony. 2004. *Imperialism, Sovereignty, and the Making of International Law*. Cambridge: Cambridge University Press.

An-Na'im, Abdullahi Ahmed. 2008. *Islam and the Secular State: Negotiating the Future of Sharia*. Cambridge, MA: Harvard University Press.

Appleby, R. Scott. 2000. Th*e Ambivalence of the Sacred: Religion, Violence and Reconciliation*. Lanham, MD: Rowan & Littlefield.

Aquinas. 2002. *Political Writings*, trans. and intro. R.W. Dyson. Cambridge: Cambridge University Press.

Arbour, Louise. 2008. 'The Responsibility to Protect as a Duty of Care in International Law and Practice'. *Review of International Studies* 34(3): 445–58.

Archer, Crina, Luara Ephraim and Lida Maxwell, eds. 2013. *Second Nature: Rethinking the Natural Through Politics*. New York: Fordham University Press.

Archibugi, Daniele. 2008. *The Global Commonwealth of Citizens: Toward Cosmopolitan Democracy*. Princeton: Princeton University Press.

Arendt, Hannah. 1959. *The Human Condition*. Chicago: University of Chicago Press.

Arendt, Hannah. 1972. *On Violence*, reprinted in Hannah Arendt, *Crises of the Republic*. San Diego: Harcourt, Brace, Jovanovich.

Arendt, Hannah. 1994 [1965]. *Eichmann in Jerusalem: A Report on the Banality of Evil*. London: Penguin.

Arendt, Hannah. 2003. *Responsibility and Judgment*, ed. and intro. Jerome Kohn. New York: Schoken Books.

Arendt, Hannah. 2006 [1963]. What is Authority?, pp. 91–141, in Hannah Arendt, *Between Past and Future*. New York: Penguin.

Aristotle. 1949. *The Basic Works of Aristotle*, ed. Richard McKeon. New York: Modern Library Classics.

Aristotle. 1996. *The Politics and the Constitution of Athens*, ed. Stephen Everson. Cambridge: Cambridge University Press.

Aristotle, 2000. *Nicomachean Ethics*, trans. Roger Crisp. Cambridge: Cambridge University Press.

Ashcraft, Richard. 1975. 'On the Problem of Methodology and the Nature of Political Theory'. *Political Theory* 3(1): 5–25.

Ashcraft, Richard. 1986. *Revolutionary Politics and Locke's Two Treatises of Government*. Princeton: Princeton University Press.

Atack, Iain. 2012. *Nonviolence in Political Theory*. Edinburgh: Edinburgh University Press.

Augustine of Hippo. 1967 [418–427]. *The City of God*. London: Penguin.

Augustine of Hippo. 2001 [410–427]. *Political Writings*. Cambridge: Cambridge University Press.

Austin, John. 1995 [1832]. *The Province of Jurisprudence Determined*, ed. Wilfred E. Rumble. Cambridge: Cambridge University Press.

Avant, Deborah, Martha Finnemore and Susan Sell, eds. 2010. *Who Governs the Globe?* Cambridge: Cambridge University Press.

Baber, Walter F. and Robert V. Bartlett. 2009. *Global Democracy and Sustainable Jurisprudence*. Cambridge, MA: MIT Press.

Bain, William. 2007. 'Are There Any Lessons of History? The English School and the Activity of Being a Historian'. *International Politics* 44: 513–30.

Bain, William. 2010. 'Responsibility and Obligation in the "Responsibility to Protect"'. *Review of International Studies* 36(S1): 25–46.

Bainton, Roland. 1961. *Christian Attitudes Toward War and Peace: A Historical Survey and Critical Evaluation*. London: Hodder & Stoughton.

Baldwin, David. 1993. *Neorealism and Neoliberalism: The Contemporary Debate*. New York: Columbia University Press.

Ball, Terence. 1994. *Political Theory: Revisionist Studies in the History of Political Thought*. Oxford: Oxford University Press.

Barnett, Michael. 2002. *Eyewitness to a Genocide: The United Nations and Rwanda*. Ithaca: Cornell University Press.

Barnett, Michael and Martha Finnemore. 2004. *Rules for the World: International Organizations in World Politics*. Ithaca: Cornell University Press.

Barry, Christian and Gerhard Overland. 2009. 'Responding to Global Poverty: Review Essay of Peter Singer, "The Life You Can Save"'. *Bioethical Inquiry* 6(2): 239–47.

BBC Online. 2014. 'Winter Olympics: Putin Cautions Gay Visitors to Sochi', 17 January, available at: www.bbc.co.uk/news/world-europe-25785161. Accessed 21 February 2014.

Beardsworth, Richard. 2011. *Cosmopolitanism and International Relations Theory*. Cambridge: Polity Press.

Beattie, Amanda. 2010. *Morality and Justice: International Relations and the Tradition of Natural Law*. Burlington, VT: Ashgate.

Beitz, Charles. 1975. 'Justice and International Relations'. *Philosophy and Public Affairs* 4(4): 360–89.

Beitz, Charles. 1999 [1979]. *Political Theory and International Relations, with a New Afterword*. Princeton: Princeton University Press.

Beitz, Charles. 2000. 'Rawls's Law of Peoples'. *Ethics* 110(4): 669–96.

Beitz, Charles. 2009. *The Idea of Human Rights*. Oxford: Oxford University Press.

Bell, Duncan, ed. 2008. *Political Theory and International Relations: Variations on a Realist Theme*. Oxford: Oxford University Press.

Bell, Duncan. 2009. 'Writing the World: Disciplinary History and Beyond'. *International Affairs* 85(1): 3–22.

Bellamy, Alex. 2006. *Just Wars: From Cicero to Iraq*. Cambridge: Polity Press.

Bellamy, Alex. 2011. *Global Politics and the Responsibility to Protect: From Words to Deeds*. Oxford: Oxford University Press.

Bennett, Jane. 2010. *Vibrant Matter: A Political Ecology of Things*. Durham, NC: Duke University Press.

Bentham, Jeremy. 2008. *A Comment on the Commentaries and A Fragment on Government*, eds J.H. Burns and H.L.A. Hart. Oxford: Oxford University Press.

Berlin, Isaiah. 1978. Does Political Theory Still Exist?, pp. 143–72, in Henry Hardy, ed., *Concepts and Categories*. Princeton: Princeton University Press.

Beyers, Michael. 1999. *Custom, Power, and the Power of Rules*. Cambridge: Cambridge University Press.

Blackstone, William. 1979 [1769]. *Commentaries on the Laws of England*. Chicago: University of Chicago Press.

Blokland, Hans. 2011. *Pluralism, Democracy and Political Knowledge: Robert A. Dahl and his Critics on Modern Politics*. Burlington, VT: Ashgate.

Booth, Ken, Tim Dunne and Michael Cox, eds. 2001. *How Might We Live? Global Ethics in the New Century*. Cambridge: Cambridge University Press.

Boucher, David. ed. 1997. *The British Idealists*. Cambridge: Cambridge University Press.

Boucher, David. 1998. *Political Theories of International Relations*. Oxford: Oxford University Press.

Boucher, David. 2009. *The Limits of Ethics in International Relations: Natural Law, Natural Rights, and Human Rights in Transition*. Oxford: Oxford University Press.

Boucher, David and Paul Kelly, eds. 1994. *The Social Contract from Hobbes to Rawls*. London: Routledge.

Boucher, Geoff. 2012. *Understanding Marxism*. London: Acumen.

Bowring, Bill. 2007. *The Degradation of the International Legal Order? The Rehabilitation of Law and the Possibility of Politics*. London: Routledge.

Boyle, Joseph. 1992. Natural Law and International Ethics, pp. 112–35, in Terry Nardin and David Mapel, eds, *Traditions of International Ethics*. Cambridge: Cambridge University Press.

Branch, Adam. 2007. 'Uganda's Civil War and the Politics of ICC Intervention'. *Ethics & International Affairs* 21(2): 179–98.

Brock, Gillian. 2009. *Global Justice: A Cosmopolitan Account*. Oxford: Oxford University Press.

Brown, Alexander. 2009. *Ronald Dworkin's Theory of Equality: Domestic and Global Perspectives*. Basingstoke: Palgrave Macmillan.

Brown, Chris. 1992. *International Relations: New Normative Approaches*. New York: Harvester Wheatsheaf.

Brown, Chris. 2000. 'International Political Theory: A British Social Science?' *British Journal of Politics and International Relations* 2(1): 114–23.

Brown, Chris. 2002. *Sovereignty, Rights and Justice: International Political Theory Today*. Cambridge: Polity Press.

Brown, Chris. 2003. Selective Humanitarianism: In Defense of Inconsistency, pp. 31–51, in Deen K. Chatterjee and Don Sheid, eds, *Ethics and Foreign Intervention*. Cambridge: Cambridge University Press.

Brown, Chris. 2010. *Practical Judgment in International Political Theory: Selected Essays* London: Routledge.

Brown, Chris, Terry Nardin and Nicholas Rengger, eds. 2002. *International Relations in Political Thought: Texts from the Ancient Greeks to the First World War*. Cambridge: Cambridge University Press.

Brown, Garret Wallace. 2009. *Grounding Cosmopolitanism: From Kant to the Idea of a Cosmopolitan Constitution*. Edinburgh: Edinburgh University Press.

Brown, Peter. 1969. *Augustine of Hippo: A Biography*. London: Faber.

Brunstetter, Daniel and Megan Bruan. 2011. 'The Implications of Drones on the Just War Tradition'. *Ethics & International Affairs* 25(3): 337–58.

Buchanan, Allen. 2000. 'Rawls's Law of Peoples: Rules for a Vanished Westphalian World'. *Ethics* 110: 697–721.

Buchanan, Allen and Robert Keohane. 2004. 'The Preventive Use of Force: A Cosmopolitan Institutional Proposal'. *Ethics & International Affairs* 18(1): 1–22.

Buchanan, Allen and Robert Keohane. 2006. 'The Legitimacy of Global Governance Institutions'. *Ethics & International Affairs* 20(4): 405–37.

Buchanan, Allen and Robert Keohane. 2011. 'Precommitment Regimes for Intervention: Supplementing the Security Council'. *Ethics & International Affairs* 25(1): 41–63.

Bull, Hedley. 1977. *The Anarchical Society: A Study or Order in World Politics*. New York: Columbia University Press.

Bull, Hedley. 1984. *Justice in International Politics*. Waterloo: University of Waterloo Press.

Bull, Hedley, Benedict Kingsbury and Adam Roberts, eds. 1990. *Hugo Grotius and International Relations*. Oxford: Clarendon Press.

Bush, George W. 2002. National Security Strategy of the United States. Washington DC: US Government Printing Office. Available at: http://ics.leeds.ac.uk/papers/pmt/exhibits/378/NSS.pdf.

Cabrera, Luis. 2004. *Political Theory of Global Justice: A Cosmopolitan Case for the World State*. London: Routledge.

Cabrera, Luis. 2009. Poverty, Inequality and Global Distributive Justice, pp. 293–308, in Patrick Hayden, ed., *The Ashgate Research Companion to Ethics and International Relations*. Burlington, VT: Ashgate.

Campbell, David. 1992. *Writing Security: United States Foreign Policy and the Politics of Identity.* Minneapolis: University of Minnesota Press.

Campbell, David. 1993. *Politics without Principle: Sovereignty, Ethics and the Narratives of the Gulf War.* Boulder, CO: Lynne Rienner.

Campbell, David. 1998. *National Deconstruction: Violence, Identity and Justice in Bosnia.* Minneapolis: University of Minnesota Press.

Campbell, David. 2001. Why Fight? Humanitarianism, Principles and Poststructuralism, pp. 132–60, in Hakan Seckinelgin and Hideaki Shinoda, eds, *Ethics and International Relations.* Basingstoke: Palgrave – now Palgrave Macmillan.

Campbell, David and Morton Schoolman, eds. 2008. *The New Pluralism: William Connolly and the Contemporary Global Condition.* Durham, NC: University of North Carolina Press.

Campbell, David and Michael Shapiro, eds. 1999. *Moral Spaces: Rethinking Ethics and World Politics.* Minneapolis: University of Minnesota Press.

Caney, Simon. 2002. 'Cosmopolitanism and the Law of Peoples'. *Journal of Political Philosophy* 10(1): 95–123.

Caney, Simon. 2005. *Justice Beyond Borders: A Global Political Theory.* Oxford: Oxford University Press.

Capra, Fritjof. 2003. *The Hidden Connections: A Science for Sustainable Living.* London: Flamingo.

Carlson, John D. 2006. 'God's Disbelief and Ours: Religious Perils and Possibilities of Human Rights'. *Religion and Human Rights* 1(1): 5–15.

Carr, E.H. 1939. *The Twenty Years' Crisis, 1919–1939: An Introduction to the Study of International Relations.* London: Macmillan.

Carson, Rachel. 1962. *Silent Spring.* Boston: Houghton Mifflin.

Carty, Anthony. 2007. *Philosophy of International Law.* Edinburgh: Edinburgh University Press.

Carvin, Stephanie. 2010. 'A Responsibility to Reality: A Response to Louise Arbour'. *Review of International Studies* 36(S1): 47–54.

Chandler, David. 2002. *From Kosovo to Kabul: Human Rights and International Intervention.* London: Pluto Press.

Chandler, David and Volker Heins, eds. 2007. *Rethinking Ethical Foreign Policy: Pitfalls, Possibilities and Paradoxes.* London: Routledge.

Chesterman, Simon. 2004. *You the People: The United Nations, Transitional Administration and State-Building.* Oxford: Oxford University Press.

Chomsky, Noam. 1999. *The New Military Humanism: Lessons from Kosovo.* London: Pluto Press.

Chowdry, Geeta and Sheila Nair, eds. 2004. *Power, Postcolonialism and International Relations: Reading Race, Gender and Class.* London: Routledge.

Christiano, Tom. 2013. 'Authority', in *The Stanford Encyclopedia of Philosophy*, http://plato.stanford.edu/archives/spr2013/entries/authority/.

Cicero. 1991. *On Duties*, ed. M.T. Griffin and E.M. Atkins. Cambridge: Cambridge University Press.

Cicero. 1998. *The Republic and The Laws*, trans. Niall Rudd. Oxford: Oxford University Press.

Claeys, Gregory. 2013. *Mill and Paternalism*. Cambridge: Cambridge University Press.

Clark, Anne Marie. 2001. *Diplomacy of Conscience: Amnesty International and Changing Human Rights Norms*. Princeton: Princeton University Press.

Clark, Ian. 2005. *Legitimacy in International Society*. Oxford: Oxford University Press.

Clark, Ian. 2007. *International Legitimacy and World Society*. Oxford: Oxford University Press.

Cochran, Molly. 1999. *Normative Theory in International Relations: A Pragmatic Approach*. Cambridge: Cambridge University Press.

Cochran, Molly. 2009. 'Charting the Ethics of the English School: What "Good" is There in a Middle-Ground Ethics?' *International Studies Quarterly* 53(1): 203–55.

Coicaud, Jean-Marc. 2002. *Politics and Legitimacy: A Contribution to the Study of Political Right and Political Responsibility*. Cambridge: Cambridge University Press.

Coicaud, Jean-Marc and Daniel Warner, eds. 2001. *Ethics and International Affairs: Extents and Limits*. Tokyo: United Nations Press.

Coicaud, Jean-Marc and Nicholas Wheeler. 2008. *National Interest and International Society: Particular and Universal Ethics in International Life*. Tokyo: United Nations Press.

Coker, Christopher. 2001. *Humane Warfare*. New York: Routledge.

Commers, M.S. Ronald, Wim Vandekerckhove and An Verlinden, eds. 2008. *Ethics in an Era of Globalization*. Burlington, VT: Ashgate.

Connolly, William E., ed. 1969. *The Bias of Pluralism*. New York: Atherton Press.

Connolly, William E. 1991. *Identity/Difference: Negotiations of the Democratic Paradox*. Ithaca: Cornell University Press.

Connolly, William E. 1993 [1988]. *Political Theory and Modernity*. Oxford: Basil Blackwell.

Connolly, William E. 1995. *The Ethos of Pluralization*. Minneapolis: University of Minnesota Press.

Connolly, William E. 1999. *Why I am Not a Secularist*. Minneapolis: University of Minnesota Press.

Connolly, William E. 2002. *Neuropolitics: Thinking, Culture, Speed*. Minneapolis: University of Minnesota Press.

Connolly, William E. 2005. *Pluralism*. Durham, NC: Duke University Press.

Connolly, William E. 2008. *Capitalism and Christianity, American Style*. Durham, NC: University of North Carolina Press.

Connolly, William E. 2011. *A World of Becoming*. Durham, NC: Duke University Press.

Cox, Robert. 1981. 'Social Forces, States and World Orders: Beyond International Relations Theory'. *Millennium* 10: 126–55.

Cox, Robert. 1996. *Approaches to World Order*, with Timothy Sinclair. Cambridge: Cambridge University Press.

Cox, Robert. 2002. *The Political Economy of a Plural World: Critical Reflections on Power, Morals and Civilization.* London: Routledge.

Craig, Campbell. 2003. *Glimmer of a New Leviathan: Total War in the Realism of Niebuhr, Morgenthau and Waltz.* New York: Columbia University Press

Crane, Gregory. 1998. *Thucydides and the Ancient Simplicity: The Limits of Political Realism.* Berkeley: University of California Press.

Crawford, James. 2013. *The Law of Responsibility: The General Part.* Cambridge: Cambridge University Press.

Crawford, Neta. 2002. *Argument and Change in World Politics: Ethics, Decolonization and Humanitarian Intervention.* Cambridge: Cambridge University Press.

Crawford, Neta. 2003. 'Just War Theory and US Counter Terrorism War'. *Perspectives on Politics* 1(1): 5–25.

Cripps, Elizabeth. 2013. *Climate Change and the Moral Agent: Individual Duties in an Interdependent World.* Oxford: Oxford University Press.

Cronin, Bruce and Ian Hurd, eds. 2008. *The UN Security Council and the Politics of International Authority.* New York: Routledge.

Crouch, Colin. 2011. *The Strange Non-Death of Neoliberalism.* Cambridge: Polity Press.

Dahl, Robert. 1961. *Who Governs? Democracy and Power in an American City.* New Haven, CT: Yale University Press.

Dalby, Simon. 2002. *Environmental Security.* Minneapolis: University of Minnesota Press.

Dallmayr, Fred. 1996. *Beyond Orientalism: Essays on Cross-Cultural Encounter.* Albany, NY: SUNY Press.

Dallmayr, Fred. 2002. *Dialogue among Civilizations: Some Exemplary Voices.* Basingstoke: Palgrave – now Palgrave Macmillan.

Dallmayr, Fred. 2004. *Peace Talks: Who Will Listen?* Notre Dame: University of Notre Dame Press.

Darwin, Charles. 1958 [1859]. *On The Origin of Species.* New York: Ballantine Books.

D'Aspremont, Jean. 2011. *Formalism and the Sources of International Law: A Theory of the Ascertainment of Legal Rules.* Oxford: Oxford University Press.

Dawkins, Richard. 1991. *The Blind Watchmaker.* New York: Penguin.

De Bary, William. 1998. *Asian Values and Human Rights: A Confucian, Communitarian Perspective.* Cambridge, MA: Harvard University Press.

D'Entreves, Alexander P. 1951. *Natural Law: An Introduction to Legal Philosophy.* Chicago: Hutchinson.

Derrida, Jacques. 1992. *The Other Heading: Reflections on Today's Europe*, trans. Pascale-Anne Brault and Michael B. Naas. Bloomington: Indiana University Press.

Derrida, Jacques. 2001. *On Cosmopolitanism and Forgiveness.* New York: Routledge.

Dershowitz, Alan. 2006. *Preemption: A Knife that Cuts Both Ways.* New York: Norton.

Dewey, John. 1927. *The Public and its Problems: An Essay in Political Inquiry.* New York: Henry Holt.

Dillon, Michael and Andrew Neal, eds. 2008. *Foucault on Politics, Security and War.* Basingstoke: Palgrave Macmillan.

Dobson, Andrew. 2003. *Citizenship and the Environment*. Oxford: Oxford University Press.

Donelan, Michael. 1990. *Elements of International Political Theory*. Oxford: Clarendon Press.

Donnelly, Jack. 1982. 'Human Rights as Natural Rights'. *Human Rights Quarterly* 4: 391–405.

Douzinas, Costas. 2000. *The End of Human Rights*. Oxford: Hart.

Dower, Nigel. 1998. *World Ethics: The New Agenda*. Edinburgh: Edinburgh University Press.

Doyle, Michael. 1983a. 'Kant, Liberal Legacies and Foreign Affairs'. *Philosophy and Public Affairs* 12: 205–35.

Doyle, Michael. 1983b. 'Kant, Liberal Legacies and Foreign Affairs, Part 2'. *Philosophy and Public Affairs* 12: 323–53.

Doyle, Michael. 1986. 'Liberalism and World Politics'. *American Political Science Review* 80: 1151–69.

Doyle, Michael. 2008. *Striking First: Preemption and Prevention in International Conflict*. Princeton: Princeton University Press.

Dunlap, Charles. 2004. Technology War: Moral Dilemmas on the Battlefield, pp. 126–50, in Anthony F. Lang, Jr, Albert C. Pierce and Joel H. Rosenthal, eds, *Ethics and the Future of Conflict: Lessons from the 1990s*. Upper Saddle River, NJ: Pearson.

Dunoff, Joel and Joel Trachtman, eds. 2009. *Ruling the World? Constitutionalism, International Law and Global Governance*. Cambridge: Cambridge University Press.

Dworkin, Ronald. 2000. *Sovereign Virtue: The Theory and Practice of Equality*. Cambridge, MA: Harvard University Press.

Eagleton, Terry. 2011. *Why Marx Was Right*. New Haven, CT: Yale University Press.

Eckersley, Robyn. 2004. *The Green State: Rethinking Democracy and Sovereignty*. Cambridge, MA: MIT Press.

Edwards, Charles S. 1981. *Hugo Grotius, the Miracle of Holland: A Study in Legal and Political Thought*. Chicago: Nelson Hall.

Ellis, Elizabeth. 2005. *Kant's Politics: Provisional Theory for an Uncertain World*. New Haven: Yale University Press.

Elshtain, Jean Bethke. 2003. *Just War against Terror*. New York: Basic Books.

Elshtain, Jean Bethke. 2012. *Sovereignty: God, Self and State*. New York: Basic Books.

Emerson, Ralph Waldo. 1990 [1836]. *Nature*, republished in *Selected Essays, Lectures, and Poems*, ed. and forward Robert D. Richardson, Jr. New York: Bantam Classics.

Emmerson, Ben. 2013. Statement by Ben Emmerson, UN Special Rapporteur on Counter-Terrorism and Human Rights concerning the launch of an inquiry into the civilian impact, and human rights implications of the use drones and other forms of targeted killing for the purpose of counter-terrorism and counter-insurgency. UN Human Rights Council. Available at: www.ohchr.org/ Documents/Issues/Terrorism/SRCTBenEmmersonQC.24January12.pdf.

Enloe, Cynthia. 2000. *Bananas, Beaches and Bases: Making Feminist Sense of International Politics*. Berkeley: University of California Press.

Erskine, Toni, ed. 2003. *Can Institutions Have Responsibilities? Collective Moral Agency and International Relations*. Basingstoke: Palgrave Macmillan.

Erskine, Toni. 2008. *Embedded Cosmopolitanism: Duties to Strangers and Enemies in a World 'Dislocated Communities'*. Oxford: Oxford University Press.

Erskine, Toni. 2009. Normative IR Theory, pp. 36–57, in Tim Dunne, Milja Kurki and Steve Smith, eds, *International Relations Theories: Discipline and Diversity*, 2nd edn. Oxford: Oxford University Press.

Euben, Roxanne. 1999. *Enemy in the Mirror: Islamic Fundamentalism and the Limits of Modern Rationalism: A Work of Comparative Political Theory*. Princeton: Princeton University Press.

Fabre, Cécile. 2012. *Cosmopolitan War*. Oxford: Oxford University Press.

Falk, Richard. 1983. *The End of World Order: Essays on Normative International Relations*. New York: Holms & Meier.

Falk, Richard. 2001. *Religion and Humane Global Governance*. Basingstoke: Palgrave – now Palgrave Macmillan.

Falk, Richard and Cyril Black. 1969. *The Future of the International Legal Order*. Princeton: Princeton University Press.

Fanon, Frantz. 2001 [1961]. *The Wretched of the Earth,* preface Jean-Paul Sartre, trans. Constance Farrington. Harmondsworth: Penguin.

Fassbender, Bardo. 2009. *The United Nations Charter as the Constitution of the International Society*. Leiden: Martinus Nijhoff.

Feldman, Seymour. 2005. Maimonides: A Guide for Posterity, pp. 324–60, in Kenneth Seeskin, ed., *The Cambridge Companion to Maimonides*. Cambridge: Cambridge University Press.

Fierke, Karin. 2007. *Critical Approaches to International Security*. Cambridge: Polity Press.

Finnemore, Martha. 2003. *The Purpose of Intervention: Changing Beliefs about the Use of Force*. Ithaca: Cornell University Press.

Finnis, John. 1980. *Natural Law and Natural Right*. Oxford: Clarendon Press.

Fischer, John Martin and Mark Ravizza, eds. 1993. *Perspectives on Moral Responsibility*. Ithaca: Cornell University Press.

Flathman, Richard. 1980. *The Practice of Political Authority: Authority and the Authoritative*. Chicago: University of Chicago Press.

Flathman, Richard. 2005. *Pluralism and Liberal Democracy*. Baltimore: Johns Hopkins University Press.

Forman-Barzilai, Fonna. 2010. *Adam Smith and the Circles of Sympathy: Cosmopolitanism and Moral Theory*. Cambridge: Cambridge University Press.

Forsyth, Murray. 1994. Hobbes's Contractarianism: A Comparative Analysis, pp. 35–50, in David Boucher and Paul Kelly, eds, *The Social Contract Tradition from Hobbes to Rawls*. London: Routledge.

Forsythe, David. 2006. *Human Rights in International Relations*, 2nd edn. Cambridge: Cambridge University Press.

Foucault, Michel. 1990 [1977]. *The History of Sexuality:* vol. 1: *The Will to Knowledge*, trans. Robert Hurley. London: Penguin.

Foucault, Michel. 2004. *'Society Must Be Defended' Lectures at the College de France, 1975–1976*, trans. David Macey, eds Mauro Bertani and Alessandro Fontana. New York: Penguin.

Franchescet, Antonio. 2002. *Kant and Liberal Internationalism: Sovereignty, Justice and Global Reform*. Basingstoke: Palgrave – now Palgrave Macmillan.

Franck, Thomas. 2008. 'On Proportionality of Countermeasures in International Law'. *American Journal of International Law* 102(4): 715–67.

Frazer, Michael. 2010. *The Enlightenment of Sympathy: Reflective Sentimentalism in the Eighteenth Century and Today*. Oxford: Oxford University Press.

Frei, Christoph. 2001. *Hans J. Morgenthau: An Intellectual Biography*. Baton Rouge, LA: Louisiana State University Press.

French, Peter A. 1984. *Collective and Corporate Responsibility*. New York: Columbia University Press.

Friedman, R. 1990 [1973]. On the Concept of Authority in Political Philosophy, pp. 56–91, in Raz J. ed., *Authority*. New York: New York University Press.

Frost, Mervyn. 1996. *Ethics in International Relations: A Constitutive Theory*. Cambridge: Cambridge University Press.

Frost, Mervyn. 2002. *Constituting Human Rights: Global Civil Society and the Society of Democratic States*. London: Routledge.

Frost, Mervyn. 2009. *Global Ethics: Anarchy, Freedom, and International Relations*. London: Routledge.

Fukuyama, Francis. 1989. 'The End of History'. *The National Interest* 16: 3–18.

Gaddis, John Lewis. 1992. *The United States and the End of the Cold War: Implications, Reconsiderations, Provocations*. Oxford: Oxford University Press.

Gamble, Andrew. 2009. *The Spectre at the Feast: Capitalist Crisis and the Politics of Recession*. Basingstoke: Palgrave Macmillan.

Garst, Daniel. 1989. 'Thucydides and Neorealism'. *International Studies Quarterly* 33(1): 3–27.

George, Robert P. 1998. Natural Law and International Order, pp. 54–69, in David Mapel and Terry Nardin, eds, *International Society: Diverse Ethical Perspectives*. Princeton: Princeton University Press.

George, Robert P. 1999. *In Defence of Natural Law*. Oxford: Clarendon Press.

Gill, Stephen, ed. 1993. *Gramsci, Historical Materialism and International Affairs*. Cambridge: Cambridge University Press.

Gill, Stephen. 2003. *Power and Resistance in the New World Order*. Basingstoke: Palgrave Macmillan.

Glendon, Mary Anne. 2001. *A World Made New: Eleanor Roosevelt and the Universal Declaration of Human Rights*. New York: Random House.

Gopin, Marc. 2002. *Holy War, Holy Peace: How Religion can Bring Peace to the Middle East*. Oxford: Oxford University Press.

Grant, Ruth and Robert Keohane. 2005. 'Accountability and Abuses of Power in World Politics'. *American Political Science Review* 99: 29–43.

Grotius, Hugo. 2005 [1625]. *The Rights of War and Peace*, ed. and intro. Richard Tuck. Indianapolis: Liberty Fund.

Grovogui, Siba. 1995. *Sovereigns, Quasi-Sovereigns, and Africans: Race and Self-Determination in International Law*. Minneapolis: University of Minnesota Press.

Grovogui, Siba. 2013. Deferring Difference: A Postcolonial Critique of the 'Race Problem' in Moral Thought, pp. 106–23, in Sanjay Seth, ed., *Postcolonial Theory and International Relations: A Critical Introduction*. London: Routledge.

Guilhot, Nicholas. 2010. 'American Katechon: When Political Theology Became International Relations Theory'. *Constellations* 17(2): 224–53.

Gunnell, John G. 1987. *Political Theory: Tradition and Interpretation*. Lanham: University Press of America.

Gunnell, John G. 1993. *The Descent of Political Theory: The Genealogy of an American Vocation*. Chicago: University of Chicago Press.

Haakonssen, Knud. 1996. *Natural Law and Moral Philosophy: From Grotius to the Scottish Enlightenment*. Cambridge: Cambridge University Press.

Haakonssen, Knud, ed. 1999. *Grotius, Pufendorf and Modern Natural Law*. Aldershot: Ashgate.

Habermas, Jürgen. 2006. *The Divided West*. Cambridge: Polity Press.

Haley, K.H.D. 1972. *The Dutch in the 17th Century*. London: Thames & Hudson.

Hall, Ian. 2006. *The International Thought of Martin Wight*. Basingstoke: Palgrave Macmillan.

Hamilton, Keith and Richard Langhorne. 1995. *The Practice of Diplomacy: Its Evolution, Theory and Administration*. London: Routledge.

Harbour, Frances. 1995. 'Basic Moral Values: A Shared Core'. *Ethics & International Affairs* 9: 155–70.

Harbour, Frances. 1999. *Thinking about International Ethics: Moral Theory and Cases from American Foreign Policy*. Boulder, CO: Westview Press.

Harris, William V. 1979. *War and Imperialism in Republican Rome, 327-70BC*. Oxford: Clarendon Press.

Hart, H.L.A. 1982. *Essays on Bentham: Jurisprudence and Political Theory*. Oxford: Clarendon Press.

Hart, H.L.A. 1994. *The Concept of Law*, 2nd edn. Oxford: Clarendon Press.

Hart, H.L.A. and A.M. Honore, eds. 1959. *Causation in the Law*. Oxford: Clarendon Press.

Harvey, David. 2007. *A Brief History of Neoliberalism*. Oxford: Oxford University Press.

Hashmi, Sohail. 1996. Interpreting the Islamic Ethics of War and Peace, pp. 146–68, in Terry Nardin, ed., *The Ethics of War and Peace: Religious and Secular Perspectives*. Princeton: Princeton University Press.

Hashmi, Sohail, ed. 2002. *Islamic Political Ethics: Civil Society, Pluralism and Conflict*. Princeton: Princeton University Press.

Haslam, Jonathan. 2000. *The Vices of Integrity: E. H. Carr, 1892–1982*. London: Verso.

Hatemi, Peter and Rose McDermott, eds. 2011. *Man is by Nature a Political Animal*. Chicago: University of Chicago Press.

Hauerwas, Stanley. 1985. *Against the Nations: War and Survival in a Liberal Society*. Minneapolis: Winston Press.

Hawkins, Mike. 1997. *Social Darwinism in European and American Thought, 1860–1945*. Cambridge: Cambridge University Press.

Hayden, Patrick. 2005. *Cosmopolitan Global Politics*. Burlington, VT: Ashgate.

Hayden, Patrick. 2009a. *Political Evil in a Global Age: Hannah Arendt and International Theory*. London: Routledge.

Hayden, Patrick, ed. 2009b. *The Ashgate Research Companion to Ethics and International Affairs*. Burlington, VT: Ashgate.

Hayden, Patrick. 2009c. Cosmopolitanism Past and Present, pp. 43–62, in Patrick Hayden, ed., *The Ashgate Research Companion to Ethics and International Affairs*. Burlington, VT: Ashgate.

Hayden, Patrick. 2012. 'The Human Right to Health and the Struggle for Recognition'. *Review of International Studies* 38(3): 569–88.

Haynes, Jeffery. 2013. *An Introduction to International Relations and Religion*, 2nd edn. Harlow: Pearson Education.

Hayward, Tim. 2004. *Constitutional Environmental Rights*. Oxford: Oxford University Press.

Hegel, G.F.W. 1977 [1807]. *The Phenomenology of Spirit*, trans. A.V. Miller. Oxford: Clarendon.

Hegel, G.W.F. 1991 [1821]. *Elements of the Philosophy of Right*, ed. Allen Wood, trans. H. B. Nisbet. Cambridge: Cambridge University Press.

Hehir, Aidan. 2012. *The Responsibility to Protect: Rhetoric, Reality and the Future of Humanitarian Intervention*. Basingstoke: Palgrave Macmillan.

Helm, Dieter. 2012. *The Carbon Crunch: How we are Getting Climate Change Wrong and How to Fix It*. New Haven, CT: Yale University Press.

Hibbing, John R. 2013. 'Ten Misconceptions Concerning Neurobiology and Politics'. *Perspectives on Politics* 11(2): 475–89.

Hobbes, Thomas. 1968 [1651]. *Leviathan*. London: Penguin Classics.

Hobbes, Thomas. 1971 [1681]. *A Dialogue Between a Philosopher and a Student of the Common Laws of England*, ed. and intro. Joseph Cropsey. Chicago: University of Chicago Press.

Hoffman, Matthew. 2011. *Climate Governance at the Crossroads: Experimenting with a Global Response after Kyoto*. Oxford: Oxford University Press.

Hofstadter, Richard. 1954. *Social Darwinism in American Thought*. Boston: Beacon Press.

Hohfeld, Wesley N. 1946 [1919]. *Fundamental Legal Conceptions as Applied in Judicial Reasoning*. New Haven: Yale University Press.

Hollis, Martin. 1994. *The Philosophy of Social Science: An Introduction*. Cambridge: Cambridge University Press.

Hom, Andrew and Brent J. Steele. 2010. 'Open Horizons: The Temporal Visions of Reflexive Realism'. *International Studies Review* 12(2): 271–300.

Hooker, William. 2009. *Carl Schmitt's International Thought: Order and Orientation*. Cambridge: Cambridge University Press.

Hovden, Eivind and Edward Keene, eds. 2002. *The Globalization of Liberalism*. Basingstoke: Palgrave – now Palgrave Macmillan.

Huntington, Samuel. 1993. 'The Clash of Civilizations?' *Foreign Affairs* 72(3): 22–49.

Hurd, Ian. 2007. *After Anarchy: Legitimacy and Power in the UN Security Council*. Princeton: Princeton University Press.

Hurka, Thomas. 2007. 'Liability and Just Cause'. *Ethics & International Affairs* 21(2): 199–218.

Hurrell, Andrew. 2007. *On Global Order: Power, Values and the Constitution of International Society*. Oxford: Oxford University Press.

Hutchings, Kimberly. 1999. *International Political Theory: Rethinking Ethics in a Global Age*. London: Sage.

Hutchings, Kimberly. 2010. *Global Ethics: An Introduction*. Cambridge: Polity Press.

ICISS (International Commission on Intervention and State Sovereignty). 2001. *Responsibility to Protect*. Ottawa: International Development and Research Centre.

Ignatieff, Michael. 2000. *Virtual War: Kosovo and Beyond*. London: Chatto & Windus.

Ignatieff, Michael. 2001. *Human Rights as Politics and Idolatry*. Princeton: Princeton University Press.

Ikenberry, G. John. 2006. *Liberal Order and Imperial Ambition: Essays on American Power and World Politics*. Cambridge: Polity Press.

International Human Rights and Conflict Resolution Clinic at Stanford University and Global Justice Clinic at NYU School of Law. 2012. *Living Under Drones: Death, Injury and Trauma to Civilians from US Drone Practices in Pakistan*. Available at: www.livingunderdrones.org/report.

IPCC (Intergovernmental Panel on Climate Change). 2007. *Climate Change 2007: Synthetic Report*. Switzerland: IPCC Secretariat. Available at: www.ipcc.ch/pdf/assessment-report/ar4/syr/ar4_syr.pdf.

Isaacs, Tracy. 2011. *Moral Responsibility in Collective Contexts*. Oxford: Oxford University Press.

Isaacs, Tracy and Richard Vernon, eds. 2011. *Accountability for Collective Wrongdoing*. Cambridge: Cambridge University Press.

Ishay, Micheline. 2004. *The History of Human Rights: From an Ancient Times to the Globalization Era*. Berkeley: University of California Press.

Israel, Jonathan. 1989. *Dutch Primacy in World Trade, 1585–1740*. Oxford: Clarendon Press.

Israel, Jonathan. 1994. *Radical Enlightenment: Philosophy and the Making of Modernity, 1650–1750*. Oxford: Oxford University Press.

Issac, Jeffrey. 1995. 'The Strange Silence of Political Theory'. *Political Theory* 23: 636–52.

Jackson, Robert. 1996. 'Is There a Classical International Theory?', pp. 203–20, in Steve Smith, Ken Booth and Marysia Zalewski, eds, *International Theory: Positivism and Beyond*. Cambridge: Cambridge University Press.

Jackson, Robert. 2000. *The Global Covenant: Human Conduct in a World of States*. Oxford: Oxford University Press.

Jahn, Beate. 2006a. Classical Smoke, Classical Mirror: Kant and Mill in Liberal International Relations Theory, pp. 178–206, in Beate Jahn, ed., *Classical Theory in International Relations*. Cambridge: Cambridge University Press.

Jahn, Beate. ed. 2006b. *Classical Theory in International Relations*. Cambridge: Cambridge University Press.

James, William. 1987 [1902]. *The Varieties of Religious Experience*, reprinted in *Writings, 1902–1910*. New York: Library of America.

James, William. 1987 [1909]. *A Pluralistic Universe*, reprinted in *Writings, 1902–1910*. New York: Library of America.

Jeffrey, Reneé. 2006. *Hugo Grotius in International Thought*. Basingstoke: Palgrave Macmillan.

Jenkins, Philip. 2002. *The Next Christendom: The Rise of Global Christianity*. Oxford: Oxford University Press.

Johnson, James Turner. 1975. *Ideology, Reason and the Limitation of War: Religious and Secular Concepts, 1200–1700*. Princeton: Princeton University Press.

Johnson, James Turner. 1981. *Just War, Tradition, and the Restraint of War: A Moral and Historical Inquiry*. Princeton: Princeton University Press.

Johnson, James Turner. 2004. From Moral Norm to Criminal Code: The Law of Armed Conflict and the Restraint of Contemporary Warfare, pp. 68–90, in Anthony F. Lang, Jr, A.C. Pierce and J.H. Rosenthal, eds, *Ethics and the Future of Conflict: Lessons from the 1990s*. Upper Saddle River, NJ: Prentice Hall.

Johnson, Laurie M. 1993. *Thucydides, Hobbes, and the Interpretation of Realism*. Dekalb, IL: Northern Illinois University Press.

Jones, Charles. 1998. *E. H. Carr and International Relations: A Duty to Lie*. Cambridge: Cambridge University Press.

Jones, Charles. 1999. *Global Justice: Defending Cosmopolitanism*. Oxford: Oxford University Press.

Kaldor, Mary. 2006. *New and Old Wars*, 2nd edn. Cambridge: Polity Press.

Kant, Immanuel. 1991. *Political Writings*, 2nd edn, ed. Hans Reiss. Cambridge: Cambridge University Press.

Kant, Immanuel. 1991 [1784]. 'An Answer to the Question: What is Enlightenment?', pp. 54–60, in *Political Writings*, 2nd edn, ed. Hans Reiss. Cambridge: Cambridge University Press

Kant, Immanuel. 1991 [1795]. *Perpetual Peace: A Philosophical Sketch*, pp. 93–130, in *Political Writings*, 2nd edn, ed. Hans Reiss. Cambridge: Cambridge University Press.

Kant, Immanuel. 1991 [1797]. *The Metaphysics of Morals*, pp. 131–75, in *Political Writings*, 2nd edn, ed. Hans Reiss. Cambridge: Cambridge University Press.

Kant, Immanuel. 1993 [1785]. *Groundwork for the Metaphysics of Morals* and *On the Supposed Right to Lie because of Philanthropic Concerns*, trans. James Ellington. Indianapolis: Hackett.

Kant, Immanuel. 1998 [1781]. *Critique of Pure Reason*, trans. and ed. Paul Guyer and Allen Wood. Cambridge: Cambridge University Press.

Kaplan, Robert. 2002. *Warrior Politics: Why Leadership Demands a Pagan Ethos.* New York: Random House.

Karp, David. 2009. 'Transnational Corporations in Bad States: Human Rights Duties, Legitimate Authority, and the Rule of Law in International Political Theory'. *International Theory* 1(1): 87–118.

Katzenstein, Peter, ed. 1996. *The Culture of National Security.* New York: Columbia University Press.

Kaufman, Whitley. 2005. 'What's Wrong with Preventive War? The Moral and Legal Basis for Preventive War'. *Ethics & International Affairs* 19(3): 23–38.

Keene, Edward. 2002. *Beyond the Anarchical Society: Grotius, Colonialism and Order in World Politics.* Cambridge: Cambridge University Press.

Keene, Edward. 2005. *International Political Thought: A Historical Introduction.* Cambridge: Polity Press.

Kelsay, John. 2007. *Arguing the Just War in Islam.* Cambridge, MA: Harvard University Press.

Kelsen, Hans. 1944. *Peace through Law.* Chapel Hill: University of North Carolina Press.

Kelsen, Hans. 1960 [1934]. *Pure Theory of Law*, 2nd edn, trans. Max Knight. Berkeley: University of California Press.

Kennedy, Caroline and Nicholas Rengger. 2012. *The New Assassination Bureau: On the 'Robotic Turn' in Contemporary War.* Carnegie Council, 6 November. Available at: www.carnegiecouncil.org/publications/ethics_online/0075.html.

Keohane, Robert. 1984. *After Hegemony: Cooperation and Discord in the World Political Economy.* Princeton: Princeton University Press.

Keohane, Robert. 2009. 'Political Science as a Vocation'. *PS: Politics and Political Science* 42(2): 359–63.

Keohane, Robert, Stephen Macedo and Andrew Moravcsik. 2009. 'Democracy-enhancing Multilateralism'. *International Organization* 63: 1–31.

Keohane, Robert, Bruce Jones, Nirupam Sen, Nancy Soderburgh and Steven Lee. 2006. Roundtable: '"A Threat to One is a Threat to All": Nonstate Threats and Collective Security'. *Ethics & International Affairs* 20(2): 219–46.

Kepel, Gilles. 1994. *The Revenge of God: The Resurgence of Islam, Christianity and Judaism in the Modern World*, trans. Alan Braley. Cambridge: Polity Press.

Kerr, Rachel and Eirin Mobekk. 2007. Peace *and Justice: Seeking Accountability after War.* Cambridge: Polity Press.

Kerry, John. 2013. Getting the US-China Climate Partnership Right. Available at: www.state.gov/secretary/remarks/2013/07/212219.htm.

Khadduri, Majid. 1955. *War and Peace in Islam.* Baltimore: Johns Hopkins University Press.

Khadduri, Majid. 2001 [1966]. *The Islamic Law of Nations: Shaybani's Siyar.* Baltimore: Johns Hopkins University Press.

King, Martin Luther, Jr. 2000 [1962]. A Legacy of Creative Protest, reprinted in Henry David Thoreau, *Walden and Civil Disobedience*, ed. Paul Lauter. Boston: Houghton Mifflin.

Klabbers, Jan. 2009. 'The Bridge Crack'd: A Critical Look at Interdisciplinary Relations'. *International Relations* 23(1): 119–25.

Klabbers, Jan, Anne Peters and Geir Ulfstein. 2009. *The Constitutionalization of International Law*. Oxford: Oxford University Press.

Knorr, Klaus and James Rosenau, eds. 1965. *Contending Approaches to International Politics*. Princeton: Princeton University Press.

Koontz, Theodore J. 1996. Christian Non-Violence: An Interpretation, pp. 169–96, in Terry Nardin, ed., *The Ethics of War and Peace: Religious and Secular Perspectives*. Princeton: Princeton University Press.

Koskenneimi, Martti. 2001. *The Gentle Civilizer of Nations: The Rise and Fall of International Law, 1870–1960*. Cambridge: Cambridge University Press.

Koskenniemi, Martti. 2011. *The Politics of International Law*. Oxford: Hart.

Krasner, Stephen. 1996. The Accomplishments of International Political Economy, pp. 108–27, in Steve Smith, Ken Booth and Marysia Zalewski, eds, *International Theory: Positivism and Beyond*. Cambridge: Cambridge University Press.

Kratochwil, Friedrich. 1989. *Rules, Norms, and Decisions: On the Conditions of Practical and Legal Reasoning in International Relations and Domestic Affairs*. Cambridge: Cambridge University Press.

Kurki, Milja. 2008. *Causation in International Relations: Reclaiming Causal Analysis*. Cambridge: Cambridge University Press.

Lake, David. 2009. *Hierarchy in International Relations*. Ithaca: Cornell University Press.

Lane, Melissa. 2011. *Eco-Republic: What the Ancients Can Teach us About Ethics, Virtue and Sustainable Living*. Princeton: Princeton University Press.

Lang, Anthony F. Jr. 1999. 'Responsibility in the International System: Reading U.S. Foreign Policy in the Middle East'. *European Journal of International Relations* 5(1): 67–107.

Lang, Anthony F. Jr. 2002. *Agency and Ethics: The Politics of Military Intervention*. Albany, NY: State University Press of New York.

Lang, Anthony F. Jr. 2003. Responsibility and Agency: The UN and the Fall of Srebrenica, pp. 183–206, in Toni Erskine, ed., *Can Institutions Have Responsibilities?* Basingstoke: Palgrave Macmillan.

Lang, Anthony F. Jr. 2007. Morgenthau, Agency and Aristotle, pp. 18–41, in Michael Williams, ed., *Reconsidering Realism: The Legacy of Hans J. Morgenthau in International Relations*. Oxford: Oxford University Press.

Lang, Anthony F. Jr. 2008. *Punishment, Justice and International Relations: Ethics and Order after the Cold War*. London: Routledge.

Lang, Anthony F. Jr. 2009a. 'The Just War Tradition and the Question of Authority'. *Journal of Military Ethics* 8(3): 202–16.

Lang, Anthony F. Jr. 2009b. Authority and the Problem of Non-State Actors, pp. 47–71, in Eric Heinze and Brent Steele, eds, *Just War and Non-State Actors*. London: Routledge.

Lang, Anthony F. Jr. 2009c. Ethics, Justice and Security, pp. 1619–38, in Robert Denmark, ed., *International Studies Encyclopaedia*. New York: Wiley Blackwell.

Lang, Anthony F. Jr. 2013a. Phronesis, Morgenthau and Diplomacy. Available at: www.e-ir.info/2013/11/07/phronesis-morgenthau-and-diplomacy/.

Lang, Anthony F. Jr. 2013b. Global Constitutionalism as Middle Ground Ethics, pp. 106–26, in Cornelia Navari, ed., *Ethical Reasoning in International Affairs: Arguments from the Middle Ground*. Basingstoke: Palgrave Macmillan.

Lang, Anthony F. Jr. 2014. Constitutionalism and the Law: Evaluating the UN Security Council, in Trudy Fraser and Vesselin Popovski, eds, *The UN Security Council as a Global Legislator*. Basingstoke: Palgrave Macmillan.

Lang, Anthony F. Jr and John Williams, eds. 2005. *Hannah Arendt and International Relations: Reading Across the Lines*. Basingstoke: Palgrave Macmillan.

Lang, Anthony F. Jr and Amanda R. Beattie, eds. 2008. *War, Torture and Terrorism: Rethinking the Rules of International Security*. London: Routledge.

Lang, Anthony F. Jr, Cian O'Driscoll and John Williams, eds. 2013. *Just War: Authority, Tradition, and Practice*. Washington DC: Georgetown University Press.

Lang, Anthony F. Jr, Nicholas Rengger and William Walker. 2006a. 'The Role(s) of Rules: Some Conceptual Clarifications'. *International Relations* 20(3): 274–94.

Lang, Anthony F. Jr et al. 2006b. Forum: 'Rethinking the Rules'. *International Relations* 20(3): 273–349.

Lapid, Yosef. 1989. 'The Third Debate: On the Prospects of International Theory in a Post-Positivist Era'. *International Studies Quarterly* 33: 235–54.

Lauren, Paul. 2007. 'To Preserve and Build on its Achievements and to Redress its Shortcomings: The Journey from the Commission on Human Rights to the Human Rights Council'. *Human Rights Quarterly* 29: 307–45.

Lebow, Richard Ned. 2003. *The Tragic Vision of Politics: Ethics, Interests and Orders*. Cambridge: Cambridge University Press.

Lebow, Richard Ned. 2008. *A Cultural Theory of International Relations*. Cambridge: Cambridge University Press.

Lecker, Michael. 2004. *The 'Constitution of Medina': Muhammad's First Legal Document*. Princeton: Princeton University Press.

Leopold, Aldo. 2003 [1949]. *A Sand County Almanac: And Sketches Here and There*, selections reprinted in Andrew Light and Holmes Rolston III, eds, *Environmental Ethics: An Anthology*. Oxford: Blackwell.

LeVay, Simon. 1996. *Queer Science: The Use and Abuse of Research into Homosexuality*. Cambridge, MA: MIT Press.

Lewis, C.S. 1943. *Mere Christianity*. New York: Macmillan Books.

Lewis, C.S. 1994. *The Discarded Image: An Introduction to Medieval and Renaissance Literature*. London: Canto Press.

Light, Andrew and Holmes Rolston III, eds. 2003. *Environmental Ethics: An Anthology*. Oxford: Blackwell.

Linklater, Andrew. 1982. *Men and Citizens in the Theory of International Relations*. London: Macmillan.

Linklater, Andrew. 1990. *Beyond Realism and Marxism: Critical Theory and International Relations*. London: Macmillan.

Linklater, Andrew. 1997. *The Transformation of Political Community: Ethical Foundations of a Post-Westphalian Era*. Oxford: Polity Press.

Linklater, Andrew. 2007. *Critical Theory and World Politics: Citizenship, Sovereignty and Humanity*. London: Routledge.

Linklater, Andrew. 2011. *The Problem of Harm in World Politics: Theoretical Investigations*. Cambridge: Cambridge University Press.

Linklater, Andrew and Hidemi Suganami. 2006. *The English School of International Relations: A Contemporary Reassessment*. Cambridge: Cambridge University Press.

Livy. 1960. *The Early History of Rome, Books I-V of The History of Rome from Its Foundations*. New York: Penguin.

Locke, John. 1997 [1663–64]. 'Essays on the Law of Nature', in John Locke, *Political Essays*, ed., Mark Goldie. Cambridge: Cambridge University Press.

Locke, John. 1959 [1690]. *An Essay Concerning Human Understanding*. New York: Dover.

Locke, John. 1988 [1690]. *Two Treatises of Government*, ed. and intro. Peter Laslett. Cambridge: Cambridge University Press.

McCarthy, Thomas. 2010. *Race, Empire and the Idea of Human Development*. Cambridge: Cambridge University Press.

MacIntyre, Alasdair. 1981. *After Virtue: A Study in Moral Theory*. London: Duckworth.

McMahan, Jeff. 2005. 'Just Cause for War'. *Ethics & International Affairs* 19(3): 1–21.

McMahan, Jeff. 2009. *Killing in War*. Oxford: Oxford University Press.

MacPherson, C.B. 1962. *The Political Theory of Possessive Individualism*. Oxford: Clarendon Press.

Mandaville, Peter. 2007. *Global Political Islam*. New York: Routledge.

Mani, Rama. 2002. *Beyond Retribution: Seeking Justice in the Shadows of War*. Cambridge: Polity Press.

Manson, Jaime. 2013. The Orthodox Church's Role in Russia's Anti-Gay Laws, *The National Catholic Reporter* Online, 13 August. Available at: http://ncronline.org/blogs/grace-margins/orthodox-church-s-role-russia-s-anti-gay-laws. Accessed 21 February 2014.

Mapel, David and Terry Nardin. 1998. *International Society: Diverse Ethical Perspectives*. Princeton: Princeton University Press.

Marcus, George E. 2013. 'What's That You Say?' *Perspectives on Politics* 11(2): 492–4.

Maritain, Jacques. 2001. *Natural Law: Reflections on Theory and Practice*, ed. and intro. William Sweet. South Bend: St Augustine Press.

Marks, Susan, ed. 2008. *International Law on the Left: Re-examining Marxist Legacies*. Cambridge: Cambridge University Press.

Marx, Karl. 1978 [1843]. *On the Jewish Question*, pp. 26–52, in Robert C. Tucker, ed., *The Marx-Engels Reader*, 2nd edn. New York: W.W. Norton.

Marx, Karl. 1978 [1845]. *Theses on Feuerbach*, pp. 143–5, in Robert C. Tucker, ed., *The Marx-Engels Reader*, 2nd edn. New York: W.W. Norton.

Marx, Karl and Friedrich Engels. 1978 [1848]. *The Communist Manifesto*, pp. 469–500, in Robert C. Tucker, ed., *The Marx-Engels Reader*, 2nd edn. New York: W.W. Norton.

May, Larry. 2007. *War Crimes and Just War*. Cambridge: Cambridge University Press.

May, Larry. 2012. *After War Ends: A Philosophical Perspective*. Cambridge: Cambridge University Press.

Meckled-Garica, Saladin. 2008. 'On the Very Idea of Cosmopolitan Justice: Constructivism and International Agency'. *Journal of Political Philosophy* 16(3): 245–71.

Mertus, Julie. 2009. *The United Nations and Human Rights: A Guide for a New Era*. London: Routledge.

Meyer, John M. 2001. *Political Nature: Environmentalism and the Interpretation of Western Thought*. Cambridge, MA: MIT Press.

Midgley, E.B.F. 1975. *The Natural Law Tradition and the Theory of International Relations*. London: Elek.

Mieville, China. 2005. *Between Equal Rights: A Marxist Theory of International Law*. London: Pluto Press.

Milanovic, Branko. 2011. *The Haves and Have-nots: A Brief and Idiosyncratic History of Global Inequality*. New York: Basic Books.

Milanovic, Branko. 2012. *Global Income Inequality by the Numbers: In History and Now – An Overview*. World Bank. Available at: http://elibrary.worldbank.org/doi/book/10.1596/1813-9450-6259.

Mill, John Stuart. 1859. A Few Words on Non-Intervention, *Fraser's Magazine*. Reprinted in *Foreign Policy Perspectives*. Available at: www.libertarian.co.uk/lapubs/forep/forep008.pdf.

Mill, John Stuart. 2008 [1859]. *On Liberty*, pp. 5–130, in *On Liberty and Other Essays*, ed. and intro. John Gray. Oxford: Oxford University Press.

Mill, John Stuart. 2008 [1861]. *Considerations on Representative Government*, pp. 205–470, in *On Liberty and Other Essays*, ed. and intro. John Gray. Oxford: Oxford University Press.

Mill, John Stuart. 2008 [1869]. *The Subjection of Women*, pp. 471–582, in *On Liberty and Other Essays*, ed. and intro. John Gray. Oxford: Oxford University Press.

Miller, David. 2007. *National Responsibility and Global Justice*. Oxford: Oxford University Press.

Miller, Richard B. 2008. 'Justifications of the Iraq War Examined'. *Ethics & International Affairs* 22(1): 43–67.

Mills, Kurt. 1998. *Human Rights in the Emerging Global Order: A New Sovereignty?* Basingstoke: Macmillan – now Palgrave Macmillan.

Moellendorf, Darrel. 2009. *Global Inequality Matters*. Basingstoke: Palgrave Macmillan.

Mollov, M. Benjamin. 2002. *Power and Transcendence: Hans J. Morgenthau and the Jewish Experience*. Lanham, MD: Lexington Books.

Molloy, Sean. 2008. Hans J. Morgenthau vs. E. H. Carr: Conflicting Conceptions of Ethics in Realism, pp. 83–104, in Duncan Bell, ed., *Political Thought and International Relations: Variations on a Realist Theme*. Oxford: Oxford University Press.

Moravcsik, Andrew. 1997. 'Taking Preferences Seriously: A Liberal Theory of International Politics'. *International Organization* 51: 513–53.

Moravcsik, Andrew. 2009. 'Robert Keohane: Political Theorist', pp. 243–64, in Helen V. Milner and Andrew Moravcsik, eds, *Power Interdependence and Non-State Actors in World Politics*. Princeton: Princeton University Press.

Morgenthau, Hans. 1945. 'The Evil of Politics and the Ethics of Evil'. *Ethics* 56: 1–18.

Morgenthau, Hans. 1946. *Scientific Man versus Power Politics*. Chicago: University of Chicago Press.

Morgenthau, Hans. 1948. *Politics Among Nations: The Struggle for Power and Peace*. New York: Alfred A. Knopf.

Morgenthau, Hans. 1960. *The Purpose of American Politics*. New York: Alfred A. Knopf.

Morgenthau, Hans. 2004. *Political Theory and International Relations: Lectures on Aristotle's Politics,* ed. Anthony F. Lang, Jr. Westport, CT: Praeger.

Morsink, Johannes. 1999. *The Universal Declaration of Human Rights: Origins, Drafting and Intent*. Philadelphia: University of Pennsylvania Press.

Moyn, Samuel. 2010. *The Last Utopia: Human Rights in History*. Berkeley: University of California Press.

Naess, Arne. 2003 [1986]. The Deep Ecological Movement: Some Philosophical Aspects, pp. 262–74, in Andrew Light and Holmes Rolston III, eds, *Environmental Ethics: An Anthology*. Oxford: Blackwell.

Nagel, Thomas. 2005. 'The Problem of Global Justice'. *Philosophy and Public Affairs* 33: 113–47.

Nardin, Terry. 1983. *Law, Morality and the Relations of States*. Princeton: Princeton University Press.

Nardin, Terry, ed. 1996. *The Ethics of War and Peace: Religious and Secular Perspectives*. Princeton: Princeton University Press.

Nardin, Terry. 1998. Legal Positivism as a Theory of International Society, pp. 17–35, in David Mapel and Terry Nardin, eds, *International Society: Diverse Ethical Perspectives*. Princeton: Princeton University Press.

Nardin, Terry. 2002. 'The Moral Basis of Humanitarian Intervention'. *Ethics & International Affairs* 16: 57–70.

Nardin, Terry. 2006. Introduction, pp. 1–30, in Terry Nardin and Melissa Williams, eds. *Humanitarian Intervention*. New York: New York University Press.

Nardin, Terry. 2008. 'Theorizing the International Rule of Law'. *Review of International Studies* 34: 385–401.

Nardin, Terry and David Mapel, eds. 1992. *Traditions of International Ethics.* Cambridge: Cambridge University Press.

Navari, Cornelia, ed. 2013. *Ethical Reasoning in International Affairs: Arguments from the Middle Ground.* Basingstoke: Palgrave Macmillan.

Neff, Stephen C. 2005. *War and the Law of Nations: A General History.* Cambridge: Cambridge University Press.

Nichols, Mary. 1992. *Citizens and Statesmen: A Study of Aristotle's Politics.* Lanham, MD: Rowman & Littlefield.

Niebuhr, Reinhold. 1934. *Moral Man and Immoral Society.* New York: Charles Scribner's Sons.

Nietzsche, Friedrich. 2007 [1887]. *On the Genealogy of Morals*, ed. Keith Ansell-Pearson, trans. Carol Diethe. Cambridge: Cambridge University Press.

Nussbaum, Martha. 2000. *Women and Development: The Capabilities Approach.* Cambridge: Cambridge University Press.

Nussbaum, Martha and Amartya Sen, eds. 1993. *The Quality of Life.* Oxford: Oxford University Press.

Oakeshott, Michael. 1991 [1961]. *Rationalism in Politics, and Other Essays.* Indianapolis: Liberty Fund Press.

O'Connell, Mary Ellen. 2008. *The Power and Purpose of International Law: Insights from the Theory and Practice of Enforcement.* Oxford: Oxford University Press.

O'Driscoll, Cian. 2008. *The Renegotiation of the Just War Tradition and the Right to War in the Twenty-First Century.* Basingstoke: Palgrave Macmillan.

Odysseos, Louiza and Petito, Fabio, eds. 2007. *The International Political Thought of Carl Schmitt: Terror, Liberal War and the Crisis of Global Order.* London: Routledge.

O'Neil, Onora. 2000. *Bounds of Justice.* Cambridge: Cambridge University Press.

Onuf, Nicholas. 1989. *World of Our Making: Rules and Rule in Social Theory and International Relations.* Columbia, SC: University of South Carolina Press.

Onuf, Nicholas. 1998. *The Republican Legacy in International Thought.* Cambridge: Cambridge University Press.

Onuf, Peter and Nicholas Onuf. 1993. *Federal Union, Modern World: The Law of Nations in an Age of Revolutions, 1776–1814.* Madison, WI: Madison House.

Orend, Brian. 2002. 'Justice After War'. *Ethics & International Affairs* 16(1): 43–56.

Orend, Brian. 2006. Is there a Supreme Emergency Exception?, pp. 134–56, in Mark Evans, ed., *Just War Theory: A Reappraisal.* Edinburgh: Edinburgh University Press.

Orford, Anne, ed. 2006. *International Law and Its Others.* Cambridge: Cambridge University Press.

Orford, Anne. 2011. *International Authority and the Responsibility to Protect.* Cambridge: Cambridge University Press.

Owens, Patricia. 2008. *Between War and Politics: International Relations and the Thought of Hannah Arendt.* Oxford: Oxford University Press.

Pagden, Anthony. 1995. *Lords of all the World: Ideologies of Empire in Spain, Britain and France, 1500–1800.* New Haven, CT: Yale University Press.

Pagden, Anthony. 2003. 'Human Rights, Natural Rights, and Europe's Imperial Legacy'. *Political Theory* 31(2): 171–99.

Paine, Thomas. 1984 [1791]. *The Rights of Man*. New York: Penguin.

Pangle, Thomas and Peter Ahrensdorf. 1999. *Justice among Nations: On the Moral Basis of Power and Peace*. Lawrence: University of Kansas Press.

Peterson, V. Spike, ed. 1992. *Gendered States: Feminist Revisions of International Relations Theory*. Boulder, CO: Lynne Rienner.

Pierce, Albert C. 2004. War, Strategy and Ethics, pp. 15–28, in Anthony F. Lang, Jr, Albert C. Pierce and Joel Rosenthal, eds, *Ethics and the Future of Conflict: Lessons from the 1990s*. Upper Saddle River, NJ: Prentice Hall.

Pinker, Steven. 2011. *The Better Angels of our Nature: A History of Violence and Humanity*. New York: Penguin.

Pinker, Steven. 2013. 'Science is not Your Enemy: An Impassioned Plea to Neglected Novelists, Embattled Professors, and Tenure-Less Historians'. *New Republic*, 6 August. Available at: www.newrepublic.com/article/114127/science-not-enemy-humanities.

Plato. 1991. *The Republic*, 2nd edn, ed. and intro. Allan Bloom. New York: Basic Books.

Pocock, J.G.A. 1987. *The Ancient Constitution and the Feudal Law: A Study of English Historical Thought in the 17th Century*, 2nd edn. Cambridge: Cambridge University Press.

Pocock, J.G.A. 1994. The Ideal of Citizenship since Classical Times, pp. 29–52, in Ronald Beiner, ed., *Theorizing Citizenship*. Albany, NY: State University Press of New York.

Pogge, Thomas. 1989. *Realizing Rawls*. Ithaca: Cornell University Press.

Pogge, Thomas. 1994. 'An Egalitarian Law of Peoples'. *Philosophy and Public Affairs* 23(3): 195–224.

Pogge, Thomas. 2002. *World Poverty and Human Rights: Cosmopolitan Responsibilities and Reforms*. Cambridge: Polity Press.

Pogge, Thomas. 2008. *World Poverty and Human Rights: Cosmopolitan Responsibilities and Reforms*, 2nd edn. Cambridge: Polity Press.

Pogge, Thomas. 2012. Interview, Carnegie Council for Ethics in International Affairs. Available at: www.youtube.com/watch?v=r9yUJLBzGX8.

Pogge, Thomas and Keith Horton, eds. 2008. *Global Ethics: Seminal Essays*. St Paul: Paragon House.

Pogge, Thomas and Darrel Moellendorf, eds. 2008. *Global Justice: Seminal Essays*. St Paul: Paragon House.

Porter, Jean. 1999–2000. 'From Natural Law to Human Rights, or Why Rights Talk Matters'. *Journal of Law and Religion* 14: 77–96.

Prager, Carol A. 2005. 'Intervention and Empire: John Stuart Mill and International Relations'. *Political Studies* 53: 621–40.

Price, Richard, ed. 2008. *Moral Limit and Possibility in World Politics*. Cambridge: Cambridge University Press.

Pufendorf, Samuel. 2003 [1691]. *The Whole Duty of Man According to the Law of Nature*, ed. and intro. Ian Hunter and David Saunders. Indianapolis: Liberty Fund.

Ramadan, Tariq. 2004. *Western Muslims and the Future of Islam*. Oxford: Oxford University Press.

Ramcharan, Bertrand G. 2011. *The UN Human Rights Council*. London: Routledge.

Ramsey, Paul. 1961. *War and the Christian Conscience: How Shall Modern War be Conducted Justly?* Durham, NC: Duke University Press.

Ramsey, Paul. 1968. *The Just War: Force and Political Responsibility*. New York: Scribner.

Ravitzky, Aviezer. 1996. Prohibited Wars in the Jewish Tradition, pp. 115–27, in Terry Nardin, ed., *The Ethics of War and Peace: Religious and Secular Perspectives*. Princeton: Princeton University Press.

Rawls, John. 1971. *A Theory of Justice*. Cambridge, MA: Belknap Press.

Rawls, John. 1993. *Political Liberalism*. New York: Columbia University Press.

Rawls, John. 1995. 'Fifty Years after Hiroshima'. *Dissent* (Summer): 323–27, reprinted in John Rawls, *Collected Papers*, pp. 565–72, ed. Samuel Freeman. Cambridge, MA: Harvard University Press, 1999.

Rawls, John. 1999. *The Law of Peoples, with The Idea of Public Reason, Revisited*. Cambridge, MA: Harvard University Press.

Rawls, John. 2007. *Lectures on the History of Political Philosophy*, ed. Samuel Freeman. Cambridge, MA: Harvard University Press.

Raz, Joseph, ed. 1990. *Authority*. Oxford: Basil Blackwell.

Reeves, Richard. 2007. *John Stuart Mill: Victorian Firebrand*. London: Atlantic Books.

Reichberg, Gregory M., Henrik Syse and Endre Begby, eds. 2006. *The Ethics of War: Classic and Contemporary Readings*. Oxford: Basil Blackwell.

Rengger, Nicholas. 2013. Just War and International Order: The Uncivil Condition in World Politics. Cambridge: Cambridge University Press.

Rengger, Nicholas, Chris Brown, Simon Caney et al. 2005. 'Reading Charles Beitz: Twenty-Five Years of Political Theory and International Relations'. *Review of International Studies* 31: 361–423.

Reus-Smit, Christian, ed. 2004. *The Politics of International Law*. Cambridge: Cambridge University Press.

Richmond, Oliver. 2002. *Maintaining Order, Maintaining Peace*. Basingstoke: Palgrave – now Palgrave Macmillan.

Riley-Smith, Jonathan. 1987. *The Crusades: A Short History*. New Haven, CT: Yale University Press.

Roberts, Adam and Richard Guelff. 2003. *Documents on the Laws of War*, 3rd edn. Oxford: Oxford University Press.

Robinson, Fiona. 1999. *Globalising Care: Ethics, Feminist Theory and International Relations*. Boulder, CO: Westview Press.

Rodin, David. 2002. *War and Self-Defense*. Oxford: Oxford University Press.

Rorty, Richard. 1989. *Contingency, Irony, Solidarity*. Cambridge: Cambridge University Press.

Rorty, Richard. 1998. Human Rights, Rationality and Sentimentality, pp. 167–85, in Richard Rorty, *Truth and Progress: Philosophical Papers*. Cambridge: Cambridge University Press.

Rosenberg, Alexander. 2000. *Darwinism and Philosophy, Social Science and Policy*. Cambridge: Cambridge University Press.

Rosenthal, Joel H. 1991. *Righteous Realists: Political Realism, Responsible Power, and American Culture in a Nuclear Age*. Baton Rogue, LA: Louisiana State University Press.

Rosenthal, Joel H. and Christian Barry, eds. 2009. *Ethics and International Affairs: A Reader*. Washington DC: Georgetown University Press.

Rosenthal, Joel H. and Ethan B. Kapstein, eds. 2009. *Ethics and International Relations*. Burlington, VT: Ashgate.

Ross, Ian Simpson. 2010. *The Life of Adam Smith*. Oxford: Oxford University Press.

Rossiter, Clinton. ed. 1961. *The Federalist Papers*. New York: New American Library.

Russell, George. 2010. UN Human Rights Council Takes Aim at New Target: United States. Fox News, 5 November. Available at: www.foxnews.com/world/2010/11/04/united-nations-human-rights-council/.

Russell, Greg. 1990. *Hans J. Morgenthau and the Ethics of American Statecraft*. Baton Rogue, LA: Louisiana State University Press.

Russett, Bruce and John R. Oneal. 2001. *Triangulating Peace: Democracy, Interdependence and International Organizations*. New York: W.W. Norton.

Sachedina, Abdullah Aziz. 2010. *Islam and Human Rights*. Oxford: Oxford University Press.

Said, Edward. 1978. *Orientalism*. New York: Penguin.

Salter, Mark. 2002. *Barbarians and Civilization in International Relations*. London: Pluto Press.

Schacht, Joseph. 1979. *The Origins of Muhammadan Jurisprudence*. Oxford: Clarendon Press.

Schmidt, Brian. 1998. *The Political Discourse of Anarchy: A Disciplinary History of International Relations*. Albany, NY: State University Press of New York.

Schmidt, Brian. 2002. 'Together Again: Reuniting Political Theory and International Relations Theory'. *British Journal of Politics and International Relations* 4(1): 115–40.

Schmitt, Carl. 1996 [1927]. *The Concept of the Political*, trans., intro. and ed. George Schwab. Chicago: University of Chicago Press.

Schmitt, Carl. 2005. *Political Theology: Four Chapters on the Concept of Sovereignty*, trans. George Schwab and intro. Tracy Strong. Chicago: University of Chicago Press.

Schneiderman, David. 2008. *Constitutionalizing Economic Globalization: Investment Rules and Democracy's Promise*. Cambridge: Cambridge University Press.

Schultz, William. 2002. *In Our Own Best Interests: How Defending Human Rights Benefits us All*. Boston: Beacon Press.

Scott, James Brown. 1934. *The Spanish Origin of International Law*, Part I: *Francisco de Vitoria and His Law of Nations*. Oxford: Clarendon Press.

Seckinelgin, Hakan and Hideaki Shinoda, eds. 2001. *Ethics and International Relations*. Basingstoke: Palgrave – now Palgrave Macmillan.

Seth, Sanjay. ed. 2013. *Postcolonial Theory and International Relations: A Critical Introduction*. London: Routledge.

Shakman Hurd, Elizabeth. 2008. *The Politics of Secularism in International Relations*. Princeton: Princeton University Press.

Shapcott, Richard. 2004. 'IR as Practical Philosophy: Defining a "Classical Approach"'. *British Journal of Politics and International Relations* 6(3): 271–91.

Shapcott, Richard. 2008. 'International Ethics', pp. 192–209, in John Baylis, Steve Smith and Patricia Owens, eds, *The Globalization of World Politics: An Introduction to International Relations*, 4th edn. Oxford: Oxford University Press.

Shue, Henry and David Rodin, eds. 2007. *Preemption: Military Action and Moral Justification*. Oxford: Oxford University Press.

Simon, Yves. 1980 [1963]. *A General Theory of Authority*, intro. Vukan Kuic. Notre Dame, IN: University of Notre Dame Press.

Simpson, Gerry. 2003. *Great Powers and Outlaw States: Unequal Sovereigns in the International Legal Order*. Cambridge: Cambridge University Press.

Simpson, Gerry. 2007. *Law, War and Crime: War Crimes Trials and the Reinvention of International Law*. Cambridge: Polity.

Singer, Peter. 1972. 'Famine, Affluence and Morality'. *Philosophy and Public Affairs* 1(3): 229–43.

Singer, Peter. 1975. *Animal Liberation: A New Ethic for our Treatment of Animals*. London: Cape.

Singer, Peter. 2002. *One World: The Ethics of Globalization*. New Haven: Yale University Press.

Singer, Peter. 2009. *The Life You Can Save: Acting Now to End World Poverty*. London: Picador.

Skinner, Quentin. 2002. *Visions of Politics, vol. I: Regarding Method*. Cambridge: Cambridge University Press.

Slomp, Gabriella. 2009a. *Carl Schmitt and the Politics of Hostility, Violence and Terror*. Basingstoke: Palgrave Macmillan.

Slomp, Gabriella. 2009b. The Origins of Realism Revisited, pp. 13–26, in Patrick Hayden, ed., *The Ashgate Research Companion to Ethics and International Relations*. Burlington, VT: Ashgate.

Smiley, Marion. 1992. *Moral Responsibility and the Boundaries of Community: Power and Accountability from a Pragmatic Point of View*. Chicago: University of Chicago Press.

Smith, Adam. 1986. *The Essential Adam Smith*, ed. and intro. Robert Heilbroner. New York: W.W. Norton.

Smith, Karen E. and Margot Light, eds. 2001. *Ethics and Foreign Policy*. Cambridge: Cambridge University Press.

Smith, Michael J. 1985. Moral Reasoning and Moral Responsibility in International Relations, pp. 33–48, in Kenneth Thompson, ed., *Ethic and International Relations*. New Brunswick: Transaction.

Smith, Michael J. 1986. *Realist Thought from Weber to Kissinger*. Baton Rouge, LA: Louisiana State University Press.

Smith, Oliver. 2011. The Ecology of History: Russian Thought on the Future of the World, pp. 113–31, in S. Bergmann and H. Eaton, eds, *Ecological Awareness: Exploring Religion, Ethics and Awareness*. Berlin: Lit-Verlag.

Smith, Steve. 2004. 'Singing Our World into Existence: International Relations Theory and September 11'. *International Studies Quarterly* 48: 499–515.

Snyder, Jack. ed. 2011. *Religion and International Relations*. New York: Columbia University Press.

Sommerville, Johann. ed. 1994. *King James VI and I: Political Writings*. Cambridge: Cambridge University Press.

Statman, Daniel. 1997. *Virtue Ethics: A Critical Reader*. Washington DC: Georgetown University Press.

Stears, Marc. 2005. 'The Vocation of Political Theory'. *European Journal of Political Theory* 4(4): 325–50.

Steele, Brent J. 2007. 'Liberal-Idealism: A Constructivist Critique'. *International Studies Review* 9(1): 23–52.

Sterling-Folker, Jennifer. 2000. 'Competing Paradigms or Birds of a Feather? Constructivism and Neoliberal Institutionalism Compared'. *International Studies Quarterly* 44(1): 97–119.

Strange, Susan. 1996. *The Retreat of the State: The Diffusion of Power in the World Economy*. Cambridge: Cambridge University Press.

Strange, Susan. 2002. *Authority and Markets: Susan Strange's Writings on International Political Economy*, ed., Roger Tooze and Christopher May. Basingstoke: Palgrave Macmillan.

Strauss, Leo. 1936. *The Political Philosophy of Hobbes: Its Basis and Genesis*, trans. Elsa M. Sinclair. Oxford: Oxford University Press.

Strauss, Leo. 1953. *Natural Right and History*. Chicago: University of Chicago Press.

Sullivan, William and William Kymlicka. 2007. *The Globalization of Ethics: Religious and Secular Perspectives*. Cambridge: Cambridge University Press.

Syse, Henrik and Gregory M. Reichberg, eds. 2007. *Ethics, Nationalism and Just War: Medieval and Contemporary Perspectives*. Washington DC: Catholic University of America Press.

Tabachnik, David and Toivo Koivukoski. 2009. *Enduring Empire: Ancient Lessons for Global Politics*. Toronto: University of Toronto Press.

Tamir, Yael. 1993. *Liberal Nationalism*. Princeton: Princeton University Press.

Tan, Kok-Chor. 2004. *Justice without Borders: Cosmopolitanism, Nationalism, and Patriotism*. Cambridge: Cambridge University Press.

Taylor, Charles. 1979. *Hegel and Modern Society*. Cambridge: Cambridge University Press.

Taylor, Charles. 1989. *Sources of the Self: The Making of the Modern Identity*. Cambridge: Cambridge University Press.

Teitel, Ruti. 2000. *Transitional Justice*. Oxford: Oxford University Press.

Thomas, Ward. 2001. *The Ethics of Destruction: Norms and Force in International Relations*. Ithaca: Cornell University Press.

Thompson, Kenneth. ed. 1985. *Ethics and International Relations*. New Brunswick: Transaction.

Thompson, Kenneth and Robert J. Myers, eds. 1984. *Truth and Tragedy: A Tribute to Hans J. Morgenthau, Augmented Edition.* New Brunswick: Transaction.

Thoreau, Henry David. 2000 [1854]. *Walden and Civil Disobedience*, ed. Paul Lauter. Boston: Houghton Mifflin.

Thucydides. 1972 [411–404 BC]. *History of the Peloponnesian War*, trans. Rex Warner. New York: Penguin.

Thomson, Janice. 1994. *Mercenaries, Pirates and Sovereigns: State-Building and Extraterritorial Violence in Early Modern Europe*. Princeton: Princeton University Press.

Thurow, Roger and Scott Kilman. 2009. *Enough: Why the World's Poorest Starve in an Age of Plenty*. New York: Public Affairs Books.

Tierney, Brian. 2001. *The Idea of Natural Rights, Natural Law, and Church Law, 1150–1625*. Grand Rapids, MI: William B Eerdmans.

Todorov, Tzvetan. 1999. *The Conquest of America: The Question of the Other*. Norman: University of Oklahoma Press.

Tooke, Joan. 1965. *The Just War in Aquinas and Grotius*. London: SPCK.

Toynbee, Arnold. 1972. *A Study of History*, 12 vols. Oxford: Oxford University Press.

Tracy, James D. 2008. *The Founding of the Dutch Republic: War, Finance, and Politics in Holland, 1572–1588*. Oxford: Oxford University Press.

Tuck, Richard. 1979. *Natural Rights Theories: Their Origins and Development*. Cambridge: Cambridge University Press.

Tuck, Richard. 1999. *The Rights of War and Peace: Political Thought and International Order from Grotius to Kant*. Oxford: Oxford University Press.

Tucker, Robert W. 1978. *The Just War: A Study in Contemporary American Doctrine*. Westport: Greenwood Press.

Tuckness, Alex. 2002. *Locke and the Legislative Point of View: Toleration, Contested Principles and the Law*. Princeton: Princeton University Press.

UN (United Nations). 2004. *A More Secure World: Our Shared Responsibility: Report of the Secretary General's High Level Panel on Threats Challenges and Change*. New York: United Nations Publications.

UNESCO. 1949. *Human Rights: Comments and Interpretations: A Symposium*, with an introduction by Jacques Maritain. London: Allen Wingate.

UNFE (United Nations, Free & Equal). 2014. The Most Shocking Map You Will Ever See. Available at: www.unfe.org/en/actions/criminalization-map.

UNGA (United Nations General Assembly). 2009. Interactive Thematic Dialogue of the United Nations General Assembly on the Responsibility to Protect. Available at: www.un.org/ga/president/63/interactive/responsibilitytoprotect.shtml.

UNHRC (United Nations Human Rights Council). 2011. Report of the Working Group on the Universal Periodic Review: United States of America. Document A/HRC/16/11. Available at: www.ohchr.org/EN/HRBodies/UPR/Pages/USSession9.aspx.

USCCB (United States Conference of Catholic Bishops). 1983. *The Challenge of Peace: God's Promise and Our Response.* Washington DC: Orbis.

US Department of State. 2010. Report of the United States of America Submitted to the UN Commissioner on Human Rights in Conjunction with Universal Periodic Review. Available at: www.state.gov/documents/organization/146379.pdf.

Valls, Andrew. 2000. *Ethics in International Relations.* Lanham, MD: Rowman & Littlefield.

Van Ittersum, Martine Julia. 2006. Pro*fit and Principle: Hugo Grotius, Natural Rights Theories, and the Rise of Dutch Power in the East Indies, 1595–1615.* Leiden: Brill.

Vattel, Emerich de. 2008 [1758]. *The Law of Nations*, Béla Kapossy and Richard Whatmore, eds. Indianapolis: Liberty Fund Press.

Vincent, Andrew. 2004. *The Nature of Political Theory.* Oxford: Oxford University Press.

Vincent, Andrew. 2010. *The Politics of Human Rights.* Oxford: Oxford University Press.

Vitoria, Francisco de. 1991. *Political Writings*, ed. Anthony Pagden and Jeremy Lawrence. Cambridge: Cambridge University Press.

Voegelin, Eric. 1974. *Order and History*, 4 vols. Baton Rouge, LA: Louisiana State University Press.

Voegelin, Eric. 1987. The *New Science of Politics: An Introduction*, with a new forward by Dante Germino. Chicago: University of Chicago Press.

Von Clausewitz, Karl. 1989 [1832]. *On War.* New York: Penguin.

Waldron, Jeremy. 1987. *'Nonsense on Stilts': Bentham, Burke, and Marx on the Rights of Man.* London: Methuen.

Waldron, Jeremy. 2002. *God, Locke, and Equality: Christian Foundations of John Locke's Political Thought.* Cambridge: Cambridge University Press.

Walker, R.B.J. 1993. *Inside/Outside: International Relations as Political Theory.* Cambridge: Cambridge University Press.

Walker, R.B.J. 2010. *After the Globe, Before the World.* London: Routledge.

Wallerstein, Immanuel. 1976. *The Modern World-System: Capitalist Agriculture and the Origins of the European World Economy in the Sixteenth Century.* London: Academic Press.

Waltz, Kenneth. 1959. *Man, the State and War: A Theoretical Analysis.* New York: Columbia University Press.

Waltz, Kenneth. 1979. *Theory of International Politics.* Reading, MA: Addison-Wesley.

Waltz, Susan. 2004. 'Universal Human Rights: The Contribution of Muslim States'. *Human Rights Quarterly* 26(4): 799–844.

Walzer, Michael. 1977. *Just and Unjust Wars.* New York: Basic Books.

Walzer, Michael. 1983. *Spheres of Justice: A Defense of Pluralism and Equality*. New York: Basic Books.

Walzer, Michael. 1994. *Thick and Thin: Moral Argument at Home and Abroad*. Notre Dame: University of Notre Dame Press.

Walzer, Michael. 1996. War and Peace in the Jewish Tradition, pp. 95–114, in Terry Nardin, ed., *The Ethics of War and Peace: Religious and Secular Perspectives*. Princeton: Princeton University Press.

Walzer, Michael. ed. 2000. *The Jewish Political Tradition*, vol. 1, *Authority*, with Menachem Lorberbaum, Noam Zohar and Yair Lorberbaum. New Haven: Yale University Press.

Walzer, Michael. 2004. *Arguing about War*. New Haven, CT: Yale University Press.

Warrender, Howard. 1957. *The Political Philosophy of Thomas Hobbes: His Theory of Obligation*. Oxford: Oxford University Press.

Watt, Montgomery W. 1961. *Muhammed: Prophet and Statesman*. Oxford: Oxford University Press.

Weber, Max. 1994 [1919]. The Profession and Vocation of Politics, pp. 309–69, in Max Weber, *Political Writings*, ed. Peter Lassman and Ronald Speirs. Cambridge: Cambridge University Press.

Wiedemann, Thomas. 1986. 'The Fetiales: A Reconsideration'. *The Classical Quarterly* 36(2): 478–90.

Wiener, Antje, Anthony F, Lang Jr, Jim Tully, Miguel Poiares Maduro and Mattias Kumm. 2012. 'Global Constitutionalism: Human Rights, Democracy, and the Rule of Law'. *Global Constitutionalism* 1(1): 1–15.

Welch, David. 2000. Morality and the National Interest, pp. 3–14, in Andrew Valls, ed., *Ethics in International Affairs*. Lanham MD: Rowman & Littlefield.

Welsh, Jennifer. 1995. *Edmund Burke and International Relations: The Commonwealth of Europe and the Crusade against the French Revolution*. Basingstoke: Macmillan – now Palgrave Macmillan.

Welsh, Jennifer. 2011. 'Civilian Protection in Libya: Putting Coercion and Controversy back into RtoP'. *Ethics & International Affairs* 25(3): 255–62.

Wenar, Leif. 2005. 'The Nature of Rights'. *Philosophy and Public Affairs* 33(1): 223–52.

Wendt, Alexander. 1991. 'Anarchy is What States Make of It: The Social Construction of Power Politics'. *International Organization* 46(2): 391–425.

Wendt, Alexander. 1999. *Social Theory of International Politics*. Cambridge: Cambridge University Press.

Wendt, Alexander. 2003. 'Why a World States is Inevitable'. *European Journal of International Relations* 9: 491–542.

Wheeler, Nicholas. 2000. *Saving Strangers: Humanitarian Intervention in International Society*. Oxford: Oxford University Press.

White, Steven K. 2002. 'Pluralism, Platitudes and Paradoxes: Fifty Years of Western Political Thought'. *Political Theory* 30: 472–81.

Wight, Colin. 2006. *Agency, Structures, and International Relations: Politics as Ontology*. Cambridge: Cambridge University Press.

Wight, Martin. 1966. Why is There is No International Theory?, pp. 17–34, in Hebert Butterfield and Martin Wight, eds, *Diplomatic Investigations: Essays in the Theory of International Politics*. London. Allen & Unwin.

Williams, Andrew. 2006. *Liberalism and War: The Victors and the Vanquished*. London: Routledge.

Williams, Howard. 1992. *International Relations in Political Theory*. Milton Keynes: Open University Press.

Williams, John. 2013. Not in My Name: Legitimate Authority and the Liberal Just War Theory, pp. 63–80, in Anthony F. Lang, Jr, Cian O'Driscoll and John Williams, eds, *Just War: Authority, Tradition and Practice*. Washington DC: Georgetown University Press.

Williams, Michael, ed. 2007. *Reconsidering Realism: The Legacy of Hans J. Morgenthau in International Relations*. Oxford: Oxford University Press.

Wilson, Charles H. 1961. *Anglo-Dutch Commerce and Finance in the 18th Century*. Cambridge: Cambridge University Press.

Wolin, Sheldon. 1969. 'Political Theory as a Vocation'. *American Political Science Review* 63: 1062–82.

Yoder, John Howard. 1994. *The Politics of Jesus: Vicit Agnus Noster*. Grand Rapids, MI: Eerdmans.

Ypi, Lea, Robert E. Goodin and Christian Barry. 2009. 'Associative Duties, Global Justice and the Colonies'. *Philosophy and Public Affairs* 37(2): 103–35.

Zaum, Dominik. 2007. *The Sovereignty Paradox: The Norms and Politics of International Statebuilding*. Oxford: Oxford University Press.

Zehfuss, Maja. 2009. Poststructuralism, pp. 97–14, in Patrick Hayden, ed., *The Ashgate Research Companion to Ethics and International Relations*. Burlington, VT: Ashgate.

Zuckert, Michael. 2002. *Launching Liberalism: John Locke and the Liberal Tradition*. Lawrence: University of Kansas Press.

Index

Note: Entries in **bold** type are substantially discussed

Agency 6
Alford, C. Fred 40, 81
Anarchy 31
Antigone 48–9
Appleby, R. Scott 187
Aquinas, Thomas 50
    On law 50–1
    On war 134–5
Arbour, Louise 45
Archibuigi, Daniele 37
Arendt, Hannah 9, 10, 21–2, 88, 117,
    124–5
Aristotle 18, 49, 158, 168–74
Atack, Ian 125
Augustine of Hippo 128–9, 134–5
Austin, John 55–6
Authority 20–42
    Practical vs theoretical 25

Baber, Walter 176–7
Bacon, Francis 26
Barnett, Michael 32
Bartlett, Robert 176–7
Bauer, Bruno 108
Beitz, Charles 13, 86, 113
Belief 180–97
Bennett, Jane 177–8
Bentham, Jeremy 55, 92, 93
Blackstone, William 55
Boucher, David 8, 79
Brown, Chris 8, 35, 140
Bull, Hedley 33

Carr, E.H. 11
Carson, Rachel 166
Campbell, David 12
Capra, Fritjof 174
Causation 169–70
Charles I and II 25
Cicero 49–50, 131

Civil War, British 25, 26, 56
Clark, Ian 33
Climate change 155–7, 174–8
Cochran, Molly 8, 14
Connolly, William 15–16, 163, 178, 182,
    192–3
Communitarianism 36
Constructivism 11
Cosmopolitan theory 6, 35
Cox, Robert 11
Cripps, Elizabeth 175–6
Cromwell, Oliver 25
Critical theory (IR theory) 11

Dahl, Robert 192
Dallmayr, Fred 78
Darwin, Charles 82–3, 160–1, 178
Dawkins, Richard 160
Dewey, John 8, 85, 192
Diplomacy 58–9
Dobson, Andrew 175
Donnelly, Jack 81
Douzinas, Costas 189
Dworkin, Ronald 100

Ecology, deep 167
Elshtain, Jean Bethke 87
Emerson, Ralph Waldo 164–5
Equality 100–3
Erasmus 129
Erskine, Toni 8

Fabre, Cécile 14, 38, 137
Falk, Richard 60
Fanon, Frantz 123
Feurbach, Ludwig 108–9
Filmer, Robert 29
Finnemore, Martha 32
Finnis, John 81
Flathman, Richard 23–5, 182, 193–4

Forman-Barzilai, Fonna 106
Foucault, Michel 79, 162
Friedman, Milton 104
Friedman, Richard 22–3
Frost, Mervyn 14–15, 36, 86–7, 191
Fukuyama, Francis 111

Gaia hypothesis 159
Geneva Conventions 143–4
Ghandi, Mohandas 125
Gill, Stephen 33
Global constitutionalism 13, 15, 34–5, 70
Global resource dividend (GRD) 114–15
Gramsci, Antonio 33
Gratian 135
Grotius, Hugo 18, 76, 81, 122
    On natural law 51–2
    On the 'impious hypothesis' 52, 151
    On just war 146–52

Habermas, Jürgen 63
Hart, H.L.A. 56–7
Hashami, Sohail 134
Hague Conventions 143
Hayden, Patrick 191
Hayek, Friedrich 104
Hayward, Tim 175
Hegel, G.W.F 19, 107–8, 188–91
Hegemony 33
Hehir, Aidan 43
Helsinki Accords 45
Hibbing, John 163
Hobbes, Thomas 16, 76, 105, 173
    On authority 26–8
    On law 54–5
Hoffman, Matthew 177
Hohfeld, Wesley 74–5
Hume, David 86, 104–5, 170
Huntington, Samuel 186–7
Hurd, Ian 32, 38
Hurrell, Andrew 33
Hutchings, Kimberley 8, 191

Ideology 9
Ignatieff, Michael 84–5
Ikenberry, G. John 2
Iliad 130
International Criminal Court (ICC) 20, 34, 35

International law 43–71
    Historical origins 59–60
    Customary 61–2, 83
International political theory (IPT)
    Definition 1–3
    And international legal theory (ILT)
        12–13
    And IR theory 10–12
    And moral and ethical philosophy
        13–15
    And political theory 8–10
Intervention 95–6
Ishay, Michelene 76–7
Islam, human rights in 78, 84

James VI and I 25
James II 25
James, William 19, 182, 193–5
Jefferson, Thomas 81
Jenkins, Philip 185
Jesus of Nazareth 127, 134, 196
Just war 134–46
Justice 102–3

Kaldor, Mary 123
Kant, Immanuel 16–17, 190
    On the categorical imperative 62
    On freedom 63–4
    On law and legislation 62–8
    On *Perpetual Peace* 63, 66–8
    On publicity 64–5
Kelsay, John 134
Kelsen, Hans 56
Keohane, Robert 2, 11
King, Jr, Martin Luther 166
Khomeini, Ayatollah 184–5
Klabbers, Jan 13
Koskenniemi, Martii 60–1
Kosovo intervention 46
Kurki, Milja 170

Lake, David 32
Lane, Melissa 174
Laws 5, 43–71
Legitimacy 38
Leopold, Aldo 166
Lesbian, gay, bisexual and transgendered
    (LGBT) rights 1, 4, 84, 162, 180–1,
    188–9

Lewis, C.S. 50, 184
Liberalism (political theory) 7
Liberalism (IR theory) 11
Linklater, Andrew 11, 14
Livy 131
Locke, John 16, 28–31, 76, 81, 106, 190
Lovelock, James 159

Madison, James 192
Maimonides 128
MacPherson, C.B. 82
Mandeville, Bernard 105
Mandeville, Peter 186
Maritain, Jacques 52, 78, 83
Marx, Karl 17, 101, 107–11, 118, 164
McMahan, Jeff 14, 137, 139
Milanovic, Branko 100–1
Mill, John Stuart 17, 92–6, 115, 190
Morgenthau, Hans 11, 31, 163, 171,
  188
Moyn, Samuel 77
Muhammad 78, 132

Naess, Arne 166–7
Nardin, Terry 8
Natural law 12, 28–31, 48–53
  Definition of 48
Natural right 80–3
Naturalism 159–60
Nature 155–79
Neoliberalism 104
Newton, Isaac 26
Niebuhr, Reinhold 14
Nietzsche, Friedrich 78
Norms 5
Nussbaum 82

Oakeshott, Michael 8, 198–9
Oldenbarnvelt, Johann 147
Onuf, Nicholas 61

Pagden, Anthony 82
Paine, Thomas 81
Peirce, C.S. 85
Phronesis 171, 173, 175, 176
Pinker, Steven 159–60
Plato 22, 102–3, 174
Pluralism 192–5
Pogge, Thomas 13, 113–15

Positivism 9
Positivist legal theory 53–8
Poststructuralism (IR theory) 11–12
Pragmatism 85–6
Pufendorf, Samuel 52

Qutb, Sayid 193

Rawls, John 13–14, 27, 63, 84, 101, 103,
  111–15
Realism 11, 188
Recognition theory 188–91
Relativism 184–8
Rengger, Nicholas 137
Responsibility 87–9
Responsibility to protect (R2P) 39, 43–5,
  68–70
Rights 74–87
  Definition of 74
  Foundations of 79–84
  History of 76–9
  Islamic conceptions of 78
  Religion and 80
Rodin, David 14, 137
Romanticism 164
Rorty, Richard 85–6
Rules 5, 42–71
  Definition 44
  Formal vs informal 45–6

Said, Edward 187
Salter, Mark 187
Schmitt, Carl 10, 187
Schultz, William 85
Scipio's Dream 50
Secularization thesis 185
Sen, Amartya 82
Shapcott, Richard 171
Shaybani, Muhammad 133
Shue, Henry 13
Simon, Yves 21
Singer, Peter 14, 101, 115–17, 167
Smiley, Marion 87–8
Smith, Adam 17, 101, 103–7
Smith, Oliver 187
Social contract 27
Sophocles 48–9
Spencer, Herbert 160–1
Strange, Susan 101, 118–19

Strauss, Leo 9
Suganmi, Hidemi 14

Teleology 169–71
Thomas, Ward 143
Thoreau, Henry David 165–6
Thucydides 130–1
Toleration 30, 192
Tolstoy, Leo 125
Toynbee, Arnold 186

United Nations Declaration on Human
   Rights (UDHR) 52, 78, 89
United Nations High Commissioner for
   Human Rights 1, 90–2
United Nations Human Rights Council
   (UNHRC) 1, 39, 70–2, 90–2
United Nations Security Council (UNSC)
   20, 38–41
Unmanned aerial vehicles (UAVs) 121,
   152–3
Utilitarianism 55

Vallodolid debate 60
Vattel, Emerich de 61
Vincent, Andrew 41, 82–3, 86
Violence 121–54
   Definition of 122
Virtue 169–72
Vitoria, Francisco de 51, 60
Vogelin, Eric 9, 186
Von Clausewitz, Karl 122–3

Waldron, Jeremy 81
Walker, R.B.J. 12
Waltz, Kenneth 31
Walzer, Michael 36, 128, 136–7, 140, 141
War 122
Wealth 100–20
Weber, Max 38
Welsh, Jennifer 68–9
Wendt, Alexander 32
Wight, Colin 170
Williams, John 88